"Chief Cook ^{and} Bottle-Washer" The Unconquerable Soul Of

Wilkie Clark

In Loving Memory Of Mama,
who taught me "the power of the pen"

Charlotte A. Clark-Frieson
Author, Entrepreneur, Educator, Public Servant

Preface Written By Alvin Thornton, PhD

Revised Edition, 3rd Printing
ISBN 0-9771401-0-5

Wilkie Clark's Daughter Enterprises, LLC
Copyright © 2005 By Charlotte A. Clark-Frieson, CEO/Founder
Wilkie Clark's Daughter Enterprises, LLC
322 Wilkie Clark Drive, Roanoke, Alabama 36274
Phone: (334) 863-4885 Fax: (334) 863-6062
http://www.wilkieclarksdaughter.net

Executive Editor: Charlotte A. Clark-Frieson
Production Editor: Charlotte A. Clark-Frieson
Cover Design: Sean Snakenberg, cover2coverdesigns

Published In the United States of America by
Charlotte A. Clark-Frieson, CEO
Wilkie Clark's Daughter Enterprises, LLC
Roanoke, Alabama 36274

Printed In the U.S.A.

Library Of Congress Control Number
2005904592

Alternate Printings:
November, 2004 First Edition: ISBN 1-4116-1809-2
April, 2005 Second Edition: ISBN 1-4116-2863-2
June, 2005, Revised Edition ISBN 1-4116-2863-2
December, 2011, Revised Edition ISBN 0-9771401-0-5

"...Clark-Frieson has shared her father with millions of readers in this explosive work! Wilkie Clark was a poor boy who became a respected civil rights leader, community activist, and business owner. Given the climate of Randolph County, Alabama in the 60s, none of the above feats were easily attained. At times Wilkie Clark spoke out when his very safety was in question. There were occasions when the very people he tried to help turned on him, but even that didn't deter him!

...Clark-Frieson's book not only honors her father, but all the strong black fathers who once were and will be again. Some segments of the book were humorous, some were sad; but the total package provided a rich history of the black community in rural Randolph County, Alabama."

Delores Thornton, Journalist, Author, and Book Publicist
Named Black Refer's Black Literary Queen, 2003 BlackRefer.com

"My mother, Charlotte Clark-Frieson has written a wonderfully inspiring book. I became very overwhelmed with pride as I read it. Pride for my grandfather, Wilkie Clark and the huge obstacles he overcame AND pride for my mother, who could have very easily let the spirit and memory of her father gradually fade away. She really put her heart and soul into this project and it shows in her writing which is overflowing with love and reverence for her father. This is one of the best books I've ever read. Good Job Mom!"

Je'Lynn Mikele Frieson, The Author's Daughter

"A well-written account of the trials, tribulations, and ultimate triumph of a very remarkable Black man who faced and overcame both legal and social roadblocks during the turbulent 1960s and 1970s. It will be difficult to put the book down once you begin to read it - so allow sufficient time to read it once you begin.

3

Though Wilkie Clark's contribution to his beloved community was recognized during his lifetime, his legacy and stature will continue to grow in the future, thanks to the wonderful book written by Wilkie Clark's daughter"

Alexandra Mugimba Thornton

"I know next to nothing of the American civil rights movement, but I can see that this is the testament of a loving daughter to her father's role in that struggle. For those who would seek to know more in detail of this part of American history I believe that this would shed light in a helpful way. As it is written by the daughter of Wilkie Clark it probably lies somewhere between biography and autobiography, but is not less valuable for that."

Professor Ian Ruxton

My Apologies

My apologies to anyone who has problems reading or understanding this book. In the event it turns out not to be a good read for you, I want to let you know in advance that I didn't intentionally not do a good job writing it.

I'm a black woman, and for that reason alone, I don't feel any compulsion to apologize to anybody for writing and publishing a book that has not been professionally edited. As a consequence of being black, I couldn't afford to pay the $6.00 to $12.00 per page most professional editors charge for their editing services. I still struggle to pay my mortgage, feed my kids, and keep my lights, water and gas on.

I had landed a publishing contract with a company who promised to provide editing services in anticipation of the publication of my book and help me market it. But they wanted me to lie; to present my dad in a light that was totally contra to who and what he really was. There was a conflict of interest. Their only interest was to package him, market and sell him; my interest is to honor him. They had some problems with my using some expletives in the book, but I disagreed. So, what else was there to do but cancel my publishing agreement. Why? Who wouldn't use foul language, when their whole life has been marked by foul stuff? The man was forced to deal with foul issues that would never have been issues if only the world had been the kind of place God wanted it to be.

So, who better than me, knows how to present my father to the world? He was what he was, and because I am a black woman, for that reason alone, I ain't changing nothin'. I'm gonna tell this. Cause it need to be told.

I am a veteran teacher with an M.Ed., and if I ain't learned in all dis time how to write by now, den I piddy all dem chillens I dun tried to teech how to reed n rite.

Enjoy and be blessed!

This book...   the sites...   the organization...
are all a labor of love and a work in progress;
and you who will read it
will determine how it all ends.
This book is my recitation of
a part of my daddy's life that I treasure...
This is the second obituary
the one I wasn't strong enough to write
when my daddy died
the one that took fifteen years to grow inside of me
the one that I have carried full term and is now
crying to be birthed
that the world might catch a glimpse
of a wonderful person.

~ Wilkie and Hattie Lee Clark's Daughter ~

Success Affirmation

I, Charlotte A. Clark-Frieson, author and finisher of the literary work herein, through this affirmation do hereby profess, proclaim and decree that I am successful in Christ because greater is He who is in me than he who is in the world. By God's grace I will not swerve to the right or left, but with God's help I shall stay on the narrow way. In other words, I shall abide in Christ Jesus — His death, burial, resurrection and ascension which will bring me through to ultimate victory.

I, Charlotte A. Clark-Frieson, earthly daughter of the late Wilkie Clark, and divine daughter of Christ the King, am more than a conqueror because He who conquered death and brought us life is in me. He, Jesus Christ, never failed. He was successful in every aspect of His ministry and calling and that same life that brings one to success, not failure, is IN ME. I rest in Christ and allow His power to rise up within me to overcome and be who God has called me to be and do what God has called me to do. It is so, so be it in Jesus' name.

Amen. Amen. Amen.

Contents

Prologue

The Impetus To Write

Wilkie Clark Remembered
An Anthology Of Praise

Resolution

Resources

WORK

"I learned that no matter what you may or may not have,

as perceived by a misguided community about what is

valuable, people understand hard work and talent

—and it can prevail."

—Maxine Waters

Preface
Wilkie Clark: A Renaissance New Black Man, Re-Defining a Community and Its People Through Words and Bold Deeds

Alvin Thornton, Ph.D.*

I consider it a distinct honor to have been asked to write a preface to a book that chronicles the life of Wilkie Clark through his daughter's diverse experiences with him. For me, he was a renaissance "New Black Man" who helped construct a community and its people through his visionary words and bold deeds. I watched and learned life-sustaining lessons from him that have served me well as I faced the challenges of becoming a man, husband, father and engaged citizen.

It is written that the value and meaning of a person to a people and place cannot be really known until the person is no longer present in the physical sense. This is true of Wilkie Clark, a member of my immediate biological family, intellectual mentor to me, and a visionary leader of local, state and national significance. He took great joy in the fact that I led an effort to desegregate the Ranch Motel Restaurant while a student at the Randolph County Training School and knew that I was actually listening to his "sermons" about the civil rights and the economic struggles of Black people. He took every occasion, family reunions, church services, monthly PTA meetings, NAACP and Alabama Democratic Conference sessions, and social gatherings to inject the urgency of positive collective and individual action by Black people to build self-sustaining institutions and positive behaviors. His words were, "If your back is not bent, those who wish to oppress you cannot stand on it;

11

stand up, stop grinning when there is nothing funny and scratching where there is no itch."

He encouraged me during my studies at Morehouse College and Howard University as I completed my baccalaureate and doctoral degrees. In me, and many others, he saw the embryonic emergence of "the New Black Men," the development of which he had devoted his life works and resources.

The pressing question is why did I and others listen to him and can we convince our young Black men to hear his words and learn from his life?

The awareness I have of the parameters of justice, equality and humanity results in no small measure from my observation of his work as a "man" of the community, a civil rights activist who acted without fear in the face of unrepresentative state and private authority, a friend to all types of people, and a father and husband. Fatherhood for him was biological and social and there had to always be a strong nexus between the two. His life and legacy deserves special recognition for posterity and as a marker for the level of man and fatherhood that the African American community will need as it faces the residue of racism and oppression and crafts cultural, economic and political institutions that will enable it to compete and develop in the next millennium. Let us display his life and pray that a sufficient number of men will observe it and learn lessons that are now so desperately needed in the face of social dysfunction and alienation, economic oppression and individual pathologies.

When Alan Locke, the great African American Harlem Renaissance philosopher and former Howard University Dean and Professor, wrote of the "New Black Man," he must have had Wilkie Clark in mind. For Locke, the "New Black Man" was first intellectually and culturally aware and committed to play a dignified role in the social construction of the reality of his community, his people and himself. He was proud of his past and committed to rediscovering it; proud of his aesthetics — his comparative physical appearance; and unwilling to relinquish his role in defining his community's constitutional and civic framework.

In many ways, his life parallels that of the great abolitionist Frederick Douglass, who emerged from raw racial oppression to be self-taught and assume a commanding leadership role in the struggle for the liberation of the Black community and the realization the American constitutional dream. These unusual attributes made Wilkie Clark a renaissance "New Black Man." With the decibel and eloquence of his voice, charismatic and commanding physical presence, and bold actions he crafted the image of a "New Black Man" and enriched the discourse about how racial and economic justice would be achieved in Roanoke, Randolph County, and the South. He had a way of speaking, walking and being that commanded the ear and respect of all, Black and White. Wilkie Clark came of age in Roanoke and Randolph County during the second decade of the Twentieth Century when "Jim Crow" racism and economic exploitation defined and limited the life experiences of African Americans and when behaving as a Black Man could be life threatening. Chattel slavery had ended only 65 years earlier and Black people in America and Randolph County were still living a dual existence as a separated people with second-class citizenship. They had few political rights that White Americans were required to respect and were marginalized economically, notwithstanding having served as one of the initial sources of our nation's great wealth, fought in its foreign wars, paid its taxes and helped build its basic physical infrastructure.

His life is about the struggle to end the marginalization of Black people and their community. He served on the trustee boards of schools for Black students and pressured boards and councils for equal treatment of Black children. As President of the local chapter of the NAACP, he fought for expanded voting rights for Black citizens; defended Black people against and unjust criminal justice and policing system; and energized the Black Church and its ministerial to play a more active role in the struggle for racial justice and economic equality for the Black community. I remember mostly his love for all children and his extended family, and the lengths to which he went to enrich both, and the disdain he had for any form of injustice and oppression. His love for people was collective and individual. All in need knew that they could approach him for assistance and that he would give even if doing so caused his family and him to sacrifice things they needed.

My oldest sister, Maggie, speaks often of Mr. Clark (cousin

Wilkie) taking her to the county seat, Wedowee, before the passage of the 1965 Voting Rights Act, to pay her poll tax and cast her vote. He not only was aware of the rights that extended from full citizenship, he also understood the need to take specific action to exercise them. I watched as he risked life and family for the greater good and learned life-long lessons of how to be a man, husband, father and citizen. For him, the U.S. Constitution and its Bill Rights were weapons in the war for justice and equality. Freedom of conscious, and the right to assemble and petition government; citizenship, equal protection, due process, liberty and the pursuit of happiness flowed eloquently and loudly from is mouth as he insisted on equal education for Black children and due process generally for Black citizens for Black people in the public and private arena.

He applied the jurisprudence of equal justice at the local level that Thurgood Marshall, through his genius, extracted from the Supreme Court in the historic Brown vs. Board of Education decision. He was like Fannie Lou Hamer, the great Mississippi civil rights warrior, who looked white supremacy, violence and death in the face and at personal risk, stood for justice for the oppressed. He also offered Martin Luther King, Jr., Richard Allen, and Nat Turner to the ministerial community as examples of the type of spiritual leadership that they should provide their congregations and communities, and found great favor in the works and writings of Booker T. Washington and W. E. DuBois as sources of how the industrial and theoretical can be combined to uplift an oppressed people.

A complex array factors shaped his personality and commanded him to assume his leadership role in the community. Through their independent life styles and familial interdependence, his uncle (Grand Pa Jack Baker) and great aunt (Lizzie Baker) taught him the importance of ownership and doing for self and family. Through his world and regional travels, which were unusual for Black people of his day, he learned of alternative racial and social formations that would permit people to coexist in a framework of enhanced humanity, mutual respect and benefit. Proximity to and interaction with the Black intelligentsia (his wife Hattie P. Clark and other area teachers) and spiritual leaders sharpened his knowledge of history and helped him craft a philosophical orientation that added reason to his actions. Although not as formally educated as these individuals, he set standards of leadership and accomplishment that few equaled. Together, they constituted the enlightened vanguard that shaped the civil rights movement in Roanoke and Randolph County.

His roles were diverse and complex and he was many things to many people— husband, father, family member, Sunday School teacher, worker, civil rights leader and entrepreneur. He let all see the love that he had for his wife and daughter. I suppose in doing so, he was modeling the essential love upon which all struggle for justice and community development is based. In the end, for our community, he was a shining prince of Douglass, King, Malcolm, and Mandela like stature who shielded his people from harm and expanded the constitutional and procedural umbrella over them. Although gone physically, he remains with us in spirit and through the expanded opportunities he made possible for the "New Black Men and Women" who emerged in his wake to take their places, with dignity, as educated, culturally proud and contributing citizens. We loved him and he loved us!

His only child, Charlotte, has written an honest, reflective, penetrating and personal account of her too short years with her father. I thank her for sharing the rich memories—the bad and good times, the sacrifices and gains, and reminders the work that is yet to be done.

———————————

* Alvin Thornton is Associate Provost and Professor of Political Science Howard University. His mother, Lillie Mae Thornton, is Wilkie Clark's first cousin. He is a graduate of the Randolph County Training School in Roanoke, Alabama on whose Board of Trustees Wilkie Clark served.

WRITING OUR OWN HISTORY

It would be a low down dirty shame,
for this generation of African Americans to sit idly by
and allow distinguished black men and women to live inspired lives
before us, then die, and pass quietly off the scene of time,
without taking the initiative or the time to preserve
or revere their historical importance for our posterity.

If publishers refuse to publish,
we have the resources to write our own histories,
tell our own stories, using our own words.
There is NO excuse.

Charlotte A. Clark-Frieson

Introduction

We who write, do so because we either want to change something or we want something to change. Because we know books change lives, we write. We want to influence the way people think about a particular issue, person, place or thing; we want to change the world—hopefully for the better. That's why I wrote *"Chief Cook & Bottle-Washer," The Unconquerable Soul Of Wilkie Clark.* I wanted to write a book that would change the world!

Before publishing this book, I always heard that black writers have a hard time getting published; big publishing houses have little interest in producing their books. Perhaps this is because many black writers focus on race and publishers don't see their books as profitable because nobody wants to read about race. Enough already!! That's their position.

I don't really give a dam how dis-interested the modern media is in publishing information about racial issues, or how tired they are of hearing about it, race still remains at the heart of a lot of American society's problems. Of all my life experiences, the one truth that has had the most devastating, profound, chilling and penetrating effect on my life, is my blackness. It has metastasized into every single aspect of my life, all my life. Even in the aftermath of Brown vs Board of Education (1954), The civil rights movement, court ordered desegregation and expanded opportunities for African-Americans, I still carry it around with me. And strangely enough, no amount of therapy, neither strenuous legislation nor infamous court decisions can ever totally heal its wounds. Any measurable degree of healing I've experienced, has come through dialogue— continuous, ongoing, never-ending dialogue and analysis of the problem. It's buried deeply in my spirit; lies heavily in my breast; it's in my heart; on my heart; like an insidious tumor, growing, eating away and gnawing at my insides; no one who isn't black, can know the extreme burden of blackness. There is one, you know. There is a social burden; an emotional burden and a spiritual

17

burden. But, the one burden that I believe that has been least explored and now merits the most of our attention at this juncture in our history is the economic burden of blackness.

I consider it nothing short of a blessing to have been born just in the nick of time to bear witness to the steep rise — and the long fall of one of the greatest movements of all time, the civil rights movement. It was more of a blessing not only to witness but also to participate in this movement. Thus, I now mourn the current "falling away" from the civil rights efforts of the past, that Black America is now witnessing.

The question arises, why was it so important for me to be a participant in this movement? And why is there now such a tremendous "falling away" from it? Immediately the answer emerges from the awareness that I had a father who not only participated but also gave me no option to decline participation. Then, the question follows, what if there had been more fathers participating, and insisting that their children participate? Thus, for me, the influence of the black man — the black father — becomes a crucial element of the continuing struggle for African-American freedom, justice and equality in this nation. The movement is by no means finished! The revolution is not over! But, it has seemingly stopped in its tracks. There is a grand finale that has yet to play itself out.

With all my heart, I believe that the civil rights movement has stalled because black fathers are not exercising the tremendous influence and potential power they have over their children. If the civil rights movement is to regain it's former momentum, black fathers must become the leaders, and must pass the torch — they must again become passionate for and about the movement, insisting that their children now take ownership — possess the opportunities that have been won through active participation in the process. Thus black fathers are crucial to the completion of the movement. Isn't it ironic that black men who took part in the civil rights movement, were fighting for the opportunity to straighten their backs up and exercise their manhood, and now that the opportunity exists, there are far too many instances of black men crippled for other reasons not akin either to the absence or presence of opportunity? In the presence of opportunity to be recognized as men, educate themselves, care for their children, obtain respectable employment, and to be a positive influence on children, don't you think it odd that so many of them seem to be working harder to avoid the responsibility that accompanies opportunity?

I always tried to hold fast to the belief that it is more desirous to lend positive verbal support and be an advocate for and defender of African-Americans causes. But I must reluctantly admit that there are times when I get mad as hell with black America for the way she has allowed herself to degenerate and wither. And while there are times when I literally want to cuss somebody out, I just have to quietly and reservedly constrain myself remembering what the bible says: "My people perish for lack of knowledge." Even at the risk of sounding self-righteous and persecutory, there is absolutely and positively no excuse for some of the junk that goes on in our culture and communities. Without question, much of it is our own fault. And as badly as I hate to lay blame on any specific thing, a large degree of our suffering is due to the passive way that many black men have approached their role as fathers.

Regrettably in 1993 at age 39, I experienced an abrupt shift in status when I was widowed after my husband's sudden death. In the 13 years since, I have evolved from a young widow to a middle-aged spinster. My extreme disenchantment with the declining image of the black man literally forced me to remain unattached all these years by choice. Don't get me wrong. It's not that I was actively pursuing or seeking a new relationship with a man. But, just in the course of living life, moving around and interacting, the black men I encountered seemed to be lacking some serious components of manhood, that were and still remain difficult to pin-point.

It seemed that no matter where I went, or what direction I looked in, all I could see were gigolo types, freeloaders, men who didn't want to work, men looking for a home—one already set up and equipped, my-baby-daddies, bums, psychopaths, imposters, drunks, dope-smokers, dope-dealers, womanizers, abusers, bar-hoppers, street-walkers, what mama used to call "whore-hoppers," and a full spectrum of personality disorders among those I encountered. Moreover, I was astounded by the number of young black misguided idiots, who'd rather risk getting sent off to the penitentiary for selling reefer and crack rock than to use their intelligence to find a decent, legal way to make a living. I found this not only unbelievable, but also disheartening in light of the fact that most of us operate under the assumption that men (the aggressors) will naturally step up to the helm and take the lead in matters of community and culture.

Despite the element of entertainment, I found vexation in the fact that many black comedians create mega-wealth by poking fun at our ignorance; our inability to obtain credit; manage debt; and our distinctively African-American idiosyncrasies; and such travesties as getting abused by law enforcement; but in reality, and with all due respect, Sommore, Steve, D.L., Cedrick, and Bernie, it's no laughing matter. It is a sad commentary on the state of Black America, and my question is, can we get serious for a minute, and deliberate about what we need to do to change the economics of being black?

Thus, I began to conceptualize this book as I tried to reckon with my disillusionment with black men. Psychologically, it was comforting to me, to be able to look back and reflect on a time when men were men. Believe it or not, there was a time, when black men were just more substantive and took more of an interest in things that had the potential to make a real difference for black advancement and black culture.

They actually cared about how mainstream America perceived our community. They understood that the way mainstream America perceived us had everything in the world to do with how we were regarded as a people. My reflective state of mind led me to look at the main man in my life, my father. Recalling how he lovingly helped me to understand and sort out my experiences with racism, I was somehow able to rationalize my disillusionment with African-American men of today. I remembered how he deliberately set out to protect me, my esteem, defend my dignity, and shield me from the emotional and spiritual abuse that accompanied many of my racist experiences. Consequently, witnessing his life is what defined manhood for me.

Thus, my purpose in writing this book is to challenge contemporary African-Americans, more specifically men, through an examination of the life of one of its sons, my father, Wilkie Clark. The remembrance of his struggle to exist as a man, to gain respectability, not only from a humanistic and social perspective, but also from an economic standpoint remains at the heart of my desire to expose a unique aspect of racism as it was practiced in the South. From this angle we are forced to look at how racism oppressed and continues to oppress African-Americans, and what kinds of strategies must be embraced to break through those barriers that continue to limit our collective progress. As you read "Chief Cook & Bottle-Washer," The Unconquerable Soul Of Wilkie Clark, some questions that might arise from this examination include the following:

1. In light of the way Society had historically regarded black men, what attributes did Wilkie Clark have, that other (the average) black man didn't have?

2. Dr. Alvin Thornton poses the following question in the preface of the book: "The pressing question is why did I and others listen to him and can we convince our young Black men to hear his words and learn from his life?"
After reading "Chief Cook & Bottle-Washer," what ideas could you formulate about why the younger men of the community listened to Wilkie Clark and placed so much faith in his wisdom?"

3. If "Wilkie Clark" or any of his contemporaries, were to return from the dead to confront us about the current status of Black America, how would you explain what has happened to Black communities? Could we justify (to their satisfaction) our current status?

4. Would you describe the State of Black America as better off or worse off than at the time of Wilkie Clark's death? Why or Why not?

5. What are the things that Wilkie Clark did regularly, that black men and boys of today do not do?

6. In the absence of his own father, where did Wilkie Clark get his values and training about manhood?

7. Where can today's women, single parents, or boys seek qualitative individuals capable of helping them define their role in their respective communities?

8. As the writer describes her relationship with her father, you come to understand that to a large extent, he is at times quite demanding of her. How do you feel about fathers being demanding of their children?

9. What is your understanding of a father's expectations of his child? Do you believe that a child has an obligation to honor the expectations of his/her father?

10. What current barriers might exist that preclude black fathers (as opposed to white fathers) from effective participation in their children's lives?

11. Do you see the role of black fathers as differing from the role of fathers in general?

12. Analyze the conditions under which Wilkie Clark maintained a job and worked during the years prior to venturing into business for himself? Was there anything required of him mentally, emotionally or physically that is not required of a young working black man today?

13. What does it ultimately take for a man to sense the urgency to change the circumstances in his life that are undermining his drive and desire to progress in his own life?

14. In general, what steps are we taking, or what steps can we take, to ensure that the historical contributions of noteworthy African American achievers are not lost to our country's history?

15. For me, throughout the development and writing of this book, the overriding issue I've sought to understand is how whole communities, neighborhoods and generations of black people can allow themselves to exist under conditions of racial and economic oppression, poverty and injustice, and NOT put forth any level of effort or express any concern or initiate any level of movement to change it?

16. The foregoing question leads me to another enigma in

regard to the kind of leaders certain localities produce, that persist in their determination to keep a race of people down despite progress and advancement in other parts of our nation.

To help you better understand the book, I suggest that as you read, you occasionally come back and revisit these questions. The questions are merely intended as points to ponder, or to generate discussions with and among other African-Americans, who truly understand black problems, and are interested in finding real solutions to the real hard-core problems of African-Americans.

I am grateful for your decision to purchase and read this book. Please be aware that a portion of the proceeds for the sale of this book will benefit the Wilkie Clark Memorial Foundation, Incorporated.

I would also appreciate it if after reading this book, you would write and post a review of the content at either of the web sites listed below:

http://www.wilkieclarksdaughter.net
http://www.charlotteclarkfrieson.com
http://www.clarkmemorial.biz
http://www.lulu.com/caclarkfrieson
http://www.amazon.com

*I*nvictus

OUT of the night that covers me,
Black as the Pitch from pole to pole,
I thank whatever gods may be
For my unconquerable soul.

In the fell clutch of circumstance
I have not winced nor cried aloud.
Under the bludgeonings of chance
My head is bloody, but unbowed.

And yet the menace of the years
Finds, and shall find, me unafraid
Beyond this place of wrath and tears
Looms but the Horror of the shade,

It matters not how strait the gate,
How charged with punishments the scroll,
I am the master of my fate:
I am the captain of my soul.

William Ernest Henley
1849—1903

FAMILY

"My family has always given me a place to be,

a place to be loved in and to love."

— *Billy Dee Williams*

~ The Impetus To Write ~

Early Recollections

All my life, mama said I was always hardheaded, just like my daddy. Mama said I was rambunctious and fast, like most little girls. Mama said I never did anything the first time I was told to do it. She'd usually end up having to raise her voice — or even holler at me — before I'd obey. I had a mind of my own! Thus, it is for that very reason that she cherished and repeatedly re-told the story about the day I did obey — *for once*. So without a **shred** of doubt, it is by God's grace and divine providence that I am even here to tell this story.

When I was four years old, my daddy, still a young man at that time, was also somewhat rambunctious. He was proud of his skill in handling a weapon. In the military he had earned the sharpshooters medal for his excellent marksmanship. Why, I had even seen daddy shoot a moving target with a pistol 50 yards away! One time, he stood on our back porch, took his pistol and shot a rabbit running like a bat out of hell across our back yard.

During those years — the late 1950's — the Stewards and Trustees were hard at work trying to complete our church — Bethel Methodist Church. Daddy had been working at the church that day, and had spotted some pigeons somewhere around the church steeple. Since the church was set less than a thirty-second walk up Riley Street from our house, he ran to the house to grab his pump shotgun. As I recall, he was going to rush back to the church and shoot at the pigeons — he was merely trying to scare them away to keep them from nesting in our church steeple.

Mama said daddy was standing there, right in our living room, trying to put a shell in the shotgun... she had already spoken to daddy once...

"Wilkie, don't be messin' with that gun in the house! That shot-gun's subject to go off and kill somebody!"

But, daddy was hardheaded too, just like me....and so, he continued to wrestle around with the shotgun...

Mama said I was excitedly jumping around like a typical

four-year-old:

"Daddy got the gun! Daddy got the gun! Daddy got the gun!"

He continued to tussle with the shotgun trying to get the shell situated; the barrel of the gun was pointed down toward the floor, but somehow, the shell must have been stuck (I'm not real sure how that all works); but concerned mother that she was, mama shouted sternly, "Charlotte, move!! Move away from that sofa!"

Mama said for once, I obeyed—immediately, when she spoke.

"Pow!!!" echoed the shotgun.

Within a split second after I moved, the shotgun had fired—reverberating throughout the house, leaving a big hole in the right arm of the sofa in the very area I had just been told to move away from. There was a hole in the arm of the sofa, as big as a basketball hoop.

Daddy, still anxious to get to the pigeons, dashed out the door, and ran to the church.

But apparently, by time he got there, it dawned on him what had almost happened. In a fit of tremors, he returned home sweating and wild-eyed, and sat down, quietly and subdued. I guess he had lost his zeal to scare the pigeons after all—

"I could'a killed that gal."

I never saw that pump shotgun in my parents' home again. Don't know what ever became of it. But, I thank God that I'm here to write about it.

This book is all about my daddy. He was a professional funeral director and mortician. In the old days, folks called people who did what my daddy did "undertakers." He was the founder, owner-manager and director of our family business, Clark Funeral Home, Inc.

In retrospect, I often chuckle because daddy (and mama) could say the funniest things! I would just double over in laughter at some of their sayings!

Whenever he was agitated about something—or he thought somebody was meddling or trying to tell him how to run his business, he would roar (oh, how he could roar like a lion) loudly, "I'm The Chief Cook & Bottle Washer Here!"

We all knew what that meant.... In a sense, he was "flexing."

But, he was certainly saying he was the "shot-caller;" he had paid the cost to be the boss; so you just better back off! At the time, it was just a funny saying to me, but now at 51, I now find myself saying it too! And remembering daddy, I still chuckle — at myself!

For a long time, I wondered where this cliché' came from. And before I learned that it actually originated in the military, I presumed it to be rooted in African-American folklore because historically, that's what African-Americans did. They cooked, cleaned and washed whatever needed washing.

Vivid are my recollections that whenever Daddy said he was the *"Chief-Cook-&-Bottle-Washer,"* everybody walked on eggshells. We (meaning my mama and me) knew not to say much more; because I certainly wasn't the one who put in the long hours, poured over the books, juggled the figures trying to pay the bills and grew gray wondering how the help would be paid. I just enjoyed the fruits. I ate everyday, had gas money to go to school, had whatever else I needed, used any of the charge cards, from Sears to J. C. Penny to Berman's to Wakefield's to Mansour's whenever I needed and just went about my business. Sometimes, I'd even be a bit sneaky about it, intentionally failing to disclose my shopping escapades. Only later, when the bill arrived, would he realize that I'd been shopping. But, he never denied me. He would gently remind me that I had come into the world on "flowery beds of ease" in comparison to himself.

He is now asleep in the peace of death, but our family still operates that small family funeral home in Alabama. Having recently marked our 36th year in business, we consider ourselves successful.

Now, understand that considering ourselves successful doesn't mean that we did everything right; that we didn't make mistakes or go through difficult times. But, it means that we're still here — and we plan to be here.

We consider our longevity to be evidence of our strength. First of all, we love what we do. We are masters at providing our service firm in our belief that no one can beat us doing what we do...we just won't allow it. We love our family business. We are infatuated with the idea of business ownership. We even love the stressful and challenging lifestyle that goes along with it. And though some may disagree, there is no other business I can think of that places one under as much pressure as our unique business activity. On occasion, it becomes so stressful until it tests our limits, and becomes oppressive. Well, one might ask, how or why in the world do we put ourselves through this constant pressure? My answer simply is that we continue this operation in memory and in honor of my daddy. Even dead in his grave, he is the motivator — the force behind my day-to-day determination do what we have always done best!

This book details daddy's trials and triumphs in trying to go into business for himself in the late 1960's... a time when the mere notion of a man like him going into business for himself and succeeding was painfully remote.... impossible because of the horrible way African-Americans were treated at the time.

Now, before I get too far into it, let me say a little more about perspective, because I wouldn't want you to get the impression that this is all there was to my dad!

My daddy was a man of many talents. He was gifted in more than a few of life's domains. Now, I don't say he was gifted because he was highly educated. He wasn't. What education he had, came from the school of hard knocks and some of it from the incredibly loving, nurturing and educated woman he was married to — my mama. But there was an inherent intensity about him that made him dynamic and fiery and enabled him to inspire others with his scholarly and eloquent manner of speaking on matters of religion and any number of other subjects. Throughout life, he received numerous accolades and awards for various accomplishments throughout our community and state. He even won an award from his family, the descendants of my great grandma Lizzie Baker, who adored him and hailed him as one of the strong pillars of the family. Perhaps, at some future time, I will explore and chronicle those aspects of my daddy's life in other writings.

Despite all I witnessed of him, I am compelled to offer this as my personal testimony to the tremendous hardship daddy experienced trying to get a business off the ground against the backdrop of racism and bigotry that proliferated throughout the south.

Always Put God First

As this story unfolds, I mustn't neglect to acknowledge

daddy as a dedicated Christian. We are Methodists. We believe in the disciplines and doctrines of the Methodist Church, particularly the sacraments. Now, Daddy wasn't always in church; on bended knee; shouting or turning cartwheels down the church aisles; falling down or laying around slain in the spirit; neither was he on the roof-tops shouting his religious fidelity for all to hear; but he was a man of extraordinary faith in God. Thus, one of the things that I have always found quite an enigma, is how he could sustain any degree of faith in the face of the shameful mistreatment and degradation we often experienced as a family trying to upgrade its standard of living. Yet, he exercised and dramatized that unbelievable faith every day of his life. He actively taught me that same faith; and everyday of his life I believe he translated that faith into action. Just by his example, I became acquainted with God in the first person. Because I knew my daddy—I know Jesus. And because I knew my daddy, to this day, I trust God to govern all of my affairs. He continues to be the force and the source for everything good in my life.

Home Is Where The Heart Is?

In addition to calling it my home, I've always defined Randolph County, Alabama as the place I love to hate. Love because it is my home — hate because it is the virtual holding tank— a proverbial chamber wherein I was held captive while growing up and forming my attitudes and beliefs about life. It lies on the eastern border of the great state of Alabama, the western border of Georgia, and almost forms a perfect square, and everybody particularly white folks, talk with a distinctive and sometimes annoying "southern drawl," that is unmistakably Alabamian.

That's right; love because it's my home. Hate —because it's so confounded hot, hot hot! Smoldering hot summers and July heat waves often make the wind stand completely still. So, you can't wait for fall and winter to cover the ground with pine needles, and multi-colored fallen leaves from the generous supply of massive oaks and tall pines that proliferate all around.

It still stands today, a sparsely populated county of around 18,000 souls, comprised of five or six remote areas that can hardly be called cities, but instead hick towns and make-believe townships including Roanoke, Wadley, Wedowee, Rock Mills, Newell, Graham and Woodland, Alabama.

As you cruise along the highways, and county roads in this little corner of the world, it is clear what the people here thrive on. The area is replete with thousands of cowboys — white men in boots and cowboy hats — who drive big diesel engine 4 x 4's with the confederate battle flag proudly displayed in their rear windows. Most own huge farms — cattle farms, pig farms and chicken farms. Many even have their own private ponds and lakes. It is an agricultural county whose vast rolling hills, valleys, meadows, flatlands, forests and woodlands, acreage and well-preserved countryside can be breathtakingly beautiful for the eyes to behold, yet hideous to the souls of the 6000-or-so black men and women who, for whatever reasons can be conceived, found and still find themselves held prisoner here, and to the hundreds of black men, who've had to literally "get in wherever they could fit in." Don't need no bars; don't need no cuffs, shackles, padlocks or keys. All we have to do is show up, and it becomes the place we love to hate. Love because this is where our mamas and daddies birthed us, or brought us, and planted us. And if it was good enough for them, then it's good enough for us. Yet hate, because despite all the struggling and straining and striving, we are yet perplexed because living here, we have not gained the level of economic peace and contentment that we feel we deserve.

After all, most of us have spent our lives, working from sun to sun. Yet, we don't have much to show for all our work. Hate— because, we educate ourselves, and prepare ourselves to climb the corporate ladder yet, we are not good enough to work in anybody's bank; we can't manage anybody's store. Hate, because we are still standing in some white man or woman's shadow — unless of course, we are willing to get up before daylight in the wee hours of the morning, get in our car, and travel to places far far from here. Hate— because we grow up here; go to school here; pay tax here; go off to college, educate ourselves, yet can't come back here and live as stand-up citizens and make a comfortable, living wage. Hate, because we long to be here, but not under just any conditions or circumstances.

No, didn't need no jail cell, no bars, no padlock, no chains. We just showed up, and the captivity was on. Captivity to the ideas that were planted in our heads, that we couldn't do any better. Didn't want to do any better. Didn't care and still don't care.

I always said, and still believe it is true today that it is a place still trying hard to find its identity. Still clinging for dear life to the vestiges of the "cotton field days" many blacks have spent their entire lives trapped in cotton mills, which were only a 20th century version of the oppressive cotton fields of chattel slavery.

We live in the city limits of Roanoke, which at one time had a bustling downtown business district where everybody congregated on Saturday. Today, that downtown business district languishes almost a ghost town. And following suit, the black neighborhoods that surround this district languish also, taking their cue from those who think they know how best to run the city.

We All Had "A Dream"

Somehow as a child growing up in Randolph County, Alabama, I sensed that my parents wanted what every other American family wanted... and were working hard to accomplish it... all the tangible "things" that signal success: a good job, a good income, a nice comfortable home, a nice car to drive, nice clothes to wear, good food to eat — not just on special occasions, but every day. This wasn't a "white dream," nor was it a "black dream." It was an "American Dream" that they bought into. But, unlike our white counterparts in Randolph County, we were about 100 years behind times in that respect, and it seems like every time we tried to do something to advance or raise our standard of living, we had to take up arms and prepare to do battle in one way or another. So as time went on, one of the lessons I learned very early was that for some reason, we weren't like the rest of America. We weren't entitled to the American Dream.

I spent my entire youth and young adult life observing as my parents would readily suspend their lives and engage in all out warfare against some racial issue that was somehow preventing them from moving forward on in life; or perhaps advancing toward the objective of the moment. They would literally get caught up in the theatre of war. Then after things settled down, they would step back into their respective roles as husband, wife, mother, father, and just take up wherever they left off.

33

As a child growing up here, and observing these things, I began to develop this terrible sense of shame and guilt about who I was; what I looked like; my nappy kinky hair, thick lips and big round nose, big flat feet.... all these things. I was beginning to perceive that they disconnected me from the American dream.

Now my awareness of another interesting fact grew only after I began to develop a more mature understanding of things. That was, the black people who had to fight hardest were those who were struggling to advance and do better. Those who "stayed in their places" really didn't have to fight because they had nothing to fight for. And, they weren't seen as instigators or troublemakers by our white counterparts the way my parents were.

Much of my daddy's warfare arose from his determination to advance and upgrade his station in life. Thus his life became what seemed like a never-ending quest for liberation.

Most of the hardship he experienced in trying to start his business was orchestrated by what I concluded to be mean, cruel and heartless people who happened to be in control of the wealth; people who had the power to grant or to withhold the resources he needed to get the business started. In most cases, they chose to withhold those resources, simply because that was the order of the day. They believed themselves to be superior to people of color and daily they exercised their belief that an African American was not worthy of any of the privileges of American citizenship. Thus, they took extreme pleasure in exercising their authority and control over people of color. Daddy was just the wrong color, plain and simple.

Every once in awhile, I still experience moments of vengeance— and even entertain thoughts of somehow seeking retribution...but, I guess I'll just have to settle for the opportunity to write and tell the world about it so that it can observe the brutal, hate-ridden and cruel circumstances under which my daddy struggled to exist as a man— because much of what he went through—most of it was so painfully unnecessary, cruel and unfair to daddy. I believe that if times had just been different, he would have faired so much better. But, I know God couldn't possibly have made a mistake by allowing him to be present in the world at that particular time, so I can only conclude that his life was all a part of God's master plan, and he was placed here by God, for such times as those.

Even though as a family we were fully engaged and committed to the civil rights struggle and the effort to secure social, political and economic justice for African-Americans, this book is not really just about racism. It is a given, that racism does comprise the hideous and distorted backdrop against which his struggles occurred; and for once, I'm not really concerned about "Black Power" either; but even though daddy's blackness was a real factor in many of his tribulations, I don't think it really had a thing to do with his success versus his failure! Deep down at my "gut level" I know there was something inside of him.... something very special that even I have a hard time explaining... yet I know it's the stuff that success is made of... something that transcends any level or degree of intelligence and reaches its destination at a point of pure spirituality. Yes indeed, it's about the unbelievable way he responded and reacted to the racism and bigotry, despite all the often-emotional beatings, and indignation he took... This book is more about what is possible when DIVINE POWER MEETS PERSONAL POWER!

"I Salute You, Daddy"

More importantly, aside from just wanting the world to know what my daddy went through to start a business during that era, the real message here is that if you want to do anything badly enough; and if your heart is pure; and you want to do it for all the right reasons, no one, no earthly power can keep you from it if you have Divine Power on your side. My Daddy was unstoppable! Unbeatable! Unyielding! Yes, daddy was that "unconquerable soul" spoken of in Invictus.

One of my favorite philosophers, Confucius said it best. "Nearly 2500 years ago when intrigue and vice were rampant in feudal China, the philosopher Confucius taught principles of proper conduct and social relationships that embraced high ethical and moral standards. Confucius' teachings and wisdom were standard scholarly education for the bureaucrats who administered the country."1 He said: "Our greatest glory is not in never falling, but in rising every time we fall." I believe that it was Reverend Jesse Jackson who later said, "If you can look up, you can get up." As the new millennium dawned, a well-known gospel singer by the name of Donnie McClurkin expressed it through a song that simply said: "We fall down, but we get up...cause a 'saint' is just a sinner who fell down.... and got up." So this book is merely my salute to my daddy for looking up and getting up; and for thoroughly implanting within me such a strong belief in this precept.

My First Crush

My life with my daddy was probably the most endearing, enriching part of my life, especially with me being a girl. You see, I think that to every little girl, daddy is unequivocally the first love. He is the prince of her life, her hero, and her knight-in-shining armor; her defender and protector. I loved — NO! I adored my daddy and there is no one who can make me believe that he didn't adore me; and I was exceedingly proud to be "Wilkie Clark's Daughter." I was so impressed by my father until, even as a young adult seeking to find love, companionship and marriage, I held every man I got involved with to a strict standard. I literally looked for a man whom I could respect and esteem just as highly as I did my father, and for the same reasons I did my father.

Somehow, even as early as the 50's and 60's when I was growing up, I think daddy understood what the sting of racism and bigotry could do psychologically to a child. So, all my life, he went out of his way to tell me that I was the prettiest, most intelligent girl in town. Mama would even chime in from time to time calling me her "chocolate doll."

I thought my daddy was one good-looking, handsome black man! Daddy had a commanding presence. He was tall, energetic, attractive and articulate. He had an enthusiasm about him that was just contagious! Whenever he would talk, he could hold everybody's attention like nobody I'd ever seen! He was a spellbinding conversationalist. When conversing with him, he could carry you on the most exciting roller-coaster ride — bigger and higher than you'd find at any amusement park in the country! There were mountains and valleys in his speech as he raised and lowered his voice, modifying the tone and pitch in perfect cadence with the thought he was trying to convey; and once he got started talking, everybody else stopped to listen to what he was saying. Oh, he knew how to get his point across! He might have even been a bit hyper. As he spoke, his lively physical presence and movements engaged his often spell-bound audiences whether one or many, dramatizing the intensity of his concern. He would wave his arms, bow his head, and step from side to side; rock and reel to get his point across. He was capable of being quite dramatic when speaking! His conversation usually centered around African-Americans and the social issues that they faced. He constantly talked about black problems and sought remedies to promote black advancement of. As far back as I can remember, everybody in town seemed to know him or had heard about him.   He somehow impressed everyone he came in contact with, perhaps because he was such an incredible conversationalist — a big talker who just loved being with other people. He had an outgoing, charismatic, magnetic personality. Many people described him as "personable" and even though I haven't quite figured out what that means, I'll buy it! He was definitely extroverted; always pleasant and kept life exciting all the time!

At times, he could be quite comical. But, there were also times when he was deadly serious. He knew how to cuss. And if you (meaning me or mama) made him mad enough, or aggravated him enough, he'd cuss you out in a New York minute! That only applied to me and mama. I always interpreted it as his way of showing "tough love." We knew him well enough to know he wasn't trying to hurt our feelings; he was actually a very intense person, and oftentimes he was just venting.

You'd better believe we knew him full well enough to know there was a difference between the light-hearted Wilkie Clark and the deadly serious Wilkie Clark. I don't ever recall him cussing anybody else out. He really had a gift for focusing his attention on others, and making everybody feel special. I find it ironic when I hear people today talk about different kinds of social issues related to the family. There are probably many current venues wherein those cussin-outs would be considered abusive. But I just think people today are too thin skinned. They can't tolerate anything.

My mama and I thought nothing of it! First of all because we knew when daddy cussed one of us out, daddy was just being daddy. Interestingly enough, he was the only person I ever knew, who could cuss you out, and it not make you mad at him! As a matter of fact there were times when getting cussed out by him was quite amusing! Actually, his unique way of cussing you out had the effect of motivating you; because it didn't make you mad at him; instead, you got mad at yourself for the same thing he was cussin you out about. The cussin-out always somehow made sense. So, for me, it made me a better person. Secondly we thought nothing of it because by mama's and daddy's decree, what went on in our house, stayed in our house, so it was nobody else's business that we got cussed out. I still swear that my daddy's special "cussin outs" is just one of the things that helped make a woman out of me. I'd give anything to have one of those right now.

I' Been Workin' On The Railroad
All The Live Long Day

My earliest recollections of daddy take me back to the time when we were just an ordinary family living in Roanoke, Alabama. My daddy worked for the Atlantic Coast Line Railroad. It was a terribly dirty job! One that took him everywhere! He wasn't at home very much. I recall how, as he prepared to leave from week to week, he would mention places like Macon, Manchester, Rome and Tifton, Georgia, Birmingham, Alabama; just wherever the railroad needed a maintenance crew daddy had to go. Sometimes, he would have to go to work as far as Jacksonville, Florida. If a train de-railed during the night, he had to get up out of bed and travel to the site and work until the wreckage was cleared.

Every Monday morning, just like clockwork, he and mama would get up sometimes at two, three and four o'clock in the morning getting ready to go to work. It was always necessary to get up extra early, because depending on where they had to go that week, the colored men would have to arrive early enough to find a colored boarding house to stay in. Because they were black, they would not have the luxury of being able to check into motels and hotels the way whites could. Neither would they be able to go into cafés or restaurants to eat. In practically every city, though, there was some nice middle-aged colored woman, who ran a boarding house for coloreds needing lodging and food. Mama would always get up with daddy. She would cook a big breakfast, and while he ate, she'd be fixing him a lunch box (sometimes enough for more than one day); and he'd be putting on his over-alls. Most of the time, I'd be in bed, but I wouldn't be asleep. He would sit down and I could hear him putting on those big brogan shoes, and he would meticulously lace them all the way up. I could hear the "click-clack" of him walking back and forth on the hardwood floors in our house.

Already awakened by their scurrying back and forth through the house I would lay in bed and listen to the sounds of him getting ready to go to work. The crackling and rustling of him donning his overalls could be heard in the still of the wee hours of the morning. I didn't want to be left out so a lot of the time, I'd get up too to see him off. Matter of fact, many times, daddy would wake me up.

"Charlotte, get up and give daddy some sugar. Daddy fittin' to go to work!"

He would say it with such enthusiasm and anticipation…. like he was going to a big gala of some kind. But, that would always be a sad time for me. There was this remarkable sense that something special was missing from my life whenever he was gone, because from my very earliest awareness that I had a father in my life, there was something "spiritual" about our relationship.

His overalls would be clean, starched and pressed to perfection. It seemed like he had 50 pairs. Daddy always sent his overalls out to the laundry to be cleaned and pressed. And every day he got up and put on perfectly cleaned, starched and pressed overalls. He kept a gold pocket watch swinging from a chain in his overalls all the time. Many times, he'd be leaving out early on Monday morning not to return until late Friday evening. On those weeks, he'd have to pack a suitcase. Into the suitcase, five stiffly pressed pairs of overalls, five shirts, five pairs of boxer shorts, that mama would have pressed to perfection, creased and all, and folded neatly, and five gall shirts, five pairs of thick work socks, and some pajamas, that Old Spice after shave and cologne that I think every man in the world wore at that time, went into the suitcase. And out the door he'd be. It was done the same way every time. So much until it became like a ritual.

Every now and then, the maintenance crew would be scheduled within driving distance, and he could come home every afternoon; but those occasions were very rare. I even remember how daddy would come in after a hard day at work, and he'd step out of his overalls, and they would stand up by themselves in the middle of the floor! And we would all just be in awe over that! He worked outside in the heat all day—maintaining the railroad tracks; laying new tracks; handling cross-ties; those overalls would be full of creosote, grease and oil, but mostly sweat from a hard day's labor on the tracks with the sun beating down on him all day long.

Ol' Mr. Shannon

I remember the first time I realized that there was something special and unusual about my daddy. It was all sort of scary. My daddy worked for the Atlantic Coast Line Railroad with a gentleman from Wadley, Alabama named Willie B. James. They were good friends. Everybody called him "Smack" and he was somewhat of a leader in his community. Now, you must understand that at that time, being a leader meant that most of the white folks who were running things, depended on you to "set the tone" in the colored neighborhoods. They depended on you to laugh often when there was nothing to laugh about. They expected you to be amused all the time; and keep the colored folks calm and complacent; steer them away from intellectual discussions that might cause any uprising or unrest. No "civil rights talk." That kind of thing.

Well, Smack was a typical colored man, humble and sort of quiet, real easy going. I think Smack was some years older than daddy. One afternoon, Smack and a car load of the other men who worked with them drove all the way over to Roanoke from Wadley just to tell my mama about how daddy scared everybody to death on the maintenance crew earlier that day, by cussing out Mr. Shannon. It was as if they had to come together outside of the job, to marvel over what had happened that day!

I had often heard daddy and mama discussing old Mr. Shannon, "Ol' Shannon" daddy would call him. From my memories of the conversations, Mr. Shannon must've been a typical southern redneck. I figure he was the equivalent of the white "overseer" of slavery days. During slavery, the overseer was usually the only white man in the fields. His task was to stay out in the field with the slaves and keep the slave master's "whip" handy making sure they worked, and stayed in their places, didn't talk too much, and didn't get out of hand. No uprisings could be tolerated! I surmised that the only difference was that instead of an actual horse whip,

Shannon's mouth took the place of the "whip."

As mama sat listening intently, Smack told her how every-body had been out there in the heat of the day, just working hard... real hard. Daddy was sweating, it was hot and they were all tired. And this man, "Shannon" was busy doing nothing but pacing back and forth, chewing tobacco, spittin, and running his mouth...

"....Niggers ain't this; Niggers ain't that; a ole sorry nigger don't want nothing; niggers don't want to work," and so on.

I remember how my mama was on the edge of her rocking chair gazing right into his mouth, as Smack related the day's hap-penings to her. Judging from the expression on her face, and the way she fixed her eyes as he talked, you'd have thought she could see all the way down his throat...

"Ol' Shannon just kept on a-running his mouth, and I could tell Wilkie was getting hot wid'im. The mo ole Shannon talked, the hotter Wilkie was git'n. Ole' Wilkie got to sweatin' out dare in all dat heat....adda while dat Wilkie thew his tools down, and unloaded on ole Shannon with both barrels! We all thought Wilkie was gonna have a heart attack or stroke out there in all dat heat."

Smack said they all thought for a moment that daddy had turned into a vicious animal of some kind....said he turned into a wolf, slobbering and foaming at the mouth, and his eyes got all bloodshot, and turned red as coals of fire. He recalled that as daddy screamed at Shannon, he could see the big jugular vein all blown up on both sides of his neck, all the way up to his temples. Using language that I dare not repeat here, and with all the viciousness and voracity he could muster, he spewed at Shannon with the force of an erupting volcano...

"Goddammit! I've had just about a-goddam-'nough of your mouth!! You don't know what in the hell you talkin about!! Man, what in the hell you mean....talkin about niggas being lazy and sorry and no-good, and not wanting to work?"

In a voice that took on the quality of thunder roaring and lightening striking, again he fired:

"Who in the hell do you think laid all this track through here.....I want to know who do you think hauled all these cross-ties out here and drove all these spikes and spread all this gravel out here — all up and down this goddam railroad track?.... My ances-tors!!...that's who ran this s-o-b — all the way across this country, out in the rain, in the cold, in the snow, in the heat of the summer time, and still had to listen to such shit as what you talking now! This whole goddam country was built on the backs of dem "niggas" — dem same dam niggas you talking 'bout so sorry — my ancestors; my forefathers! Dammit, the longest day I work out here wid you, you bet'n not never let me hear you talkin' 'bout a sorry nigga. What 'n the hell is you talking about?!! What in the hell is you doin?!!"

Smack James said, about the time this all got started, it was lunchtime, so he and some of the other crew had already stopped work to eat their lunch. But daddy in his industrious, busy way was still at it; and when he got wound up and let go on ole Mr. Shannon, Smack said he almost lost his sandwich. He was scared to death! He had never seen such a side of my daddy — loud, aggressive and vicious.

Mama and I never doubted the truth of what was told, because we knew that when daddy was truly mad, there was a thunderous quality about his voice that could frighten either the bravest or the whitest of men. And he didn't care — really! The mild-mannered, easy-going Wilkie Clark had transformed into a deadly rattlesnake, his fiery words became the venom that spewed forth from his mouth as he struck back in defense of his dignity! None of them had ever seen this side of daddy. As they reported to my mama that evening, they all marveled, "Ol' Wilkie sho got ol' Shannon tole today, yeah he did!"

But, all those "colored" men on the maintenance crew were scared to death, and they steered clear of daddy for quite some time after that. They probably thought he was crazy! See at that time, a "colored" man just didn't talk to a white man that way; especially your boss man — the man that handed you your pay-check.

Somehow, I knew even back then that my daddy just didn't belong there. He knew it too. He just couldn't hold his peace. Smack said he was sure daddy would get fired that day. But, he said, "Ole Shannon didn't do nothin' but drop his head and walk off."

I remember only too well what my daddy said:

"Hit ain't a dam thing they can do to me for speaking my belief. He spoke his. Furthermore, I'm a dam good worker and I know it. I never seen anybody that can do good work, that can't find work to do." That was just one of many railroad stories that I heard about my daddy. I thank God for allowing my daddy to survive that incident. God was good to daddy out there on that dangerous railroad. He watched over him day in — day out. Over his eighteen years there, he survived some near fatal mishaps. There, he sustained several serious injuries for which he was never compensated. I remember him being severely burned around the bottom of one of his legs while working on the rail gang after one train wreck; and I clearly recall him telling how he came within an inch of losing his life at another wreck-site, when a derailed train car almost crushed him to death. I also remember him having to have surgery on his left knee after being injured on the job, but I give God all the glory for sparing his life. That's why I know my daddy was touched by the hand of God.

The Pittsburgh Courier: Reading Was A Key Element Of Family Time

Working on the rail gang was back-breaking manual labor. In spite of all, daddy was faithful to that job— despite the fact that the work imposed a severe test of both bodily and spiritual strength. He would always say, "You have to work easy when you have your head in the lion's mouth; once you get it out, you can tell him to go to hell." So, I guess his head was in the lion's mouth. He left home every day; and we could always predict his return with amazing accuracy. I can remember as a child no more than six or seven years old, running out to the car to meet him, and him picking me up — holding me under my arms, and tossing me up and down repeatedly. Then, he'd give me a big bear hug and a big sloppy kiss on the jaw. And all was well.

Most days, he'd head straight for the bathroom; take a bath; come out smelling so good! Then, he'd settle down with newspaper in hand and he and mama would orally review the news. They were both avid readers. When they got to reading, you would think a political debate was going on between the two of them, but that is how they kept abreast of the issues affecting black folks at that time. They were particularly fond of The Pittsburgh Courier, which was a black newspaper that had to travel all the way from Pittsburgh, Pennsylvania to Alabama. A very good friend of the family, Horace Whittaker delivered The Courier every week, and when Horace brought The Courier, mama and daddy would literally scramble over it; then whichever one of them got hold of the paper first, would divy out the sections to the other. They'd read that paper from cover to cover. Often, mama would have to help daddy with the words, but he would read those articles aloud, and then, they'd discuss, paraphrase and interpret what the article was saying.

After I got older, I learned why reading the Courier was so important to them. A man by the name of Edwin Harleston started publishing The Pittsburgh Courier in 1907. Harleston was a security guard, but he wanted to write. Three years later, Robert Lee Vann became the editor-publisher, treasurer, and legal counsel for the paper. Under Vann's direction, The Courier gained national prominence and became the country's most widely circulated black newspaper with a national circulation of almost 200,000. The Courier sought to empower blacks economically and politically, and almost everybody who was anybody, wrote for it, and read it. The editor(s) were continuously spearheading vehement protests and campaigns against institutional racism. In the 1930's the paper began a nationwide protest against the "Amos n' Andy daily radio serial. It helped influence black voters to shift their political allegiance away from the Republican Party and to support the Democratic candidate, Franklin D. Roosevelt. From it's inception in the early 1900's The Courier hosted the works of such greats as Marcus Garvey, W.E.B. Dubois and James Weldon Johnson. In later years, Elijah Muhammed wrote a column. Zora Neale Hurston was hired to cover the murder trial of Ruby J. McCollum. By the 1960's the civil rights movement had really started to gain momentum. The Courier bore witness to many of the events. With such lively figures as Malcom X, Dr. Martin Luther King, Jr., and others, they had strong motivation to read this paper.

Often, there was lively conversation and sometimes even argument, about what the NAACP was doing or about people like Dr. Martin Luther King, Jr., Stokley Carmichael and H. Rap Brown; or organizations like the NAACP, The "Black Muslims," SNCC, and every issue imaginable. Sometimes, they agreed; sometimes, they didn't but they seemed to really enjoy each other's company while doing it.

Quality Time With The Kids

Other afternoons, daddy would be in more of a playful mood. In our neighborhood, there were lots of other kids growing up. On the north end of our street were the Walkers, Deitre and Arnita, living on the old Riley place. Then later after they moved out, the Esters who didn't have any kids our ages; then there was our house, then, the Rossers. They were raising Jeffery who was not their child by birth, as their own son. Everybody in the neighborhood called him "Polly." The next family was Ms. Ella Mae Traylor's family: Vonzella, Dorothy, Joe, Carolyn and Virgil. Then there was Harry and Carrie Winston, who didn't have any children of their own, but who had a niece, Judith Carole, who visited often. About midway the street was the Watkins' family, with lots of girls who were several grades ahead of most of us, and Henry (LuLu) Watkins who was just a little older. Also, there was William and Minnie Bell Winston who had an army of kids, not only of their own, but their grandchildren, great grandchildren, nieces, nephews, and you name it they had it. On the south end of the street were the Watkins, the Johnsons, Coley and his older sister Jean, the Heards who didn't have any children of their own, and the Joneses, Ronnie, Carole, and Linda. Everybody would joke about the Winston kids because there were so many of them. We would say they had to sleep in shifts, because there were so many children in the house; or they had a house but they needed a barracks.

Daddy treated them all just like they were his own, and they admired and respected him too. All the kids called daddy "Mr. Wilkie." Seems like all the kids everywhere knew who he was, too. I cannot count the afternoons when what seemed like every kid in the neighborhood would be in our yard playing softball, or whatever the game of the moment was.

Daddy would come in after a hard day at work, take his bath, change clothes, then next thing you know, he'd be out there in the yard pitching balls to us, or either batting balls with his big strong railroad arms and have all of us kids running all over the yard and out in the fields like rabbits chasing down his home run hits! We were just kids, and oh how we would marvel at how hard and how far he could hit that ball! When the ball met the bat, it sounded like an explosion!

And we would all marvel, "Oooohweeee!"

Then we'd take out running after the ball. We'd swiftly return to throw him another pitch, just to have the same thing happen again. Sometimes, we'd spend the entire afternoon just chasing daddy's hits. I wouldn't take nothing for that part of my life.

During those days, I remember being a very happy child. Because daddy and mama worked very hard, seems like we had so little time together as a family, but the time we did spend together was always precious. They both kept me well entertained. They taught me how to be content as an only child, and how to entertain myself when I wasn't in their company. Mama and daddy encouraged me to spend time alone in my room, reading. Anything they wanted me to know about, they bought me a book about it, and told me to read. That included the things that were difficult for them to talk to me about.... facts of life, like getting my period, and even sex and venereal diseases, and such. They could find books about every subject.

Otherwise, we had amusing and interesting conversations, went joy riding on Sunday afternoons, visited with other family, friends and acquaintances and just enjoyed our family time together.

Our neighbors and good friends were the Burneys and the Rossers, Mr. and Mrs. H.T. and Susie Rosser, whom everybody called "Miss Sue." They were also my god-parents. They lived on the opposite side of the street, just a rock-throw from our house. They were all very chummy. H.T. was known all over town as "Lightening." He was also known for his ability to make money. He had a reputation for not being able to read a lick, but folks said he really had the knack for making money. They said that everything he touched turned to money. He had a taxicab business in town. There were three or four black men who were partners in this taxicab business: Lightening, Mr. Booker Williams, and Mr. Charlie Cameron.

"Goin' To Town"

On Saturday mornings, everybody looked forward to "going to town," where they would meet and greet each other. "Going to town" usually coincided with payday, or first & third of the month check day. Because Roanoke was a mill-town, Thursday was universal payday. But, everybody usually went to town on the Saturday morning after payday. Mama loved going to town! And because she couldn't drive herself (she never really got comfortable with driving, and never got a license), everybody in the family had to go to town to take mama to do her shopping for the house.

While the colored women did their shopping, the colored men usually would congregate on the sidewalks, and exchange pleasantries. There would be vigorous laughter and loud talking. I often got the feeling that they talked loudly for the benefit of the white bypassers — so they would know they weren't being conspired against. We had a busy downtown! One of mama's favorite stores was IGA, which later became Super Value. As we traveled down Main Street northwest from "East Roanoke" toward the downtown business district, this was the first store on the right in the first downtown block. The good thing about this store is that they had their own "store parking" lot adjacent to the store, just south of the block. But it was tight parking. Often, daddy and I would sit out in the car, while mama went in the store. I don't know why it was, but I just hated going with mama to shop for groceries. It took too long! Well, in this block, there were a lot of interesting stores — every one of them open for business. There were beauty salons for the white women on both sides of the street — but not for us. The white women could walk into the beauty salons and have their hair done, and as we walked down the sidewalk, we could see them sitting there in the salon chairs or under the hair driers. In this block, we also had the Martin Theater; there were two or three nice shoe stores; we even had a Belk Gallant's; and a Top Dollar Store. There was another store called "McConnell's." There were two banks downtown— one was the Commercial Bank of Roanoke, and the other was the City Bank and Trust Company. On the other side of downtown Roanoke, there was a City Pharmacy, where they had a very interesting soda fountain. All the white kids would be in there sitting up on stools, and eating hotdogs, sandwiches, and drinking sodas. Although the smell of the food, and the sight of other children drinking sodas always beckoned me, I had always been warned that I was NEVER to go in there.

There was a five and dime store. It was the ONLY place

47

downtown where you could get water. But, we always had to drink out of the colored fountain. It was ugly, and beaten up. Although I don't remember every detail, mama always told me that I was such a rambunctious and inquisitive child that I would always embarrass her in the store by demanding to drink the "white water." She said from the time I was a little girl, she had always had to pull me by the arm, and practically drag me out of that store— yelling and screaming bloody murder, because I was determined to drink the "white water;" and she didn't want to disturb the white folks, or cause a scene in that store.

At the end of the block, there was a quaint little café called "Sam Robunkas' Café." Everybody talked about how good the food was in that café. And, if you happened to be downtown Roanoke on a breezy day, the breeze would carry the tempting aroma of the variety of southern dishes they were serving there. The food smelled so inviting that one could only imagine what was behind the forbidden front doors of the cafe. I had never had a chance to eat any of it, because they definitely did not serve coloreds. If coloreds wanted to eat Robunkas' food, they had to go to a dilapidated area around back, and request their food and then carry it out. But, they couldn't sit in the restaurant and eat. For that reason, we didn't do ANY eating out. We went grocery shopping, and mama cooked and we ate at home. Somehow, I don't think I ever fully got out of my system, the desire to one day get a chance to eat the food at Robunkas' Café. I guess it could be thought of as some kind of a pathological "forbidden fruit" syndrome that I experienced.

I never shall forget this one particular Saturday morning, when I was about nine or ten years old. Mama wanted to do her routine shopping ritual. We knew all her stops by heart. The first was IGA, so daddy drove into the parking lot, but this time, we all went in the store with mama. As mama was checking out, I walked on out of the store and headed toward my daddy's Pontiac. Daddy had a 1957 Fire Chief Pontiac. That two-toned blue car was his absolute pride and joy! On this day Mama and daddy were still lingering in the store, waiting for the groceries to be bagged. So, already out the door, as I got in sight distance of the car, I saw a white man in an old beat up truck back into daddy's car.

In my rambunctious way, I got real excited and started yelling...

"Daddy! Daddy! Come quick! That man in that truck hit your car!"

Daddy had finally come out of the grocery store, and was walking toward the car. Mama was yet lingering in the store. The man then pulled forward, and started to drive off.

But I was still yelling and screaming!

"You hit my daddy's car!"

Daddy slowly walked around his car, and was visually inspecting it, unaware that by this time, the white man had put his truck in park, and gotten out with a double-barrel shotgun in hand, as if he was fully prepared to open fire on both of us!

The gunman ordered me to shut my mouth...

"You just better shut up, and git in that goddam car!"

I was startled! And even though I was a mere child when this happened, I was old enough to remember the look of utter fear on my daddy's face, and the feeling I had that this man would have killed both of us, and probably walked away from the situation "Scott free."

I recall that incident with great hesitancy, because it was probably one of the most revealing experiences of my life. It revealed to me, just how little value was placed upon black life at that time, and how easy it would've been for both of us to be gunned down over a mere incident we didn't even cause. It revealed to me how little concern there would have been for our safety, and how nobody in that parking lot that day would have willingly bore witness to anything that might have happened that day.

That was a typical Saturday morning in Roanoke, Randolph County Alabama, for a black family trying to live life as any normal family would — only to have that life complicated by such perplexing experiences as this.

When I reflect back on this event, I know my daddy did all he could do under the circumstances to protect himself and me. He didn't say one word to the gunman. But he very calmly said to me,

"It's alright honey — he didn't hurt anything."

This was the only thing that de-escalated the angry white gunman. I thank God for sparing both of us on a day that could have turned tragic.

Time To Water The Street

In addition to being the day to go to town, Saturday was also the day to work in the yards and water the streets. It seemed to me that my daddy was the inspiration for everybody's pride in our street. Despite simple houses, outdoor toilets, and dirt roads, everybody took pride in keeping the neighborhood nice and clean. Everybody planted grass, and it was almost as if they competed with each other to have the prettiest yards. Since we lived on a dirt street, to calm the dust and dirt, Daddy and Lightening would stand outside in front of their houses, and turn on their hose pipes, and shoot water all up and down the street. At that time, if a car drove by, it stirred up enough dust keep you dusting for days. Dust would fly all into the house, and everywhere. I remember as a youngster, how we could just sit in the house, and see the dust particles flying through the beaming sun rays. The dampness helped keep dust and dirt from flying into the house. I can just imagine as daddy and Lightening stood there with their hoses, shooting water up and down the street, he was probably thinking, "One of these days, we'll be like everybody else and live on a paved street where we won't have to waste all our precious water this way." By time they got through watering the street, the sun would be going down.

Sunday School

Every Saturday night, "Lightening," would come to our house to review the Sunday school lesson—just as regular and predictable as clockwork.

He was a member of First Baptist Church, and Daddy was a member of the Bethel Methodist Church, and not having a mature orientation to the way things worked, I always had a hard time trying to figure out how and why the Sunday School lessons at both churches were the same! They would get their Adult Sunday school books out. Both books had different backs and different titles, but they had the exact same stuff in them. These two fellas would read aloud and go over the lessons, reading every scripture, and just generally have their own living room lesson going, just the two of them.

Since they were all so chummy, sometimes when they'd start, mama would get up and walk out to "Lightening's" house and sit on the front porch with Miss Sue. But, sometimes, mama would stay at home and keep sitting in her rocking chair while daddy and "Lightening" read the Sunday School lesson. I think she tried hard not to get involved in the lesson but the school teacher in her couldn't help it. Every now and then, one of them would make a horrible mistake in reading, and she just couldn't help but correct them. At times, the mis-pronunciation would be so flawed, until I could catch mama snickering out of the corner of my eye. They'd look up at her, correct the error and keep on reading. The lesson would sometimes last way into the night.

But, I finally figured it out. At that time, neither of them were very good oral readers, but I think daddy could probably read a lot better than "Lightening." Both of them wanted to be able to join in the discussion at Sunday school and comment on the lesson the next morning. So they spent every Saturday night rehearsing and preparing themselves. Now, it goes without saying, that after several years of this Saturday-night ritual, they both got pretty darn good at all of it — reading, understanding the scriptures and discussing the lesson.

I do believe that it was during these sacred moments of studying the word of God, that daddy made a philosophical discovery that would influence the way he behaved toward others, for the remainder of his life; and that was the question posed by Cain in the book of Genesis: "Am I my brother's keeper?" It was probably there in our living room, at 217 Riley Street, when I was a mere child, that both Daddy and Lightening Rosser came to the conclusion that most assuredly, it was God's divine and perfect will, that they were destined to become their brother's keeper.

Proud To Be Wilkie Clark's Daughter

I remember how as a child I would just beam all over because everybody in town would always say, "You Wilkie Clark's daughter, ain't you?"

Or if they weren't sure of who I was, they would say, "Ain't you Wilkie's daughter? I thought that was you! Your name is Charlotte! Yeah, I know you...."

And they would be swift to conclude with, "Your daddy is such a fine man. And he is such a nice person!"

The way people would say that just made me feel so important! As a child, I don't really think I understood the significance of that. But, later I began to realize that throughout the African-American villages of my community, I got that kind of treatment because people loved and respected my daddy, before he ever went into a business of any kind. It made me proud just to be his kid.

But I Did Have a Mama Too

At this point, I certainly feel a need to make one thing crystal clear, because I know me. When I get to talking about my daddy, you'd think I didn't have a mama! I don't want anybody reading this to think that I didn't have a mama. But, indeed I did! In her peculiar way, Mama was just as bright and magnetic as daddy was. But, she was packaged differently. She had a totally different set of gifts. Yes, Mrs. Hattie Lee Peters Clark! Needless to say, I was also called "Mrs. Clark's daughter," too. And it always amazed me how everybody knew me — even if I didn't know them. Better not be seen out somewhere misbehavin. Heck no! Mama and Daddy would get the news before I could hit the front door! To close friends, I was "Pete & Wilkie's daughter." I just know it felt awfully good to be somebody important's daughter. To know that I was somebody special ONLY because of who my daddy was — that was just too cool!

Needless to say, I had no problems whatsoever with my own self-esteem. I am in sympathy with the numerous children today who will spend their lives in a continuing battle for identity because they have not enjoyed the rewards and blessings that come with an endearing relationship with their fathers.

With the deterioration of the "family," as I've always understood it; with so many youngsters burdened by issues of sexual abuse, mistreatment and neglect, physical abuse, poor self-esteem, poor or NO self-concept, it has always been difficult to understand how any of these issues could exist. When I was growing up, my daddy showed great strength of character and he passed that on. He took his role as husband and father to the extreme. My daddy

52

was a determined man. To amplify how strong he was in this determination, he would often use humor. He would comment to all our friends and acquaintances

"I done told Hattie Lee, when I die, she better bury me ride out dare 'side dat front walk; dat way, whoever come to dis here house will still have to come by me..."

Everybody would get a big laugh out of that, but right now, remembering that joke makes me wonder if I should have buried him there on our home place! He was determined to wear the pants in his house; to be the bread-winner; and the "shot-caller;" in essence, he was determined to be respected. He took care of the business for the family. No matter what predicament the family was in, or what its financial position was, daddy was commander. He often remarked to his friends that, "I bet'n not never hear tell of Hattie Lee going nowhere, askin' no white man for no money....if she need to borrow some money from the bank, tell me — I'll go ask for the money! What'n the hell kind of man lets his wife run around beggin other men for money?"

Whenever he uttered these oft-repeated words, he would say it with such force and vigor, until we'd dare not violate this principle. He made the money and brought home his check and turned it over to my mother insisting that she be meticulous in keeping the bills paid and running the house — not that mama didn't work; she was a professional woman too!

Mama was a school teacher. She was the coordinator for the elementary education department at the Randolph County Training School, and had the respect of all of her colleagues. But, despite the fact that she had more formal education that he did, daddy still commanded respect from both of us. And, he carried himself in such a compelling way that we couldn't help but to respect him. Mama took care of me, and him; she cooked; and she supported him in his endeavors. He commanded his post as the leader in the family. At the same time, there was a delicate balance between commanding and reciprocating; because, he gave us the same degree of respect that he demanded from us.

By daddy's decree, he was the "spokesman" for the family. Even though mama may have had more formal education, and even if he didn't know quite what to say, he was determined to learn the proper and most appropriate way to address ANY issue confronting our family and speak with authority about that issue. He was protective of us; our home; our dignity. He was a man of great faith, and it is by his fatherly influence, that I, too am suffused with the same degree or perhaps even a greater degree of faith in a higher power who engineers all life's affairs.

So, With My Pen, I Honor You

So, it is with much love and respect, that I dedicate this book in memory of my daddy, the late "Wilkie Clark" — unusual name for an unusual man. He was born March 8, 1920; and he died on July 29, 1989, at 69; and in the years since his death, I like to refer to him, reverently as "The Late Wilkie Clark." Even as he sleeps I hold him in the highest esteem, because he earned my utmost respect. Wilkie Clark; my father....my first love.....my friend.....my mentor.

SELF-DETERMINATION

"If I didn't define myself for myself, I would be

crunched into other people's fantasies for me,

and eaten alive."

—*Audre Lorde*

Background

In this section, I want to set the back-drop for this writing. It is important to me for you to understand why I am writing it; and what my mission is.

Around 1987, I was 33 years old. That's about the time my mama started talking to me about things she wanted me to do when she and daddy would no longer be alive. In my mind, as I often did, I pondered how in the world she thought I would be able to accomplish all of these things single-handedly — after all, I was an only child. Even though I was married and had two elementary school-age children, the family was very small, so I often lamented the fact that after mama's and daddy's deaths, my allies would be few. As they grew older, I began to foresee my future fate. I often wondered how I would make it. How I'd handle the six other properties they had accumulated; how I'd single-handedly manage a funeral home business. From time to time, I resentfully would chide my parents for sentencing me to life as an only child. Being their daughter was difficult because they were both very demanding.

As a youngster, I spent a lot of time with daddy, and enjoyed being with him. I wanted to follow him everywhere he went unless he specifically told me that I couldn't go. Then, I'd be mad. He didn't want me to be one of those prissy, frilly girls, prim and proper, or a little fragile flower. He wanted me to be tough; being around him made me that way. He taught me things like how to ride my bicycle; by age eleven I could drive a stick and could drive his old big truck almost as well as he could. I could do things like mow the grass, and stuff like that. Mama wanted me to be with her in the house, doing "girlie" things, but that just wasn't me. When mama demanded I come in and help her do dinner or clean the house, I'd get so mad! I'd pout for a while, but then I'd hurry in and get it done so I could spend time with my daddy; hanging out with him shaped my attitudes and beliefs for life. He seemed to be totally fearless in every situation, and little by little, under his strong influence, I became fearless, too.

Tug-Of-War

They both demanded perfection from me. Knowing that we had a family business, I often felt like they played "tug-of-war" with me. I felt I had to try do what mama wanted me to do, just to please her; but also I felt I had to do whatever daddy wanted me to do, to please him; and try to stay out of the middle; because it always seemed like each was jealous of any attention that the other got from me. Can you imagine that? Two parents jealous of the attention the other is getting from their only child!

That's just the way it was. I went to school and got a Masters Degree in Education. That was for mama, who was a teacher. She loved teaching and emphatically believed that was all a black girl could aspire to at that time. But, I worked my butt off at Clark Funeral Home from the time I was 15 years old; and in my early twenties, I was licensed in Alabama as a funeral director; and by the time I was 27 years old, I could single-handedly do everything that had to be done, and was practically running the funeral home on my own. That was for daddy. For as long as I could remember, he indoctrinated me that no black person could get ahead working on a job for somebody else.

I believe that from a very early age, daddy understood that true liberation for the black man, was inextricably tied to economic liberation. As long as the black man had to depend on the white man for his livelihood, his food, his sustenance, his shelter, he would never be free to pursue his civil rights. He felt you had to make your own way; you had to create and seize your own opportunities, because the world was not about to give you anything. He preached economic independence and declared it every time he had the opportunity; so for that reason, I fell in love with entrepreneurship. As a matter of fact, he indoctrinated me so thoroughly until I became a sucker for practically every opportunity that came along . And there were lots of them! I could see promise in every one! You name it, I joined up: Amway, Shaklee, Bee Pollen, WeCare, Herbalife, Dick Gregory; and you know who my best good customer and cheerleader was? You've got it....daddy! Not only was he my customer, he was my success coach; and he'd want to tell me how to promote my product. He'd say, "This is what you've got to do to sell your stuff... now, here's your sales pitch...." And he could sell anybody almost anything. It seemed like he had a natural ability for understanding what it took to get people to commit to buy things. Without spending even a day in a business school, he somehow had mastered the psychology of selling! He was just gifted in that way! He also understood the reverse psychology of selling. He used to always tell me, "anytime you hear a salesman talking, he's talking for himself...." "You have to think BEFORE you buy."

It is ironic, that he never used that ability to profit, though I truly believe he could cultivated his skills and profited, if he had wanted to. Well, ultimately following the beaten path, I sought to perfect myself as a funeral director, because he mentored me in funeral service. As far as my orientation to the funeral home business, he and mama both literally took me in hand like a piece of clay, and molded me into exactly what they thought a young lady funeral director should be. They squeezed, mashed, mauled me, groomed me, dressed me; they taught me how to walk and talk; how to act; what to say; more importantly what not to say... I mean, I had to rehearse my scripts, until it literally melded with me.

Amazingly, mama and daddy were both as different as night and day. Mama was all about education. She really did not believe in business — especially if you were black. She felt that teaching was the most secure thing a young (black) person could do at that time. Mama was seven years older than daddy, and I believe that being older, her memories of the depression coupled with her experiences with racism and bigotry had somewhat limited her thinking. But, daddy— NO WAY! I was going to go to Howard University, study law, and come back to Roanoke, and join him and liberate our people! My dream was to become a journalist, because I loved writing, and it was a skill that just came naturally to me. Mama, in the "preachy" way she would often talk to me, would say:

"Charlotte, you don't see no black nappy-headed girls on that television giving the news; I want you to go to school and take something where you can get a job and take care of yourself; have a check coming in every month... children are being born every day. Somebody's going to have to teach them.... there will always be a demand for teachers; you are going to be as poor as Job's turkey listening to your daddy's foolishness about going in business."

Now, I never understood how poor "Job's turkey" was, but I always kept her words in the back of my mind, and I definitely didn't want to be that way, (whatever that was).

A Philosophy Of Education

Daddy despised educators — not that he personally disliked any of them. But he hated hypocrisy and felt that many (or most of them) demonstrated an attitude of hypocrisy. He often expressed to my mother how black teachers talked a good game, but did not practice what they preached. He thought that with all their polish, education and knowhow, they had an essential role to play in the civil rights movement; but few would ever volunteer to help. When OR IF they did, it would always be "on the down-low." Often times, they would pay their money for a membership in the NAACP. But, they would always conclude the transaction with, "I want to help, but you can't let anybody know I'm a member." Or, they would come up with some other lame excuse for not wanting to be openly involved.

Even as a youngster, I fully understood —and somewhat agreed with his thinking, and often wondered why black educators seemed to be so afraid of civil rights. Equal rights for blacks just made so much sense to me, and seemed so right and so fair until I couldn't understand why people didn't want to participate and help my daddy. His philosophy was that black teachers had no backbone.

He would say, "They have all that education —and no backbone —no guts." He said they were "Uncle Toms" who were subservient and subordinate to their "Negro" principals, who were also "Uncle Toms," because they quietly and reservedly worked in inferior schools, and would not stand up and speak out against the deplorable conditions in the black schools. But, I understood that he said those things because he was a strong civil rights leader but could never persuade many black educators to get involved in the movement for equality. He would often mock the male teachers of that day saying things like:

"...They have their big fine degrees, and their fine houses and furniture, but I bet you couldn't put nare one of 'em in a shit-gun and shoot 'em to the City Council Meeting or to the Board of Education."

(I'd be thinking to myself, "In a shit-gun!! What in the hell kind of gun is a shit-gun?"

Mama would scold him by saying, "Wilkie, you know those teachers can't go over there to that school raising hell and that's where their pay is coming from! Now, you know better than that!"

Mama and I would just laugh it off -- because we knew he didn't mean any harm. He was just frustrated, because civil rights was a huge burden that he took to heart, and he needed a lot of help that was very often lacking. But, I also believe that this only served to further validate his philosophy that because they were held in captivity by the mere necessity to hold on to the source of their livelihood, they were literally muzzled and couldn't afford to speak out on any issues. So, they learned how to be subservient and accepting of whatever was dished out to them. His attitude was most evident as I prepared to receive my Masters Degree in Education from Auburn University. Several years earlier, I had completed an undergraduate degree in Special Education for children with behavior disorders. In the course of my frequent discussions with him about various aspects of my training, I could tell that he just didn't think much of it at all. Recalling a youngster who had attended school in a nearby system, he had once commented, "There was a young'un over there at the school couldn't nobody do nothin wid... They eventually made him the shit-house captain! Dat was the only way they could do anything wid 'em. Now you tell me, who in the hell want to teach somebody like that?"

I had always gotten a big laugh out of that story. But here I was about to receive my M.Ed. I was in my early 30's and as we readied ourselves to drive down to Auburn's campus for my commencement exercises, Daddy confronted me:

"Now that you have earned your Masters Degree, what are you going to do with it?"

Knowing him as I did, I knew he was trying to provoke my thinking in some way, but I was totally caught off guard. At that time, I was working as a teacher for the public school system in nearby LaGrange, Georgia; I replied,

"I'm going to get a raise."

"How much of a raise are you going to get?"

"About a thousand dollars."

Daddy hit the ceiling! You would have thought I had "burnt up a church and killed a baby!" (another one of his sayings). But, I was surely in for another one of his cussin-outs.

He yelled, "What in the hell did you say? A thousand dollars? You are a dam fool! You dun spent all that dam money runnin up and down the road — back and forth to Auburn University to get a Masters degree and all you are going to get out of it is a thousand dollars? Hell! What in the hell did you go down there for? When you get a Masters Degree you s'pose to have some sense. Getting a Masters Degree means you s'pose to be able to think on a higher level than the average person; I wouldn't let nobody know I had spent all that dam money to go to a public school and get in a dam prison camp! That's all you're in! ...spendin your time with a bunch of hoodlums that ain't gonna amount to nothin! You got a Masters degree and you still got to punch a dam time clock; you still got to jump when somebody else says to jump! You ain't bettered yourself worth a dam. If you had any sense, me and you could jump right down there under that hill (meaning the funeral home) and we could make that little $25,0000 a year you making. But, you listenin to yo Ma!"

I now believe when he scolded me that day, the part that he did not say was:

"You have let me down. My dream for you was to go to Howard University, major in Political Science, get a Law Degree, and come back home, set up a law office in the Funeral Home and help me in the fight to liberate black people in Roanoke, Alabama."

I wasn't the least bit intimidated by that cussin out. As a matter of fact, my eyes were opened. See, I was so well indoctrinated by then that I fully understood his line of reasoning; and I actually felt ashamed of myself for "thinking inside that box." He actually saw the relative gains afforded by my obtaining my M.Ed. as nothing because I was still held captive. I really felt that I had let him down. Because I wholeheartedly knew what he was saying was TRUE!

Daddy was an optimist. Mama was cynical. Daddy was altruistic; mama was very cautious and prudent. Daddy was a philanthropist; mother was frugal. Daddy is the one who put the "fight" in me. I never shall forget, when I was about to graduate from high school, he told me:

"Yo teachers tell you that when you graduate, the world is waiting for you with outstretched arms. They don't tell you that there's a hammer in each hand waiting to knock hell out of you...."

Mama wanted you to foresee every pitfall in life, before you got to it, so you could anticipate all the detours and follow the smooth route. Daddy was a dreamer; mama was well grounded — sometimes too well grounded! She was from Missouri. You had to "show her the money!" It is amazing to me how these two very different individuals blended so well and captured my heart. I was so much in love with both of them that I adjusted my life and made all kinds of personal sacrifices to please them— just because I was in love with them.

The Promise

Now, as if my life hadn't already been hard enough, just trying to live in the world and please both of them at the same time, here she was again, telling me what I must do —had to do — after their deaths:

"I don't care what you do, Charlotte, but, don't let Randolph County forget your daddy; the sacrifices he's made; the extraordinary deeds he's done in the interest of the black constituency in Randolph County. You'll have to keep the NAACP going. I want you to build that Wilkie Clark Community Center...."

Didn't she know that when she and daddy were no longer on earth, I'd be left alone? Who in the world would help me? How did she expect me to accomplish all these things? She was being unreasonable! But, the way she spoke, she was so sincere, resolute in her confidence that I would carry out all these motherly decrees, edicts and mandates. Well, little did I know at the time she was talking to me, that the next two years would bring both their deaths and departure.

I knew and fully understood why she felt that way. I felt that way too. You see, my daddy was a hero of sorts in our community. Especially between the 50's, and late 1980's. To us, his was one of those untold stories of ordinary African-Americans doing extraordinary things in his own community; going about the business of breaking down racial barriers in the "dirty south." I figure every community probably had at least one black hero. Their stories just didn't get told.

But, mama made me promise her that I would do something to keep his memory alive. She didn't concern herself with how I was to do it — as long as it was done. So, I promised her I would. Thus, this book is the result of that promise. Both mama and daddy died in 1989. Mama in February, and Daddy later that same year in July. I was so deeply devastated and grief stricken over their deaths, until it took me two years just to resume some semblance of normalcy in my life. When they died, I was overwhelmed in ways that I still can't count. Now, all of a sudden, I had a teaching job in Georgia and a family business to run — solo! Talk about a juggling act! It was a one-woman show!

As I look back over my life, I still don't know how I did it. It was ONLY by God's grace and the help of my beloved husband Clarence Frieson, Jr., whom I also lost four years after their deaths, that enabled me to survive. Not only do I owe this debt of gratitude to my beloved late husband, Clarence, but I owe a tremendous debt of gratitude to two very dear friends, The Reverend William Allen Dean, and Mr. John Ceroy Bell, who were steadfast friends who stood by my side and helped me manage the company in the aftermath of daddy's death.

Consumed — bad choice of words. No, OBSESSED with the promise I had made to my mother, I believed the ultimate way to keep my promise to her was in my obligation to the business that daddy had started 20 years earlier — to keep it going. Declaring the funeral home to be an earthly monument to daddy's life and works, the first thing I did (for purely sentimental reasons) was appended the word "memorial" to the business' name — so that all would understand that my persistence in continuing the business operation was an act of remembrance.

Subsequently, I became inundated with it; engrossed in it. I concentrated all my effort on the pursuit of excellence in the mortuary field. Already well-versed in every aspect of the mortuary business, how much more could I absorb? But, you'd be surprised what a big head can hold with strong enough motivation. I was tenacious — driven — POSSESSED! In 1992, I even got bold enough to resign my teaching position. What in the world was I thinking about?

But, as the years passed, I became more and more vexed by my realization that merely operating the business alone, was not the key to creating a memorial to my daddy; because he was so much bigger than just a business. Clark Memorial represented way more than just providing goods and services to our community — much much more. There was much more to my daddy that made him great — he was more than just a great businessman. In order to become a great businessman, he had to first be a great man. And it was all of these things I had to try to capture, and project if I was to remember him adequately. Clark Memorial — much more than a place where people brought their dead or a mere company — had to become an institution. It had to somehow tell daddy's story; a story of struggle, triumph, adversity, ingenuity, creativity and most importantly courage and finally transition.

In the years that followed their deaths, I nearly worked myself to death trying to be all that daddy was in my community; trying to emulate him; imitate him — which wasn't really all that hard to do, because folks say all the time that I'm just like him. But, I still wasn't moving any closer to the promise made to my mother. Over the years, I prayed and prayed that God would give me a vision; show me how to do it; tell me how to best honor my father. I waited to hear from God. From time to time I would re-visit the matter. But I could never make a start on anything for too long, because if it didn't feel right to me, I took it as a sign that it wasn't from God, and I'd scrap it and start over. But finally one day, fifteen years after his death, shortly after my 50th birthday, God finally revealed to me what I had to do, and I was in complete agreement. In order to appropriately remember my daddy's impact on the world I would have to write a book; build a website; and form an organization.

So, it was actually around October 2003, that I birthed the idea of this book, the web site that I maintain in his honor, and the Wilkie Clark's Daughter Organization. The web site was totally perfect to me because it is both tangible and intangible — sort of spiritual. It is a little corner in space, with the potential to touch people all over the world. It would allow me to somehow capture my daddy's spirit — in word and deed, just the way he captured so many hearts as he went about his life. I have tried to make it a compassionate site — the way daddy was. It's about helping others overcome their adversity; about overcoming your fears and doubts; and moving toward your dreams and goals — even when you don't quite know how you'll come out.

Now, understand I have approached this task with dread, because I am so much older now than I was when they first died. And I, too am confronted with fears. Fears that I'm too old to start something new; fears that I've started too late. I should've done this 15 years ago; I need to be concentrating on my retirement; I need to be focusing on succession planning for the mortuary business. But, I have had to constantly remind myself that after almost 20 years of back-breaking manual labor for the Atlantic Coast Line Rail Road my dad celebrated his 50th birthday the month after he opened Clark Funeral Home, which was like a re-birth for him! He ran 20 more years as fast and as far as he could. And that's what let's me know I can do the same!

Another case in point: Imagine, if you will, the famous sculptor, Gutzon Borglum, born March 25, 1867 at Bear Lake, Idaho. Borglum had a dream of carving images out of a mountainside. He was passionate about his art. He went to school in both San Francisco and Paris. And in the meantime, he completed many other projects and received numerous honors for his animated life-sized bronze statues. But, he never abandoned his biggest dream — to carve images out of a mountainside.

Finally, in 1927, at age 60, he began to work on the sculpture he ultimately became most noted for, Mount Rushmore — a magnificent sculpture depicting the busts of three famous American Presidents: Washington, Jefferson and Lincoln. This world-famous sculpture was hewn out of Mount Rushmore in the Black Hills of South Dakota. Each Statute was about 60 feet tall!

He worked on them for 14 years. Eventually, he died at age 74 before he could finish; but look at the result of the 14 years he invested in starting the task!

The journey of a thousand miles must begin with the first step. Many times, in pursuit of our dreams and goals, we have to just walk out on our faith alone. When we start out, we may not even be able to visualize the end of the dream; but, have you ever thought about the possibility that God may not always intend for you to complete it? Instead, your purpose may be to merely make the start. It may not always be God's will for you to finish everything you start. But, that doesn't preclude us from making the start. I do believe that my dad was a perfect example of that, as was Dr. Martin Luther King, Jr. Dr. King even foretold in his I Have A Dream speech that "..I may not get there with you, but we as a people will get to the promised land...."

Right here, I think it is most fitting to recall a favorite poem that was first introduced to me by one of my daddy's dearest and best friends the late Horace Whittaker, who could always come by and say just the right thing at just the right time, just when I needed it most. It is entitled: "The Tapestry Of My Life"

My Life is but a weaving
Between my Lord and me
He chooses all of the colors
And He works on steadily.

Oftimes he weaveth sorrow,
And I in blinded pride
Forget that he sees the upper
And I, only the underside.

The dark threads are as needful
In the Weaver's skillful hand
As the threads of gold and silver
In the pattern He has planned.

Not til the looms are silent
And the shuttles cease to fly
Shall God unroll the fabric
And reveal the unknown why.
Author Unknown

With all these facts in mind, the integrity of my desires remains undaunted not only to complete my daddy's dream, but to keep the promise made to my mother. I believe this is my destiny. And I believe that through me, they both will be immortalized. As of the writing of this book, I have not reached the place where I truly want to be. But, every day I focus my attention and some of my effort on moving toward that goal.

This book is just a feeble attempt to detail the aspects of his life that I found most inspiring. In particular, his quest to own and operate his own business during the mature years of his life is the major inspiration for this book; because witnessing his struggle and triumph is what inspires me today to continue to operate that business. Now, understand that we aren't a fortune 500 company. And I don't think we have to be in order to claim our rightful place in history.

We certainly weren't rich–at least not financially. Not even affluent; but, I can attest to the fact that we were abundantly blessed. Through the income made by that business, my parents gave me a good solid education at one of Alabama's finest universities, helped keep food on the table, and in the years since daddy's death, has helped me to educate two children, and a grandson. More importantly, it enabled us to help a lot of other people along the way. We have recently marked our 36th year in business. And, I believe this longevity can be attributed to the virtues we saw and admired in my daddy.

I truly believe that because his story remains powerful enough to inspire and move me fifteen years after his death, then, it will certainly touch your heart and motivate you, too.

One doesn't have to guess that the most difficult aspect of going in business for himself, was getting the money to start the business, which he eventually did get through an SBA direct loan — but he had to jump through hoops to get it— and then, when he did finally get it, it wasn't near enough of a loan to give him a fair start, or to make him competitive in the market.

I have often wished that I had had the knowledge and the education then, that I have now. I would have insisted that he decline what little money they offered him, and demand that SBA either give him what he needed or give him nothing. My sincere belief is that what SBA tried to do, first was to discourage him from pursuing the loan; then when they saw that he was not going to quit, it seems they then made their objective to set him up to fail.

Under normal circumstances, I believe EVERYBODY who tries to go in business for themselves probably encounters some obstacles — unless they're already wealthy. But, add to that the barriers that were created by the kind of racial discrimination we endured in the 1960's; it was like climbing the rough side of a mountain that never reaches its peak. In my heart, I just don't believe it should have been that way in the land of the free and the home of the brave.

I was no different from most little girls growing up in a two-parent family. I was my "daddy's girl." And my daddy was my hero. In my eyesight, he was the strongest, toughest, most wonderful man (THE ONLY MAN) in the world! But, can you imagine what it felt like for me, at age 12, 13 and 14 to see such a man reduced to tears? Well, during those early years, when he was trying to get his business off the ground, I saw that. This journey toward business ownership seemingly became a never-ending battle; sometimes, so brutal — often adding insult to injury after injury after injury. Not injured in the physical sense, his feelings were often hurt; his intelligence questioned and his integrity insulted. Everybody he had to deal with was white; and it seemed that they could and would with all due deliberation, say some of the meanest, most insensitive, unthoughtful, and cruelest things to him, to try to humiliate and quell the spirit. But, with each battle I saw him made stronger and stronger in his determination not to be denied.

Quite naturally, being so madly in love with my daddy, empathic and impressionable — when I sensed that he was hurt, I was hurt. If he cried, I cried. Because he wanted this so badly, I wanted it just as badly for him. I could sense that this was something terribly important to him; something he wanted so badly but couldn't get because he was a black man who had to somehow prove himself to white people who already didn't believe in a black man's ability to plan and successfully follow through on his plans; who already didn't believe that a black man had sense enough to run a business; to solve problems; to press his way.

From that day to this, these experiences have been permanently etched in my mind — and not in a positive way. Thus, one of my goals in writing this book is to use my daddy's story to inspire and encourage other people who truly want to transform their lives, either by going into business for themselves or by way of any other type of endeavor that has the potential to help them advance spiritually, academically socially, or economically. For daddy, it was about breaking into the business world!

68

FIRST STEPS

"I knew someone had to take the first step

and I made up my mind not to move."

—Rosa Parks

> ## Setting Forth The Purpose & Direction For The Wilkie Clark Memorial Foundation, Inc. aka "Wilkie Clark's Daughter Org"

My father was a man who had a deep and strong belief in organization. He was sold on the strength of numbers. Probably long before the word "co-operative" came in vogue in the business world, he was talking about forming co-operatives with others in the funeral profession. But, they just couldn't see or imagine the possibilities!

Many stood by and watched as my father, caught up in his own transformation into a "new black man," began to grow in his understanding of what it would take to renovate his life, and work toward the re-shaping of his neighborhood and community as he learned new ways of thinking and behaving—ways that contradicted anything he had ever seen or heard before. On the journey from a rambunctious young black man with an insatiable zeal for life, to a mature citizen of the world, his profound life experiences somehow transformed him into a champion for an oppressed people, particularly on the local front. Much of what he did, was accomplished by way of his strong belief in organization and association. It was largely through his organizational ties that he began to make his ascent.

He Learned From The Pros

How did he come to understand and appreciate the need for African-Americans to organize? I think it probably all started back in the late fifties and early sixties.

I vividly recall being a child, and riding in the back seat of the car as daddy and mama traveled to Birmingham, and to Atlanta, Montgomery, Tuskegee, and other places throughout the Southeast to NAACP meetings. There, they would do all kinds of things that I didn't quite understand. But, I was made to sit in the meetings and listen. There would be chanting of songs. Daddy called them "Freedom Songs:"

"Which side are you on boys, which side are you on?
Which side are you on boys, which side are you on?
Don't be no Uncle Tom for Mr. Charlie!
Don't listen to his lies!
If ever we are going to be free
We have to organize!"

I remember how daddy would come home and have his NAACP meetings, and teach the people these chants. And they would sing along with him in the meetings. As time went by, there were other songs taught and used as a way to motivate black people to get involved in the movement:

We shall over come, We shall overcome
We shall overcome some day.
Oh Deep in my heart, I do believe
We shall overcome some day.

Another favorite that he taught me went like this:

O Freedom! O Freedom!
O Freedom Over Me, Over Me
And before I'll be a slave
I'll be buried in my grave
And go home to my Lord,
And be free!

I also recall being 9 years old when we got our first television—a black and white console. It wasn't long after that, that Dr. Martin Luther King, Jr., began his illustrious pilgrimage as a civil rights leader. As news of his dynamic leadership strategies began to spread, Daddy became more and more enraptured by this movement.

How well do I recall, daddy buying every single one of Dr. Martin Luther King's recorded sermons and civil rights speeches. At that time, they were recorded in LP Albums. He would sit for hours in our living room with the record player, and play these sermons over and over again. I would observe him as he listened — not only with his ears, but with his soul and spirit. He played them so much until he knew every one of them verbatim. It was as if listening to the voice of Dr. King, convicted him in his heart. And wherever he heard the voice of Dr. King, whether on the record player or on a live television newscast, you'd better hush up! Uh Oh! Better not say anything. He'd snap on you!

"Shut up! Dammit, don't you hear Dr. King speaking?"

As far as daddy was concerned this was holy ground. You dared not to speak or violate his order of complete silence! So we all had to listen...to the message of freedom....

If the television volume was down, and Dr. King (or any civil rights leader) flashed on the television, he'd anxiously re-focus his attention:

"Hurry-up! Hurry-up! Turn it up! Turn it up! Turn it up! There's King! Let's see what King is doing now!"

"Aw! They're marchin'! That's what I'm talking 'bout!"

"Just listen to him!" (King)

He would just snap, crackle and pop with excitement. The civil rights movement had his total attention. So, he listened, he watched, and he learned. He learned the issues; and he learned how to present the issues — with eloquence.

He often read the order issued by the United States Supreme Court on May 17, 1954 when it handed down the decision in Brown versus Board Of Education. He read it so much, until he could quote it verbatim. He loved to quote this decision:

> *"We come then to the question presented: Does segregation of children in the public schools solely on the basis of race, even though the physical facilities and other "tangible" factors may be equal, deprive the children of the minority group of equal educational opportunities? We believe that it does." Brown v. Board of Education of Topeka, 347 U.S. 483 – 96 (1954). pp. 488 – 92.*

As he mastered these ideologies, he made efforts to apply them in his own community. Every time he went off to a meeting, he would bring new knowledge back into the community and make an effort to implement it. He compelled black men and women to stand up and be counted, and participate in this aggressive movement toward freedom. He began to challenge the racial inequities on the local level. Often misunderstood, he pressed on — often alone.

Anointed to Lead

As the 1970's dawned, black men and women of Randolph County began to see and appreciate daddy's many admirable works and wanted him to be remembered and recognized for the things he had done and was still doing for blacks in Randolph County. African Americans had started to grow tired of being mistreated because of race. Most of them were members and volunteers with the Randolph County NAACP Branch, which under daddy's heroic leadership, was taking many BOLD steps to improve the quality of life and socio-economic status for African Americans throughout Randolph County.

Many African-Americans still feeling the sting of racism and bigotry in Randolph County, while supporting the efforts, nevertheless feared that if the NAACP were allowed to meet in their churches, there would be trouble. There were many black churches where the NAACP was not welcome to hold a meeting or put on a fund raising event. After all, times in Alabama hadn't changed all that much. Many whites not only misunderstood the NAACP, but hated it. Many churches were still fearful at the thought of "Civil Rights" groups using their facilities to hold meetings, and the NAACP needed a permanent "home" of its own, where it could hold its meetings, meet its objectives in the community, and not have to put church overseers in a position wherein they felt threatened.

Daddy saw a need not only for a place to hold meetings, but also for a center of operations, because leadership of the organization carried with it, a heavy administrative burden that necessitated having access to an office where official business could be taken care of and records could be housed. Running the NAACP was almost like a full-time job—one that didn't pay. Up until that time, daddy had personally documented, housed and archived 25 or more years worth of civil rights activities in Randolph County; much of it related to the struggle to achieve black poll-workers, press for the hiring of black police officers, encourage voter registration, implement aggressive voter education programs, address issues of police use of deadly force, and the numerous education issues that he was being called on to investigate under the aegis of the NAACP.

Aside from the need to have a base of operations in the black community wherein civic issues could be addressed, there were other needs as well. After losing our school grounds and facility to court-ordered desegregation, we were now without a community-based gathering place. The black school had always been a center of community activity. However, having lost access to our school facilities, there wasn't even a decent place in town wherein black organizations could host a large event or fund raiser; put on a talent show; or just gather and fellowship outside of the church. So, there was then, (and still is now) a critical need for such a facility—community based and community controlled. A place where we could assemble without having to ask the white man's permission to meet and deliberate about our unique circumstances and issues. Thus, such concerns as these were at the heart of the drive to purchase a permanent location that could be owned by "the black community."

Indeed, daddy's strong support base dramatized their firm belief that his admirable record and courageous works deserved an earthly monument that could be left behind so that others who followed would know of the struggles that were engaged in the name of growth, progress and empowerment, especially for African-Americans, the poor and the underprivileged.

Just to mention a few of them by name, they included: Wilkie Clark, Hattie Lee Peters Clark, Robert Joiner, Jr., James and Catherine Davenport, Adella O'Neal, Ruby Lois Molden, Reverend Lathonia J. Wright, Juanita Wright, Roy and Willo Terry, Lillie Thornton, John Ceroy and Cynthia Bell, Earnest and Annie Lois Heard, Hershell and Juanita Holliday, Lawrence and Rosie O'Neal, James I. and Mary E. O'Neal, Arthur Ray and Barbara E. Pate, and numerous others who are not named here. They began to work and move in that direction. Taking a giant leap of faith, and with the financial and moral support of black people all over Randolph County, they purchased the property formerly known as the (defunct) York Rite Masonic Lodge Hall (later the "Blue Bird Café") located at the corner of Longshore and Riley Street. At that time, their desire was to purchase property so that the local NAACP would always have a home in Randolph County. The two-story lodge building was old and in need of a lot of repair. Together, they dreamed of renovating this building and converting it to an office and activity building. There were visions of a community library and an archives building wherein the historic events and memorabilia from local historical events of interest to the African American community could be housed. Despite a multiplicity of ideas and perspectives on their vision of this project, they were all in agreement that this property would one day be dedicated as the "Wilkie Clark Community Center." Their movement in this direction is well-documented in many forms, and throughout assorted issues of the local newspaper, The Randolph Leader which from time to time carried updates about various events related to this effort.

Even those of the younger generation at that time embraced the idea, and sponsored a summer camp that they named in his honor, being the first "Wilkie Clark Community Center Summer Camp," for black youngsters, which was held during the Summer of 1989.

But for various reasons along the way, they were stalled and their dream complicated by other factors. There were setbacks, and roadblocks that slowed their progress. For some, it was the illness and subsequent death of some of those who were actively involved in the effort. On the other hand, the bureaucracy of the NAACP National office prohibited it's local branches from property-ownership, which further complicated the issue. Yet those who remained were faithful to the pursuit of this goal.   So as to avoid conflict with NAACP nationals, the property was ultimately purchased in the name of the "Wilkie Clark Community Center," and a new organization was born. Later, the group decided the building needed to be re-roofed, but needed to borrow the money. Since daddy was willing to take the risk to borrow the money, to meet the lending requirement of the bank, the deeds had to be made out in his name. A loan was negotiated at Colonial Bank, and other material was purchased to complete the roof.

At that time, little could any of us have foreseen daddy's forthcoming death, in July of 1989. However, as it came to pass, daddy died with the property still titled to him. Heavily burdened with our grieving, we did not pay much attention to the building at that time, since it was largely abandoned and not in use. Several months later, the building burned to the ground, we believe at the hands of a vagrant seeking shelter from the cold. But, we never lost sight of the vision.

In light of all the action previously taken, and so much evidence and documentation to support it, what better way to create a memorial in honor my father than by way of a newly created, updated, re-vamped organization named in his honor?

Once it became apparent to me that the organization was an integral and essential part of the effort to memorialize daddy, with the help of my family, daddy's baby brother, and my children, I personally took up the banner and task of seeing to it that my daddy would be remembered, not only locally, but around the world. That's why I have named my collective business enterprises after him. We call it the Wilkie Clark Memorial Foundation because we believe he was a major contributor to the growth and progress of the African-American community during his lifetime and because we are the initiators of this movement to archive the history of African-Americans in Randolph County. It is a non-profit corporation. At the time of this writing, we are in the process of seeking 501c status from the Internal Revenue Service. With the formation of The Wilkie Clark Memorial Foundation, Inc., we will now move with all due speed, to transfer the deeds to the Foundation, and appoint a full board of Trustees to oversee its operation and use. I envision this Foundation as a community based ministry of inspiration and empowerment, which will seek to raise community consciousness on every front, and inspire people to set a course for their own self-empowerment, economically, socially and spiritually.

So today, building on the action taken by that visionary group in the 1980's, our vision extends far beyond what that small group of visionaries saw. With our neighborhoods working together, our aggressive goal is to acquire the adjoining properties, and expand their original vision by erecting a community based, and community supported archives center that will be located at the corner of Longshore and Riley Street in Roanoke, Alabama. We foresee the erection of a grandiose structure within which the entire African community can proudly display the life histories of all of the great men and women who helped to shape our neighborhood, as a reminder to those who come after us that we, too have made a difference in our own community. We believe that preservation of this rich history will serve as a beacon and a point of inspiration and encouragement to future generations of black youth who will grow up in our community.

In addition to serving as an archives center, we foresee this agency as a fully operational, full-time and fully staffed personal empowerment center, wherein, people from all walks of life can come to receive knowledge, wisdom, know-how and to find power for living in the context of a world that is becoming increasingly difficult for African-Americans to live in. In summary, the focus of this program will revolve around the black constituent in Randolph County becoming pro-active in its own economic development and destiny. It's about cleaning up our neighborhoods. While it is not about divisiveness, or separatism, but it certainly is about black pride. Where there is no community pride, no economic development there is an atmosphere of bleakness. It's about becoming landlords (as opposed to slum lords) and property-owners instead of renters; job providers instead of job seekers. One of the major strategies we will employ will be that of archiving the great works of the "new black men" of the past and present, such as my daddy, and so many others who, like him, left their footprint on the sands of time, right here in our local community. It begins right here with the writing of this book. It is vital that we understand that my objective is not to set aside our faithful institutions such as the NAACP, the ADC, our local churches, and other great organizations, but to embrace, and to incorporate them in this great community-based infrastructure.

At the heart of our mission is my desire to bring to life and to embody those aspects of his character that resulted in change for the better for individuals, for the neighborhood, and even for the world. Anchored by the philosophy that it is impossible to serve God, without serving man, which is also ratified in God's holy word (i.e. "inasmuch as ye have done it to the least of these my brethren, ye have done it unto me.") we now seek to recreate and resurrect his spirit in the form of an organization that will reach out to help humanity, to lift and make whole, unrestricted by locality or nature of need, beginning at home and spreading abroad. The book, which is only the first phase of our initiative, presents the life of my father as a guidepost for coming generations of young black men and women who will come of age within the numerous failing black neighborhoods and communities throughout the rural south (or perhaps across America).

While we know there may be others perhaps equally worthy of similar honor; while we know that daddy was no saint and by no means are we trying to bestow sainthood upon him; we nevertheless want the world to know and recognize him for being the man that he was for touching lives in the way that he did.

It is my utmost prayer that through the work of this this foundation, the name "Wilkie Clark" will go down in history as being synonymous with "service to humanity" because that is what he was about.

I foresee all of our services revolving around the idea of creating and bringing "new energy" into the neighborhood by inspiring creative ways for individuals, families and communities to elevate themselves to their rightful place in the world, the way Wilkie Clark did. At times, the effort involved struggle, sometimes it involved the agony of defeat, but he emerged from the experience whole, complete, and victorious. And that, my friends, is what matters most.

We (his family) feel that we can best represent him and fulfill the aggressive mission of our organization by focusing our efforts in three key areas. They include business development, benevolent outreach and community action. These are the theaters in which he operated during life. And here is where we choose to be.

Of particular interest to me is the area of business development. With respect to business development, I visualize our mission as one of helping the disadvantaged meet the huge challenges that bombard them daily as they struggle within failing communities, to free themselves from generations of poverty and lack. We will unite with them, and stand firm with them, to encourage and foster economically strong neighborhoods through the purchasing of homes or investment properties, the starting of new business ventures, the nurturing of business ideas. We are committed to act as a comprehensive and compassionate resource for anyone wanting to be in business for themselves. We will seek to achieve our goals by involvement in research, education, and outreach. I want to encourage you to go to the website, http://www.wilkieclarksdaughter.info or www.wcmf.citymax.com, where you can get more background information and insight into our motivation for helping to achieve a strong economic foundation upon which our neighborhoods can thrive and survive.

We are not only praying but we're believing God for national and world-wide support for this initiative. I ask readers of this biography to partner with us by pledging to support this initiative. We believe that if we can persuade just 1,000 individuals who think and believe as we do, to commit to supporting this effort by pledging a minimum of $10.00 per month, we can make a massive impact in our community, and perhaps the world. So, we humbly solicit your donations, which will help us to implement our aggressive "Clark Initiative" in honor of my father. With this initiative, it is our objective to develop an organization and a support base that will serve to raise the standard for every African American neighborhood in our county, and to inspire other communities to embrace similar initiatives. I truly believe this can be accomplished through the provision of education, resources, and support, and continue the compassionate and benevolent work that he was so well noted and remembered for. There is not a day that passes by, that I don't drive through my neighborhood right here in Roanoke, Alabama and observe bright young energetic entrepreneurs standing on the street corners, peddling their product. The fact that at their youthful stage in life, they already recognize the value of the dollar is admirable; the fact that they are diligent enough to be persistent in doing it is a virtue; the problem is their product. It is destructive — not only to themselves, but to their clientele and the neighborhood. But, I fully understand why they do it. They don't see that they have a snowball's chance in hell of making a dime on a decent job, for decent wages in our environment. One that they have grown to understand and view as their adversary. They are young black boys, who see no other way out. "Wilkie Clark's Daughter" proposes a wonderful opportunity to minister to these youngsters, and show them a better way; help them find a better product; move them to a better location... But it all starts with education—a special kind of education that is not being adequately addressed through the public schools, in the homes, or in any other social institutions.

Just look around you. Who's really doing anything constructive to help the aspiring small business owner? It's hard to go in business. It's hard to get the money to get set up. It's hard to get people to tell you anything — or give you any information they think will help you advance. It is the spirit of compassion that my father had for so many "underdogs;" that same compassion that I have for you that makes me wish for your success and makes me not want to see any person deprived of the resources you may need to be successful in life.

It's important that you understand, that while my dad's struggles were steeped in the racial prejudices and mis-conceptions of that day, I acknowledge that your struggles may have a totally different origin in this day. While some may STILL BE racially motivated, others may involve gender issues, money or other funding issues, poor "people-skills," difficulty accessing information, lack of know-how, limited business skills, personal inhibitions, academic weaknesses or any number of issues—all of which can be addressed, and corrected! I know you can overcome any of these!

So, let's explore these areas, and see what can be done to help you achieve your goal of starting, improving or expanding your own business.

As of the writing of this book, I am in the process of organizing a board of volunteers who will personally and collectively commit themselves to providing needed assistance and serve as a compassionate resource to individuals seeking to start or develop existing businesses. In addition to business development, I also envision this organization as a resource for personal development.

It is a fact that a lot of businesses fail because their owners lack versatility. They are like horses with blinders on. They can't look to the left or to the right; they have to go one way. Likewise, some people can't wear but one hat; they can't do but one thing at a time. For example, you may be the key person in your business and you may be good at typing, but terrible with accounting. That means you have to hire extra help to do a job only because YOU don't know how. I envision a network that can offer immediate training or consultation in whatever kind of business know-how you may need; possibly something as simple as "balancing the checkbook," something most of us could probably use.

Other examples include: budgeting, preparing financial statements; typing skills; basic accounting; basic bookkeeping; tax accounting; employees; etc. Sometimes, just an intensive one-on-one seminar or workshop with an expert who already knows and has been there is all you need to pull yourself out of a rut. I would ultimately like to be able to offer you assistance in any area of need that will help you solve your problems and move forward. At the present time, I am consulting with experts in business administration to develop a list of key areas where we can jump-start our members on personal development (i.e. personal motivation, people-skills, basic computer skills, keyboarding, etc.) As this organization evolves, I am inviting and urging your feedback, ideas, and criticisms, which we can all explore through my forum at "The Executive Suite," which you can access through the web site. So please join the organization, and then join the forum and give me your ideas. I want to make this the best resource for self empowerment and self-development in the world!

It is important for you to know that as we work to put into place, the infrastructure to make these services available, I am also developing a related company Wilkie Clark's Daughter Enterprises, LLC, which will ally itself with The Wilkie Clark Memorial Foundation and help to promote the foundation. Although our website is still under development, we invite and encourage you to visit often, to keep informed about what's new and how we are progressing. We can be found at: http://www.wilkieclarksdaughter.info/Projects.html. I have already started to enlist the help of many trained people from all over the country, who have the expertise and know-how to help us achieve our goals individually and as a community.

As we continue to move toward the opening of the Foundation headquarters, we are asking our community to embrace and adopt our vision for this wonderful archives center. We are asking you to prepare by volunteering to work or serve in some capacity in this Foundation, and become a part-owner with us. We will be soliciting your participation, and your input as we move to bring this vision to fruition.

As we move to bring this new institution into existence, we ask others to prayerfully consider other African-Americans that you believe worthy of a place of honor in the archives center, and begin moving toward preparation of documents, photographs, and other tangible evidence of the great work they may have done to contribute to the growth and progress of our community.

Lastly, in honor of my father, the late Wilkie Clark, and in remembrance of his compassionate and benevolent spirit which I witnessed throughout my life with him, I propose that this organization will honor and immortalize him by providing a ministry of benevolence and emergency relief, in addition to Civil Rights activities which remain a high priority on our agenda as well.

In the coming months, we solicit your prayers and your support as we continue to move toward the implementation of our aggressive plan of action, that whatever the outcome or result, God will receive all honor, and glorification as a testimony to his goodness. With your help, we can and will do just that.

IMAGINATION

"Dream big dreams! Others may deprive you of your material wealth and cheat you in a thousand other ways, but no man can deprive you of the control and use of your imagination."

—Jesse Jackson

The Historical Significance Of
Wilkie Clark AND Other Missions Of The
Wilkie Clark's Daughter Organization

"Those who have no record of what their forebears have accomplished lose the inspiration which comes from the teaching of biography and history."

Dr. Carter G. Woodson, Father of Black History

History has done an unforgivable injustice to the African American communities and culture. The true horrors of racism have never really been told. Nor have black Americans ever fully been given credit for their courage and commitment to overcome the spiritual and economic ravages of slavery and its aftermath.

But, how can we sit by and allow extraordinary African-American men and women to live, achieve the impossible, and then die without recording, or lauding their great contributions to our progress?

In large measure, the testimony of their lives translated into hope for those of us who bore witness to their amazing spiritual resilience and intestinal fortitude.

Thus, I am on a crusade to ensure that the historical significance of my daddy is well documented and affirmed in Randolph County, Alabama.

Who was this man — Wilkie Clark? Daddy was a self-made man, who over his lifetime, transformed himself from a dirt-poor sharecropper, to an outstanding entrepreneur and outspoken, audacious civil rights leader, and humanitarian. I was an innocent bystander, and eye-witness to practically every event that led to his greatness. I saw it develop and evolve with the passage of time. Because he came to be regarded by many as "the man who stands up for the black people," I was thrust into a position of being the eye-witness to every kind of racial mistreatment imaginable. Anytime there was a racial incident of any nature, it was brought to daddy's attention. Consequently, I became his chief assistant as he would require me to meticulously document each and every incident. He came to know the community so well until it seemed that his finger stayed on the pulse of Randolph County. From my perspective, I cannot conjur up images of anyone who devoted more time, energy and effort, to trying to better his community than he. Though he probably never thought much of it, I, and numerous others thought he was amazing! People talked — he listened. Not only would he listen, he responded. He talked— people listened. I've seen instances of Black people in the community who were sick, and had no money for medical care. I've heard him telephone the Mayor and Hospital authority, and demand that emergency services be dispatched immediately to take care of the sick. Though I never counted, he probably broke the world record for attending City Council Meetings in Roanoke, Alabama. He was an encourager of people who had no reason to be encouraged. He had a righteous indignation for injustice of any kind and aggressively vocalized it. Often, people would ring our doorbell in the middle of the night. He always got up and talked to them. Sometimes it involved some-body being put in jail; he'd get dressed and go sign the bond — no charge. Over-time, he began to take on the image that people gave him. He was a champion of oppressed black people.

Why is it so important for me to memorialize my dad 15 years after his death? Let me answer by illustration. As daddy's reputation as a civil rights leader spread, he was met with resistance. Frequently when trying to address the city council or other official bodies in our community, he was met with arrogance. White city officials would literally try to ignore him or disregard his presence at their meetings. Seemingly unmoved and uninhibited by any of their efforts to publicly humiliate him, he would say quite flamboy-antly, "Hell, you don't have to recognize me; I recognize myself...." and you'd better believe, that was his attitude! I said that to say this: While recognition from others is not all that important to me, I do believe that when a person gives as much of himself to their com-munity as my daddy gave on both a public as well as a very private level, he deserves recognition. And I have sense enough to realize that if I don't make that happen, he will be denied his rightful place in the annals and archives not only of this local community, but of this world. I don't know a single human being who before or since my father, gave so much of themselves to their communities as he did publicly or privately. He wanted to make a mark on his com-munity. He wanted his life to mean something. And I, his biggest fan, believe that it did. I believe he succeeded in establishing meaning and purpose for the time he spent on this earth.

Though he couldn't boast any formal training from any of the prestigious black universities, daddy was conscientious in scholarly pursuits. He vigorously sought and pursued every level of knowledge from any source with the potential to liberate him from ignorance. He studied diligently — and read everything — from every newspaper covering our region — to the works of Dr. Martin Luther King, Jr., Dr. Benjamin E. Mays, and other scholarly writers of the time.

Daddy was imbued with attributes strikingly profound and real. Something that I find lacking in so many shallow people today, most of whom are only concerned about themselves, and couldn't care less about the greater good. And rather than to use that to elevate himself, his core instinct was to use his gifts to help other people. He was substantive. Though he never had a single class in philosophy, again, I am again compelled to turn to Confucius.

One of Confucius' disciples, Fan Chi asked about "humanity." Confucius' answer was to, "love men," a phrase that literally means "be concerned about others."2 The disciple Zeng Zi said that Confucius's teaching was "loyalty and reciprocity;" one should do one's best for others and identify as much as one can with the other person. When I analyze the deep level of understanding of human issues with which Confucius interacted with other men of his time, I see my daddy. He dramatized this every day of his life. He shaped his life by his love for his fellow man in such a profound way that in return, most men reciprocated that love with love. He was a man truly worthy of recognition.

Shortly after my father's death, only because there were African-American city councilmen namely, Michael Joiner and Mack Arthur Bell, who pressed the issue, our street was named after my father. And of course, our then Mayor Henry V. "Spec" Bonner made a few short remarks at the funeral service. And that was it. Daddy was dead — and as far as the city fathers were concerned, he was done, and they were done with him— he was a thorn out of their sides. A few years later under a subsequent administration, somewhere in our community's very recent past, there were discussions about establishing a museum. But, do you think I was ever approached by any of the officials about including my father as a prospective figure in this (proposed) museum? No! And what that simply confirms for me is that decades after all the unrest and controversy over civil rights, after all the mixing and de-segregating that white Americans still maintain very fine lines of distinction and demarcation between us and them. What is important to us - is not important to them!

Our heroes are their headaches and heartaches. To them, Wilkie Clark was nothing but a loud-mouthed trouble-maker — that "old NAACP nigger," is what they called him behind his back " — always goin round trying to start somethin'." But, you'd better believe, they learned to respect him to his face; and I can guarantee you this: regardless or what any of our current leaders outside the African-American community and culture may think or feel, as far as OUR community was concerned, my daddy was a champion — with a capital "C." Much like a legend, to this day, black people (and some whites) walk up to me and say: "I sure do miss your daddy," or "Wilkie was a hell of a man!" "I bet if your daddy was here, so and so wouldn't be happening in Roanoke." He will NEVER be forgotten. So, what that also signifies is that somehow, the contributions of African-Americans to the growth and progress of their respective communities are still regarded as mediocre at best. But, I believe they warrant recognition and placement in the history of our towns and cities. Therefore, not only is it necessary but urgent that we (their offspring) begin to be more aggressive and adamant in demanding that they are not again written out of history; but rather that they not only be included and recorded in history but applauded for the great courage they displayed for such times as they lived in.

So, for me, merely having a street named after my daddy is not enough. I am in pursuit of more — much more than just a name on a street sign. It is my utmost desire that both The City Of Roanoke, and the Randolph County Commission, issue proclamations conferring historical distinction upon my father posthumously. I do not believe that a monument or historic marker placed on his property, or some other mark of distinction placed in a prominent location in Randolph County, is asking one bit too much. And I believe that any or all of these symbols of historical distinction would result in a most tasteful and appropriate way to honor him throughout Randolph County, Alabama. I want my community — black and white — to come together and help me make this happen, not because it's black thing — or because it isn't a white thing — but merely because it's a right and proper thing to do. I believe this is a more than fair exchange for all the unconscienable, reprehensible, mean spirited, humiliating treatment that my daddy endured as a black man trying to exist as a free man in Randolph County, Alabama and help others do the same.

The next reason nearest and dearest to my heart is that I want my children, Wilkie Sherard Frieson, and Je'Lynn Mikele Frieson, to know who this man was. This man who because they were so young when he died, has largely been a figment of their imaginations, yet was kind and generous enough to bequeath them all his worldly goods, including Clark Memorial Funeral Service. This man, to whom it was so important that they know he was determined to leave them something of value to remember him. I want him to be as real to them as he is to me.

Lastly, because, unlike many people who might have gone into business and made a few dollars, upgraded their standard of living, and transformed themself into a champion for progress, he refused to forget his beginnings. Unlike George Jefferson, daddy never forgot who he was, or the journey. The average person's sole motivation for going into any kind of business venture is profit. Then, just like the Jeffersons, they strive to move on up and move on out. Their goal is to forget everything they knew in their former life. No, unlike the often self-centered, egocentric George Jefferson, my daddy spent a lot of money, gave most of his resources away, and devoted most of his life to helping other people. That was his quest. And even if daddy had achieved great wealth during his lifetime, he still probably wouldn't have been in a position to leave his family much, because he was a man so marked by compassion and generosity, that he gave away most of what he had to help other people advance; particularly those whom he saw as oppressed, disadvantaged — those he often referred to as "the underdogs." Now, it is not my purpose here to rattle off a long list of names of people he helped or the countless deeds or favors he did for this one or that one. That would serve no earthly or heavenly purpose and I would not dare breach the confidence they placed in my daddy. Many of them are still here today and I believe they would graciously affirm what I'm saying here! Furthermore, if one searched the records diligently, there is no question in my mind, that a lot of evidence would surface, to support my writing. Therefore, understand that my only desire is to use the most tasteful approach, the most appropriate and fitting way of sharing these aspects of his character and spirit.

I believe that historical distinction, honor, and praise are due to The Late Wilkie Clark for the courage he showed in the face of unsurmountable, undeserved and sometimes life-threatening opposition in pursuing freedom, justice and equality not only for himself, but for the black constituent in Randolph County, Alabama; also for the courage and persistence he demonstrated in pursuing his goal to liberate himself by starting his own business. While I know my daddy will be remembered for many things, I think he would most want to be remembered for that one achievement of which he was proudest; and that was transforming himself from a poor black boy from "Springfield," Alabama who couldn't even finish high school because he had to sharecrop to help feed his family to a business owner-operator, beloved and respected for his self-less and compassionate works bestowed on those in the community where he lived. There are some people who couldn't care less about owning a business; in their opinion business ownership is not "all that." But, of all the good that my daddy did in his life, HE viewed it as his greatest achievement in life. And he pursued it vigorously because he viewed it as the most effective vehicle for black economic freedom and empowerment. So, for him—it was. I want him to be remembered and honored for that; for having a dream; and having the courage to pursue it; despite All the odds against him. That became his passion. And, because my mother and I loved and admired him so much — WE MADE IT OUR PASSION TOO. Because I firmly and steadfastly believe that passion is the one attribute that is necessary for anybody to succeed in business, and my daddy was the epitome of that, I propose to take his historical distinction and use it to show others the way.

I believe that he merits public memorialization in a way that will make him known throughout eternity — for as long as any earthly symbols of distinction stand—for as long as this book remains in print, and his name resides on the domain that I maintain in his honor to inspire an appreciation for him and his business adventures by others who will be impacted and inspired by its content — let him be long remembered, for the many works wrought that so eloquently spoke for him.

Let him be remembered through the creation of this community-based network designed to promote and encourage black business ownership; one wherein anyone wanting to raise their economic standards can do so, without the resistance my daddy met in the 1960's. Let his life and works serve as a constant and tangible reminder that we, too can cultivate the human qualities that will enable us to overcome! Let us remember him by making it easier for somebody else who desires to over come. Let us remember him by creating an economic fellowship where ideas can flourish and blossom; where we have nothing to gain by your failure; but everything to gain by your success!

Let us remember him by offering ourselves and our services as a comprehensive resource and education outlet for individuals with a wide range of business interests who want to raise our standards in our respective communities. In his name and in his honor, let doors and opportunities be opened to us, instead of slammed in our faces.   Let us remember him through a membership organization and support base, through which monetary grants may be sought and awarded in his name to those who seek to better themselves.

As we work to implement this "Clark Initiative," our hope is that a renaissance will occur in the African-American neighborhoods; that we will witness a new awakening as we lead our communities into this millennium. That our communities will not only come alive but that they will survive and thrive.

This is but a small part of what we are working to accomplish through the memorialization of the late Wilkie Clark, and the establishment of a Foundation in his honor. Certainly you can see the need for it. My prayer is that you will also see the need to support it.

Business Ownership
An Escape Route From Poverty For African Americans Or Just An Illusion of Affluence?

Many African-Americans turn to thoughts of business ownership as an escape route from our "generational curse of poverty and lack." And while it's okay to view it as an escape route, I would ask, is it as much a vehicle toward abundance as a vehicle toward empowerment?

My only admonition is that you just bear in mind that no matter how you choose to view it, it is no picnic.

Anyone considering business ownership needs to know the real deal. And if you are a minority, you REALLY must consider carefully and weigh every aspect of your desire to be in business. If you are thinking about entering the business world, you need to understand both the logistics — and the statistics.

Both of these terms have to do with numbers. How many, and how much... because in the end, the bottom line will be a number: how many customers you won; how much of your product or service you sold; how much you got paid; how much it costed you to make whatever amount you made.

Logistics has to do with figuring out numerically what your potential is for succeeding based on the kind of business you are trying to go into, as relates to the population who will have a demand for your product or service. In other words, before you open the door, you need to know exactly how many people will want what you are selling? How many competing businesses exist in your general market area and what is the probability that they will patronize your business versus any competing businesses? In logistics, you will have to look at the total economy of the location you want to go into with your business. What kinds of jobs do people have? Will they be able to afford your product or service? Are they already using your product or service, or will you have to create a market for it?

You must be able to answer that and similar questions numerically. In the business world, this is called a "logistical study." Statistics has to do with the prior actual buying and spending trends or patterns expressed numerically. How many people have previously bought this product or service you now want to offer? How did the product sell? Was it hot? OR was it not? What was the price? At it's highest? At it's lowest? If it was hot, how long was it a hot product? If it was not, then what unique thing do you plan to do to change that trend? What specific plan to you have to create interest in it? Have you tested it? If not, how could you test it?

Based on all this and a lot of other data, you have to come up with your formula for success.

You also need to know that a very high percentage of people who start their own businesses fail miserably. You need to understand why they fail. You need to know that the majority of failing business do so because of poor planning. An old cliche' I've often heard about businesses that fail is that "they don't plan to fail, they fail to plan."

What will sustain you as you make that transition from a previous "wage earner" to being the last name on the payroll ? and the one who usually doesn't get a pay check? There may be times, when you'll ride the economic wave; on the flip side of that coin, there will also be those economically slack times when you may run the risk of losing everything you've invested. And whether times are economically fat or lean, on practically any day you'll be met with any number of incidental expenses that will add to the cost of making that money. By the time you finish counting up what it has cost you to make that money, you may profit $100.00. You'll be raising cain to profit $125.00.

I cannot emphasize enough, that business ownership, while very rewarding, it's more than just a notion. It is a real mental challenge that has the potential to totally consume and rob you of every ounce of the life force within you, destroy you spiritually, burn you out emotionally, mentally fatigue you, and physically drain you.

Just like my daddy said, "the world will await you with open arms" — make you think they're happy, even anxious for you to do your thing—strut your stuff; but remember, they'll have a hammer in each hand, ready to knock the hell out of you; so from the jump, you've got to be made out of the right stuff or you'll get your butt kicked.

Once in business for yourself, if you survive for any length of time, you'll learn to be tough and thick-skinned; to be ready for every possible pitfall that awaits you; be ready to withstand all kinds of criticism— not only the criticism of your known adversaries, but of your thought-to-be friends and supporters. Go ahead right now, and start thinking about how you will protect yourself against that kind of thing, because if you don't have a meticulous plan, you can forget all the other advantages and perks that accompany business ownership; You won't survive the mental, physical, emotional and spiritual ravages it will work on you. On the other hand, once you are prepared in all the above domains, then you are certainly ready for the excitement, the rush, the sheer thrill, the exhilaration of entrepreneurship.

Entrepreneurs are truly a special breed. We're all made of similar stuff. We may have different ideas about what we want to do, or how we want to do it; but, at heart; we are over-achievers, workaholics, self-starters and self-motivated risk-takers; and we thrive off of new challenges.

That's the kind of man my father was. And even though he didn't make a million dollars, he didn't die rich, he didn't leave me a million dollars, he came along at a time when all odds were against him and I think he did darn good. When I think about daddy, he had no choice but to be successful. He could not afford to fail in business, because the opportunities for recovery from failure were so bleak and so few–actually non-existent. At all times, there was probably double, even triple motivation at work in him, driving him in that direction; laying in a course for his success. What were these compelling reasons for him to succeed?

Mainly, because daddy was a man on a mission. First of all, being a black man, he had no choice, because at the time he came of age, as outspoken as he was; as passionate as he was about the racial climate of that time; as much disdain as he had for any kind of racial mistreatment; if daddy had stayed on a job of ANY KIND, no question in my mind, he would have been killed! We knew that, and I believe he knew it too.

Daddy was on a mission to prove the white man wrong. There were all the stigmas attached to being black; all the pre-conceived ideas about blacks not having any sense; being mentally inept, dumb; lacking the ability to direct himself; ignorant; stupid; clowns, akin to the ape or the gorilla or whatever animal they wanted to compare us with. He was ever so passionate in his hatred of this stigma. How he wanted to prove that wrong and then be able to brag about it, where the white man could hear him loud and clear! Where he could "gloat" over it, and have the white man be ashamed and embarrassed for ever thinking that way about us. He was so serious about this that even as a little girl, I could just feel those vibes emanating from him.

Not only was there a battle to change the white man's thinking about blacks, but there was also an even greater battle to "de-program" blacks from all that "white-wash" that the white man and the stigma of racism had placed in them that worked against their self-respect, self-worth, and self-esteem.

Here was a black man, my daddy, trying hard to inspire a people in a community who had been beaten down on every hand, and in every way imaginable; who lived as second-class citizens; who'd been told all their lives they were not even as good as the most ruthless, criminal, trashy, white man or woman on earth; that even educated, they were nothing; as PhDs, educators, preachers, they were nothing; nothing they could do could ever equal any white achievement. Here also was a black man raising a young daughter, and needing his daughter and his wife to honor and re-spect him as the leader and commander in his family; how could he command their respect, when he was leaving home every day clean, and return filthy from the dirt of oppression; from the dirt of a job that was so demeaning and so demanding that no white man would consider doing it. Leaving home a man, and returning a boy, subjected to the daily verbal harassment and mistreatment and abuse of such as old Mr. Shannon? Who was no better. Whose only redeeming quality was his whiteness.

I also believe that there was within him this overwhelming passion to make himself an example for other black people, so they could see that they didn't have to stay where they were. That all they needed to do was change their minds and attitudes, and be-lieve in themselves; reject the mind set the oppressive "white man" had brainwashed them with, that they couldn't do any better — that all the colored women could do was go into the affluent white homes and wash and cook and baby-sit their children; that all the colored men could do was sweep floors, clean toilets, and swing off the back of the city garbage trucks. That it was possible for them, by way of business ownership, to raise their own standards, and not wait on the white man to decide when it was time for them to come of age, raise their standards of living and existing.

Lastly and most importantly, I think even above and be-yond all of that, daddy was just an entrepreneur at heart. He was destined to be his own boss, black, white, purple or polka-dot. Certainly this must be what Dr. Martin Luther King, Jr. had in mind when he spoke about judging individuals not on the color of their skin, but on the content of their character. Until one experiences that kind of rejection, race-based pre-judgment (prejudice) doesn't hold much meaning. But, here is the point at which the power of Dr. King's statement is dramatized. From the time he was a young adult, my father had within him the desire, the character and the makings of a successful entrepreneur. But, white America denied him that; they couldn't see that, because they were too busy looking at the color of his skin. Simply put, he was pre-judged. And that alone, forced him to defer his dreams. But it was his destiny. And that was the one thing that white supremacy could not deny him.

Some people can punch a time clock— entrepreneurs are not made that way. They intrinsically know that they have something special to give to the world and they are determined to give it. Ultimately, that is what drives them out of the day-to-day rat-race and into business. After all, that's where they can shine and create the backdrop to showcase their own unique talents. I think that at the core of all we do, is the drive to serve humanity and inspire others. That is precisely the way I saw my daddy. And these are the personal attributes I saw in him that I believe made him so successful and popular with so many people. More than just my hero; he was my inspiration; my motivation. And even today, 15 years after his death; he continues to inspire me because today, I operate the business HE devoted the last 20 years of his life building; He still inspires me — to write books and build web sites in his honor...

COURAGE IS THE CAPACITY TO
CONFRONT WHAT CAN BE IMAGINED

You are bigger than anything that can happen to you.
The obstacles you face are only mental barriers
which can be broken by adopting a more positive approach.
Reality is something you can rise above.
You don't have to be a puppet
manipulated by outside powerful forces;
You can become the powerful force yourself.
Courage is resistance to fear, mastery of fear —
not absence of fear.
This is where you will win the battle —
in the playhouse of your mind.
Visualize what you want.
See it, feel it, believe in it.
Make it your mental blue print,
and begin to build.
See things as you would
have them be instead of as they are.

Adapted From
"Reality Is Something You Can Rise Above"
By Max Stein

In Loving Memory Of My Dad, The Late Wilkie Clark

95

AGGRESSIVENESS

"I had to make my own opportunity. . . .

Don't sit down and wait for the opportunities to come;

you have to get up and make them"

—*Madame C. J. Walker*

What This Book Teaches

Certainly, there has to be a moral to this story. Otherwise, why write it? I can think of a million lessons that people of all ethnic backgrounds could learn from this personal account of my daddy's life. But, in this chapter, I'll try to limit my discussion to those most important to me. You have to bear in mind that this is all very personal to me. Of all the writing I've done in preparation for publishing this piece, this has been by far the most difficult of chapters. After at least twenty-five or more false starts, I'm pressing toward the mark. One reason for the difficulty is because I had to think long and hard about what I wanted people to get out of this.

Separating The Good From The Great

You see, on a very basic level, everybody probably feels that there is some individual they know, who is special to them and who merits special recognition. We are always conferring recognition on somebody for something. Usually, there are very personal reasons for this....we like them...we know of a few good things they may have done....or maybe they were just good to us and we feel obligated to reciprocate. I would imagine that everybody probably feels their own father or mother worthy of special recognition. There are a lot of men and women who can be considered "good" people. But, there is a point at which the "good" must be separated from the "great." What made him so great? So, here is where I attempt to enumerate the reasons why I believe my dad is so deserving of the recognition I seek. In an effort to establish this, for once, my attention turned away from what I myself would get from it. Forget about the closure I sought. Forget about retribution. Forget about the purging of my soul. Even forget about my desire to immortalize my daddy. Here is where I had to dig way down deep inside myself trying to get to the heart of the matter. My answers gradually emerged as I questioned myself about what lessons I would have wanted my own children (particularly

97

my son) to learn from my daddy's life. What did I need for him to learn by observing my daddy's life — and what had he missed by my daddy not being in his life? What important life lessons did he miss, that only time spent in the presence of my daddy would have been capable of teaching him? In an effort to pull this discussion together, my mind returned to former thoughts about how deeply I regretted that my son never really had a chance to grow up around daddy, because at some level, perhaps a spiritual one, I knew that just merely being in daddy's presence alone would have provided for my son, so many "teachable moments."

The Kind Of Lessons Children Learn From The Significant Adults In the Lives

What is a "teachable moment?" This is a "lesson" that you don't deliberately set out to teach kids; but a situation arises that produces a perfect example within which to impart that virtue or moral lesson. As my mother used to say, to learn by association. At every opportunity, no matter how small, daddy took time with me, just to teach. And great instructor that he was, there was a lesson in every life event, and he took time to point these things out to me in his own unique, charismatic way, and make certain that I understood and got the point of the lesson. This is one of the most precious elements of child rearing that I so often find is clearly missing from the lives children today. They have so little understanding about how to live life....successfully. So, we see them continually making ridiculous mistakes, that lead them down a life long path of destruction.

How African Americans Should Regard Community

I feel so fortunate that my daddy taught me — even persuaded me how important it is that African Americans learn to operate as a community; to move together as a community; to unite in our effort to better ourselves. What I find so shameful is that this is a lesson that many black communities still have not learned, because so many of us, in a futile effort to still try to embrace white thinking patterns, feel that we don't need to be connected with other African Americans in our community, to achieve our common goals. We don't care about community. We are not bothered by the fact that an overwhelming number of our people are fairing poorly.

As long as "me and my house" are doing well, we got ours, now you get yours. Just think about how much farther along we might all be today, if years ago, we could have moved together as a community under a strategic plan of action. We still have not realized that what works for the majority, (of which we are not a part) does not work for us.

We have more churches in our community than you can count. And in many respects, that is wonderful! Commendable! Yet in other respects, it's shameful. Because, every one of them is marching to the beat of a different drummer. Every one of them has a different agenda. Facilitated by our slightly improved economic status, we have much nicer buildings; padded pews; plexiglass (often-engraved), lecterns; thickly padded carpeted, centrally heated and cooled facilities. We sing long and loud about "serving this present age our calling to fulfill," yet, many of our churches show little or no concern about addressing the social issues of this day. Every now and then, we go to the kitchen and cook a grand meal, distribute a few plates for the hungry, and raise a few dollars for the sick, but we don't begin to scratch the surface when it comes to ministering in our communities. In the midst of all these churches, and bible-toting missionaries, we all still live in drug-infested communities, where we seem to have blinders on, to the immorality that walks the streets night and day. We turn up our noses, and walk right past it, and walk right into the church and close the door behind us. We shut them out, and shut ourselves in. And our communities continue to deteriorate.

Why We Have Not Overcome

So, what's the most important thing to be gotten from all of this? There are many concurrent themes scattered amongst these pages. If we were to pinpoint 1954 (Brown vs. Board of Education) as our frame of reference, in spite of nearly 50 years of progress, we as a people still stand on shaky ground, socially, educationally, economically and politically. And, I won't even try to comment on the religious status of African-Americans, because that would take another whole book. The main question we must ponder is in light of our disjointed history as a people, how do we fix our broken selves? How do we capture the attention of misguided young black men and women? How do we impress upon them the idea of modifying their priorities? Taking the "high road" to success, rather than the "low road."

How do we shield and protect ourselves from the repulsive stigma of racial stereotyping that continues to plague our culture. How do we come out of all this in one piece?

So, summarized here is my sequential listing for fixing what's broken:

1. Acknowledge the damage that American Society has done to us;

2. Reject society's view of our culture;

3. De-program ourselves (this includes our cultural institutions; our lodges, clubs, churches, community groups etc.);

4. Re-define ourselves (this includes our cultural institutions; our lodges, clubs, churches, community groups, etc.);

5. Declare our Independence from former definitions of ourselves;

6. Dare to ACT on all the above; create new — unconventional ways of setting and achieving goals;

7. Pass It On.

What It Will Take To Overcome

As I reflect on everything I've tried to share with you about the unconquerable soul of Wilkie Clark, the above list of actions appear to repeat themselves throughout the events of his lifetime.

For my own son, the very core of my spirit is pierced by the awareness and the deep regret that I was unable to teach him how to be a man, especially a strong, courageous, protective man such as my father was. I could show him love, I tried to make him tough, I tried to show him "tough love;" tried to show him the nurturing, mothering love. I tried to make sure he learned from his mistakes. But, I couldn't teach him how to be a man. I tried to teach him virtues like honesty and integrity; but couldn't teach him how to be the strong, determined, persistent, unyielding, proud and insightful black man that is such a rare breed and so desperately needed in our communities today. In order for a boy to become a man, he's got to see a man. That just was not there for him. Even as I looked around and about my community in search of a role model for him, there was none. Not one. Unlike my dad's uncles, whom you'll read about later in this book, after my husband's death, his own brothers, so embittered by Clarence's death, went right on back to their lives, and forgot that there was a young boy here who might have needed a male role model in his life, or confidant.

The Real Men Must Come Out Of The Closet

Consequently, if the majority of decent African-American men are hiding somewhere in the closet, who is left for our young black boys to emulate? Only those they see on the street corners. Thus one of my greatest fears is the possibility that the young men who will surely become the future decision-makers and leaders of our respective communities will continue to be so heavily influenced, enchanted and fascinated by this hip-hop, gang-banging, glock-toting, cap-busting corruptible culture. What kind of nation will we find ourselves living in? If nothing else, I pray that I've succeeded in effectively planting a tiny seed of understanding of the degree to which daughters are empowered when their relationship with a spiritually and morally strong father has been undergirded by a healthy, trusting, loving form of attention, unconditional acceptance and positive affirmation.

The Need For Strong Father-Daughter Relationships

One of the most hurtful events of my adult life came when I learned that at the fragile age of 14, my daughter, Je'Lynn had become pregnant. Everybody around me was telling me that pregnancy wasn't the worst thing that could have happened to her, yet while acknowledging that, I was nevertheless devastated by the news. Everybody tried to persuade me to accept the fact that this was commonplace in this day, and no big deal. But, the only thing I could see was how this would place upon her young immature shoulders a mountainous adult responsibility that she was not mentally, emotionally nor intellectually ready for. How it would rob her of most of her own remaining adolescent years and curtail her ability to take full advantage of what educational opportunities were available to her. I found myself wondering how I could have prevented this. As I looked back over our lives, again, I recalled her daddy's sudden passing when she was only 10 years old.

Clarence was a loving and nurturing father both to Je'Lynn and Sherard. As a matter of fact, she was more attached to him than she was to me, because he doted on her and made her his "princess." He had many nurturing qualities most men are afraid to reveal, much like those I saw in my dad, but was abruptly snatched from our lives far sooner than any of us expected. I suppose that somewhere in my mind I should have understood and anticipated the impact his death would have on her. But, not having experienced the deprivation of my father's presence at such a young age, I assumed my daughter would grow up emotionally strong, because I was that way. Why couldn't I stand in the gap and be the portrait of inner strength in her life? Worst assumption I could have ever made! I was sadly mistaken. Now that I've had lots of time to reflect and think it through, I've concluded that as my daughter entered puberty and missing the affection and affirmation of her father, she somehow lost herself in an unhealthy relationship with an older boy, who merely used her for sex the same way a lot of black girls get used for sex ... because they are seeking something their mothers can never give them. It's the kind of strength, empowerment and security that evolves over the course of a sustained healthy and loving relationship between a father and his daughter. The kind that I had, for 35 years. Regrettably, hers was an abusive relationship that resulted in the birth of my beautiful grandson, whom we call "Kenzie." Though I love him dearly, I regret the circumstances under which he was conceived.

Here's is yet another black man-child, growing up in my home where regrettably there is no strong father to nurture him, accept him, love him, shield, protect and empower. My concerns: Will he understand who he really is? How will he learn his role in life? How will he develop his sexuality? How will he develop the manly instinct to defend and protect, so he can be the commander in the family that he will one day create? Will he learn how to confront life's problems and obstacles? How will he learn to be a problem-solver? "An over-comer?"

Now, I occasionally find myself weeping for my daughter who has missed something so special, that she will never have the chance to experience. And because she missed that, all I can hope for her now is a future with the right man – one with a good heart, who will love, accept, affirm, and empower her the way I know Clarence would have if only he'd been here in her life. I believe the influence of a strong father (or significant male) in her life would have reinforced her emotionally with the strength she needed at 13 and 14 to reject the notion of engaging in an empty physical relationship at such a fragile stage in her life; or to involve herself in any kind of abusive relationship; it would have allowed her to see that her father did not abuse her mother and likewise, compelled her to reject any kind of treatment other than kind treatment as unacceptable; the strong influence of a father who could have affirmed her importance, her beauty, her deserving better than some shallow sexual experience with a boy to whom she meant nothing but a good time behind closed doors.

In spite of everything that happened in our lives, today, I take pride in Je'Lynn's total transformation and accomplishments. She has emerged a wonderful young lady who is both refined and astute. She is a loving Christian mother, and is well-focused on securing a bright future for herself and her young son. I am honored to have her as my daughter.

A Constant Ever-Present Force
To Be Reckoned With In the Home

I pray this book will dramatize to African American men that if we as a community are to contribute to the growth and progress of our great nation in a way that equals or exceeds that of our forefathers, it's just not enough for fathers to merely be present in the home; but they must be active, particularly with their daughters. They must play an active role in shaping their daughters' understanding of who and what they are. They must spend time with them; talk to them; be friends with them. The relationship can't be allowed to merely exist only in a superficial– or tangible way. It can't just be about giving financial support; or paying court-ordered child support; it's about continuous emotional and mental support as well as a kind of intangible support that facilitates their emergence as self-sufficient, problem-solvers and creators of their own destinies. This is something that no judge can order. For that matter, why do we need a legal system crafted by white men to tell us how to be good to our black children? How can some white judge sitting on some bench, who probably never drove through our community, tell us what is best for our children? Why do we need anyone outside our own family, telling us how to take care of our children? I can just see daddy in my mind— how he would frown upon the idea of any man outside the black race dictating how we interact within black families!

The Importance Of The Black Man
Must Also Be Affirmed
And Good Black Fathers Must Be Praised

While American society frowns upon and tends to look down upon its black men, it must, none-the-less acknowledge and accept responsibility for the role it played in making the black man what he is. For, the black man—whatever he is—is what American society has made him. Perhaps the more appropriate word to use here is "programmed" him to be.

Let's face it. America, and more particularly the state of Alabama, has unfinished business with its black men and boys because American society has done a real number on the black man dating all the way back to captivity and enslavement. He comes into the world already bruised and scarred. I recall one of my daddy's favorite anecdotes that he often shared that went something like this:

"On March 8, 1920, the day I was born, the mid-wife said: "Lue Ella, you got a boy!" Mama asked, "What color is he?" The midwife replied, "He's jet black!" "I was in trouble, and been in trouble ever since..."

Somehow daddy understood that without any of the other baggage that just comes along with living life, the way of the black man was already rough, crooked and watered with tears. Many others have written about it, like Dr. Earl Ofari Hutchinson, In Praise of Black Fathers, (2000 Family Digest Media Group), but, somehow, the message seems to be getting lost.

According to Dr. Hutchinson, America has already attempted to obscure the black father from our view. It has neglected to recognize, acknowledge or take responsibility for the tremendous and deep seated emotional damage that has been done to his psyche. Beginning with the separation of the black man from his family in slavery, white America deliberately sowed throughout the African community seeds of separation with the intention of dividing and isolating black men from their families, severing relationships, all with the intention of weakening him; weakening the emotional bonds between boys and their fathers, mothers and siblings.

If you read the shocking historical accounts of the mistreatment of slavery, you learn how children were brutally torn from their fathers and sold; how the slave masters generally refused to grant permission for slaves to marry. The enslavement process was long and tedious and deliberate.

White America stole strong black men from their native land, and set out to break them like breaking in wild horses. The mind had to be broken down, bit by bit until every ounce of his will to be free and in control of himself was shattered.

Over a period of many generations, he was systematically de-programmed by means of one brutal whipping and scolding after another until finally reprogrammed to accept this new condition of dis-empowerment, little by little and bit by bit, he succumbed.

Now, under such oppressive circumstances how could black families function as a unit? How could black fathers function as leaders in their families while held captive? But somehow, oddly enough however, in SPITE of the dysfunctional histories of our families, many black men nevertheless rose to the occasion of fatherhood – displaying both strength and courage.

Yet, you don't hear about them because nobody bothered to write about them. So, there began a growing myth of the black man propagated by die-hards still intent on diminishing and invalidating the potential strength and power of black men. As a result of this growing myth, black men even today, are feared, shunned, scorned, isolated, and avoided, particularly in corporate America, wherein lies real economic liberation. You need to know that contrary to the myths that have been perpetrated, black fathers did and DO have families that they care about. Often risking life and limb they made sacrifices to liberate their wives and children from bondage, sometimes heroically rescuing them. Others bought their freedom. Driven by a sense of love and loyalty and desperate to fulfill their responsibilities as fathers, they made their marriages legal after Emancipation.

Sadly but truthfully, even though blacks represent a smaller portion of the general population, we see far too many instances wherein for some black families, black men do desert their homes; do make babies that they don't take care of; they fill the jails and prisons; they join gangs and commit acts of violence; they die young from drugs, alcohol and disease; and from conception to adulthood are forced to run the gauntlet of American abuses. But I pray that the message here is that it doesn't have to remain that way.

So that we can face the uncertain days that lay ahead for Black families it is not only imperative, but urgent that we tell the stories that celebrate the victories and triumphs of our people; stop talking about defeatism and despair; rather about optimism and hope, and most of all about success. In the words of Dr. Earl Ofari Hutchinson, "We must finally lift the cloak of invisibility from Black fathers."

While I partially agree with Dr. Hutchinson's assertion that the biggest problem is how society looks at Black men and how Black men look at themselves I take issue with the first part of that statement. To me, what is MOST important, is how black men look at themselves. If black men don't like they way American society has stereotyped them, then it's up to black men to openly, loudly, boldly and actively reject it. We have to paint that new portrait, which is where redefining ourselves becomes important.

We can not afford to allow American Society to tell us who and what we are. And in my assessment, black men have been too quick to yield and settle for whatever brand is seared onto them by American Society. This tendency to yield is what I believe threatens the very fabric of the black family as it ought to exist.

Finally, another important lesson here, is that we must impress upon society, how important it is to look for and examine carefully the roots of the extreme anger within so many black males, which often manifests itself in negative outcomes. During his lifetime, I saw this same anger in my father— almost every day, in some form or another. But, I surmise that daddy learned very early how to "fight city hall."

He understood that in order to validate his manhood, it was necessary, even urgent that he learn all he could about this oppressive system, and find a way to defeat it, within the parameters of THAT OPPRESSIVE SYSTEM. For him, it meant getting involved in the struggle for civil rights; it meant being a good citizen; it meant adhering to Christian principles; doing everything in the right way. He set about to deliberately make these attitudes and behaviors a part of his character. Amazingly, none of these actions overshadowed or diminished his masculinity, because at the same time, he openly, candidly dramatized his righteous indignation with racism and oppression by vocalizing it whenever and wherever he saw a need to do that — sometimes, it was ugly; vigorous; occasionally in a soft-spoken but matter-of-fact manner, always done with respectability and a cordial demeanor. This is one lesson, that I believe has somehow eluded so many young black men, who don't understand because they've never been taught, how to wage war. Daddy didn't wear black leather, and big chunks of gold jewelry bling-blinging about his neck; didn't have not one gold tooth; never attacked anybody with a glock or an oozie and didn't ride around with a flashy car, or jewels, or diamond rings. He was just daddy; but he was a hell of a man. He was a soldier — from the heart.

Speaking Truth To Power

Throughout this book, I have made numerous references to oppression, mistreatment, economic disadvantage, social isolation, bigotry, hatred, inferiority, white superiority, poverty. These are all conditions under which my father existed and operated for most of his 69 years. The world continually chanting his demise; reminding him of his inadequacies; verbally dooming him to eternal enslavement...working diligently to secure it.....attempting to burn onto his mind an acceptance and a willingness to exist under these evil pre-conceptions with a branding iron of trickery and deceit. Representing lies as the truth and truth as a lie.

He existed in a world where what practically everyone else perceived as truth, was in reality a lie; a deceptive trick of the devil. In his reality, few people other than himself, saw it for what it was, or realized it was a lie. But rooted and grounded in what he saw as truth; going against the popular train of thought, he opted to acknowledge that which for him represented truth. Shutting out everything else that looked like, sounded like, or in any way resembled a lie, he chose to ignore the lies and deception and to acknowledge his reality.

"And ye shall know the truth, and the truth shall make you free." (John 8: 32)

"And judgment is turned away backward, and justice standeth afar off: for truth is fallen in the street, and equity cannot enter." (Isaiah 59: 14)

When one lives in such a world as my daddy did, so heavily populated by those whose vision was clouded and dimmed by generations of lies conceived in hatred and perpetuated in bigotry, what reason would he have to believe in himself or his potential to succeed at anything? How could he challenge or overcome such overwhelmingly disproportionate odds? Unless one is born into the African-American race and understands the psychology and intricate workings of the black mind, they can not fathom what I am talking about, without at least a partial explanation.

You see, my daddy not only had to overcome the stigma of racism that was already inherent in the psyche of white oppressors all over the south. But, he had to overcome the deep, penetrating, violent self-hatred that had historically been implanted within the psyche of so many blacks all over this country. A self-hatred so evil, vicious and violent that it caused us as a people to develop faults in our personalities; faults that inclined us to rejoice in committing acts of betrayal against each other; to discuss each other in demeaning ways; to reject any notions of supportiveness, unity and racial cohesiveness; so evil that before we would rejoice in our brother's successes, we would rather set a trap to cause his failure; so evil that we would endeavor to aid our oppressor by perpetrating vicious lies to make it easy for the oppressor to discredit and belittle, ultimately causing him to believe that he does not deserve the liberation he seeks; make him feel guilty about his desire to be liberated, economically or otherwise.

When discussing economic advancement among blacks, there was a phrase often repeated throughout the civil rights community that described the corruptible attitudes and thinking of blacks toward each other. It was often repeated in meetings and other public gatherings. That statement was: "the white man's ice is colder." This oft-repeated phrase was used as a reminder to African-Americans that our quest for economic advancement was dependent upon our willingness to help each other in our business endeavors. But instead, African-Americans were often helping to sabotage our own businesses, because when one of our own would go into business, rather than to support that business owner, we'd drive further and pay more to buy it from a white business owner. Despite that intellectually, we know that ice is ice and we know that one block of ice is just as cold as the next, as a carry-over from that perception of black inferiority, there was always that lingering mind set that whatever the white man did was better. Whatever word proceeded out of the white man's mouth was gospel. If the white man endorsed it, it was a superior product. Thus blacks whose backs were still bent to the will and the words of American society, is what gave them power. After all, how could the black man succeed in any business, when his own people refused to support it? Certain that he could not count on white trade, he often still found himself at a loss, because frequently he couldn't even corner the black market either.

How does one beat that?

Knowing that he had all these things working against him, one has to wonder, how he did it? My daddy, I mean. What gave him the courage to risk everything he had accumulated in life on an idea that had the potential to destroy him financially and permanently? In spite of his limited exposure or preparation for running a business, inferior knowledge, what made him so undaunted and relentless in pursuing his dream.... a dream that no-one else believed in but him? How was it that he could remain so steadfast in his determination to follow through on it with everybody predicting his failure, throwing stumbling blocks in his pathway, and constantly taking stabs at his self-esteem, inventing reasons to discourage him? What rare breed of courage did it take to forge ahead into the uncertain days that lay ahead when there was no reason to believe....seemingly untouched...unmoved by the degrading and sometimes scornful spirits of those whom he encountered? I submit that in reality it certainly was not courage. For as surely as I journey backwards in time within the deep recesses of my mind and re-examine the challenges that confronted daddy through the eyes of that little girl who sat and watched him with adoration — what I saw operating in my daddy at that time was not courage. It was faith. That young girl who sat and observed carefully as instructed by her father, sometimes saw fear in his eyes; sensed the intense trembling of a man who no doubt was treading unchartered waters, but assured only by his faith in a higher power, he went forward. Remind you of anything you've heard before? "In the fourth watch of the night, Jesus went unto them, walking on the sea. And when the disciples saw him walking on the sea, they were troubled, saying, "It is a spirit;" and they cried out of fear. But straightway, Jesus spake unto them saying, "Be of good cheer; it is I; be not afraid." And Peter answered him and said, "Lord, if it be thou, bid me come unto thee on the water." And he said, "Come." And when Peter was come down out of the ship, he walked on the water, to go to Jesus." (Matthew 14: 25-29).

Focused only on that thing down inside of him that was planting within him the assurance that he was not too ignorant; that he was not stupid; that he did have the ability to think for himself and solve his own problems, and that he was not alone, he treaded those unchartered waters. I contend that daddy was just made out of all the right stuff. The stuff I have reference to is the human qualities he possessed. It was the things you could "feel" and "sense" about him. He had a reputation that preceded him. He had spent the first 49 years of life working on that, even during his railroad days, he worked steadily on it. He had started building that reputation when he was at home with his mother. He didn't have any money; but what he had which was far more valuable that money was a good name; he was a man of integrity; he had a good heart; he had humility; he had love and compassion for humanity; and had a desire to serve God by serving others.

He had discipline; and he had purpose; he understood his mission; he had common sense, something that we might also refer to as "wisdom;" he had a desire to better himself; he had honesty and genuineness. Some educators would call these "life skills;" others would say "character." In the business world, we often call these "people skills;" or "PR." Daddy had just the right amount of care. He cared about others. But he didn't care enough to allow anybody to get in his way. Whatever you choose to call them, they are at the heart of this movement that has swept America, to "teach" character to large numbers of children who seemingly enter school with no shred of decency. But, can schools really impart these lessons to children in a way that they can be internalized? These lessons are indeed virtues that I believe are best taught and translated by way of the influence of a strong and steadfast man who is constantly in the life of a child.

Well, I predict that one day in the future some little black boy is going to open his eyes and begin to question why he exists in the state he does. I foresee that he will be confused and perplexed, and want to know how it is that he was allowed to degenerate into the miserable state he will find himself in. He won't even understand the circumstances that landed him there. There won't even be in existence a "Wilkie Clark" to tell him about the "Princely" heritage he enjoyed until stolen from his native land and brought to this country as a slave; and how his strong family ties were broken by a ruthless white man determined to dehumanize him and turn him into a piece of property; how his father was maliciously and cunningly separated from him, for fear that he'd be rescued; that cultural ties and strong religious foundation of his ancestors brought him down through generations of bondage and slavery; and how a new nation was borne and built on the blood, sweat, tears, and the backs of his ancestors; and how a handful of "new black men" of the 19th and 20th century began to take risks by straightening up their backs and standing tall and establishing self-sustaining institutions that would stand as earthly monuments to their work in strengthening the neighborhoods. He will not understand how amid an inconceivable new wave of permissiveness, promiscuity, immorality and indecency the concept of "father," and "mother," and family somehow diminished over time and delivered him to the despicable place wherein he will find himself. Perhaps in that decisive hour, this book will be laying around for him to catch just a glimpse of who he really is. That day, my friends, is already upon us.

He will not understand why he is lacking in the virtue of self-discipline that are so necessary for survival in the world of the future. He will not understand why he has been shown no value in the idea of educating himself in preparation to compete in American society. He won't understand why he doesn't know, value or have a relationship with his heavenly father — or his earthly father for that matter.

He will look for someone or something —anyone or anything to blame his misfortune on. Having lived life without a strong, steadfast man in his life, will have wreaked havoc on his mental state, his attitude, and his prospect for succeeding in life. And never having experienced the sheer spiritual energy, the life force, and strength gained just by virtue of having had a strong man in his life, not just any strong man ? the one we refer to as "father" he won't even understand why.

Now, sadly enough you can rest assured that society will view him as one who is a disappointment to the community not having lived up to his potential; a burden; as incapable of pulling his fair share of the economic load; a predator; and he will be labeled as a failure. But an even sadder commentary is that despite the claim that he has failed the neighborhood, in reality it is the neighborhood that will have failed him.   So, I lay out my daddy's life as a point of reference and a point of inspiration that any young man or woman can re-visit and use to help them find their way.

I fear that many black youngsters will drown in a sea of ignorance, because our stories — stories of victory and triumph have never been told to them. How can they develop virtue, when they are raising themselves, and have no role-model in the home – or in the neighborhood for that matter, as a point of reference? How can they build self-sustaining institutions if the only black men they see are the ones who are standing on the street corners, peddling drugs; How can anyone expect them to be law-abiding citizens when they don't know what good citizenship looks like? If the only black men they know are the ones who desert their homes, how can they know what loyalty feels like? If the only men they know, make babies that they don't take care of, how will they know what "responsibility" walks like? If they only men they know are those who fill the jails and prisons, join gangs and commit acts of violence, how can they know anything other than that? The men who die young from drugs, alcohol, and disease; and who from conception to adulthood are forced to run the gauntlet of American abuses are fast becoming fashionable to the up and coming generations of youngsters in our society, because this is what we let them see.

We are remiss in our responsibility to these youngsters as long as we treat our heroes, and sheroes, triumphs and victories as closely guarded secrets.

My spirit is vexed by the huge economic and digital divide separating the African-American community from mainstream America and preventing startling numbers of people from living the lives that I believe God wills for us to live. Not having traveled extensively, I can only comment on my immediate surroundings throughout East Alabama and West Georgia, where I do travel extensively. I get weary, seeing my people oppressed by conditions of lack and disparity, a people so despondent that they can't even ignite a fire within their own minds or muster up the will to challenge these deplorable conditions. So, they just stand or sit there in one place, and allow time to move them from one degree of disparity to another. It hurts me to think that they have allowed themselves to sink into a mode of acceptance of this totally unacceptable state of being; largely because they have been brainwashed to believe they have no choice.

It seems the only relief they seem capable of focusing on is to gradually self-destruct by anesthetizing themselves with cigarettes, drugs and alcohol, which makes them even less attractive in the marketplace. They follow the same old routines and rituals day in and day out, 365 days a year, year after year after year until before you realize it, a generation has come and gone, and the cycle begins again. The powers that be don't care. It ain't them.

The black family as an institution has feebly existed under the threat of extinction ever since our ancestors in Africa were taken into captivity. As a result, there is a lot of dysfunction and faulty perceptions about living life in general; about relationships, about survival; and about what it takes to live life successfully. Kids are no longer being taught those virtues that in the 1950's and 60's facilitated the emergence of the "new black men."

Virtues like discipline, self control, self-respect, pride, honesty, decency, humility, kindness, doing unto others as you would have them do unto you; that's what I'm talking about. Those intangibles that our ancestors treasured. Even though public schools have made feeble attempts to embed the teaching of these concepts into a few moments a day in the school setting, youngsters need to see these take on another form other than an announcement over the intercom. It is essential that they be observed every day in the lives and works of the strong men in their lives, who have the power to create the most penetrating impressions.

The old plantation is recreated in the textile mills and sewing factories of today, replete with the slave master, overseer and all. And the only incentive for casting ones self into this scenario is to satisfy a momentary need. The need for a check. American society has placed within the African-American spirit, a very distorted view of success.

So, now, we find ourselves living in an age where nobody want's to invest any time or energy to accomplish anything. We want everything quick, fast and in a hurry. A lot of folks who are not in business, only see the superficial side of business ownership— and thereby assume it to be a panacea. It isn't. They think it's easy. It isn't. Oh, we've learned how to make it look easy; but it ain't easy.

A lot of folks see business ownership as a way out of a dead end job; or the answer to their financial woes. Often, people look at me and their impression is that I'm rolling in money because I'm in business. And they long to do what I'm doing because of this very faulty mis-perception.

They can't even discern the enormous cost of maintaining the business, which is sometimes more overwhelming than I want to think about. But even more compelling than that, they can't even begin to comprehend what one black man endured, just for the mere privilege of availing himself of what was considered an American concept that would afford any man or woman the privilege to advance as far as he or she desired — the "Free Enterprise System."

Many times, what people view as accomplishments are very shallow things. The younger generation in particular tends to base their perception of success on how many long black limos you have sitting in your garage; and how much gold you can wear around your neck or in your mouth. But what we all have to understand is that success is relative. What do I mean by success is relative? Well, what I mean is that success must be considered in relation to, or in comparison with the previous conditions under which one existed prior to going into business. When one considers a black man who came from nothing, with nothing other than his own intellect, sheer will and determination, and who by the grace of God, emerges a better person, we can consider that success. Furthermore, true achievement and success actually are works in progress; they build character; they test your patience; and sometimes vex your spirit. And they call for extreme courage. For that reason, we should be teaching our communities to hold black businesses in high regard, as historic markers and institutions denoting tremendous achievement. This is how I regard my daddy. He was a mover; a shaker; a true "history-maker." At day's end, that's what all true entrepreneurs are made of. In the 1960's my father, a black man born in the heart of the "Old South;" born with NO advantages, NO exposure to the business world, and only out of the sheer will to change his life, better himself, liberate himself and his people, put himself in position to help hundreds of people in his community. A man with an unstoppable spirit, with unbelievable compassion for others, and genuine desire to elevate himself spiritually, he met and overcame every challenge; and ultimately prevailing, started his own business. It was his proudest life accomplishment. I contend that the same degree of faith and courage, that it took for those black men of slavery times, to rescue their families from bondage, is the same courage it took for my daddy to overcome and break through his barriers en route to business ownership.

Many people today see business ownership as a "ticket" out of a life of entrapment; out of a life of the routine and mundane drudgery of going to a dull, unexciting job, doing the same thing day after day; never having the opportunity to grow, expand, or get ahead in life. For daddy, a black man in the 1960's business ownership put you in a place like none other. It afforded him a taste of freedom— not just from the time restraints of a regular 9 to 5 job; but in that day, it meant freedom to speak; and freedom to express himself — truthfully and honestly, instead of having to restrain himself from commenting on political issues affecting black people; freedom to join and support organizations that were working to fight the oppressive state of existence for black Americans. In those days, there were times when just being on a job itself was oppressive; mean-spirited bosses and supervisors often had free reign to take their personal frustrations and bigotry out on the first black subordinate they saw.... Yes, indeed, for daddy, being in business afforded him a taste of freedom.

Now, tell me, what are you willing to go through? What are you willing to put up with? What are you willing to sacrifice, to experience a taste of freedom?

What price would you be willing to pay for that kind of liberation?

Today, freedom may not necessarily relate to the liberty to speak out and express yourself; but it may mean freedom to make meaningful decisions related to the work you do; freedom to be creative and to create; freedom to change directions; freedom to expand, grow... perhaps just the freedom that comes with being the "Chief Cook and Bottle-Washer" in your own company.

Read Wilkie Clark's story, and see if you are made of the right stuff!

"Choose a job you love,
and you will never have to work
a day in your life. "

Confucius (551 BC - 479 BC)
Chinese philosopher, administrator, and moralist
Analects, 5th century BC

ADAPTABILITY

What most successful blacks learn is that most everything can, in fact, be learned — how to talk, how to dress,
how to groom an image for success. The important thing
is to recognize what is not known and then learn it.

—Audrey Edwards and Craig K. Polite,
from Children of the Dream

The Story
"Giving Service Above Self"
"Where Courtesy Dwells and Service Excels!"
*"We Specialize In Helping Families Celebrate
the Precious Gift Of Life"*

Today, there is hardly anybody in the African-American villages of Randolph County, Alabama, who wouldn't instantly recognize the above "tag lines" and link them to Clark Memorial Funeral Service in Roanoke.

To our family all these "tags" are words we have used to characterize our unique business activities. February 18, 2005 marked the 36th year since the founding of Clark Memorial Funeral Service. For us, it is a time of contemplation as well as reflection, because it causes us to look back at the life of it's founder, my father, the late Wilkie Clark.

Clark Funeral Home stands as an earthly monument to the racial and economic struggles of Wilkie Clark, whose life, I believe bears witness to the unfailing, unfaltering grace of God, by and through whom we rise above our circumstances, no matter how they oppress us.

Today, my family and I continue to operate Clark Funeral Home because of our deep love for daddy and everything that Clark Funeral Home represented TO HIM. For us, it has NEVER been about trying to make a lot of money— because in reality, after 36 years in the death-care industry, we've come to understand so much about this business — and one of the realities is that the cost to operate a small-scale "mom & pop" funeral home — in a rural community serving a handful of economically oppressed African families — is so enormous, until we do good to break even. But, FOR US, it's about the love, respect and reverence that my children and I have for my father, and his courageous effort to meet unsurmountable odds to achieve a goal in life. It's also about respect and reverence for his motivation for doing so. His life and struggles continue to inspire me; they ignite in me the same kind of faith that sustained him and my mother. This is something the two of them instilled in me that nobody can take away.

That is why since July of 1989, we have operated as Clark MEMORIAL Funeral Service.

My daddy often had some strange — BUT WISE sayings. He would often say, "...Hell, you don't have to recognize me; because I recognize myself!" In keeping with the spirit of that philosophy I am not as concerned about recognition from others as I am about my commitment to recognize him. WE KNOW our own history in our community. And that is why we take this opportunity to pause and acknowledge our business and the impact it has had in our community. And we cannot fail to point to our founder, father, and grandfather, as the inspiration for that.

Oh! How I wish that I had started writing this biography 15 years ago, when he was still fresh in the minds of so many African-Americans, throughout the county, state, and southeast region! Oh! how well they could help me re-construct his life and innumerable works. How I wish that the late Ernest Heard, Jr., his childhood friend was still alive to tell about how as young boys, roaming the vast hills of Wehadkee, High Shoals, in Randolph County, they would sit together and muse over their future fates; as little black boys without a snowball's chance in hell of succeeding in life, but both having a deep desire to overcome their rudimentary existence. Oh! how deeply I regret waiting until I have only my memories of our personal relationship as father and daughter.

I know precious little about those days at Wehadkee. But, all my life, daddy would often take me on long drives through the county to revisit the "Springfield" community. The velocity with which we would move down the road was reminiscent of a funeral procession — slow and deliberate as if to fulfill a need to thorough-ly absorb every intensive and sorrowful moment of the journey. On these slow drives, he would point out landmarks and re-live his childhood.

"Right here, is the place I left from when I came to town....."

"Look over there, Charlotte, right out yonder is the Noel Foster Place. That's where my mama sharecropped. I wanted to go to school so bad; but if dat white man told mama, 'Lue Ella, you keep dem chillun out of school and work dem fields;' she had to do it. Dat's why I couldn't go to school." Deliberately choosing not to look directly at him, I could nevertheless catch glimpses of big tears welling in the inside corners of his eyes as we cruised the area.

He'd always tell me, "Don't never forget from whence you

came; don't never forget the bridge that brought you over."

He was born March 8, 1920 in Carrollton, Carroll County, Georgia. From all accounts, his mother, Lue Ella Baker was the only girl in a large family of boys. They were the children of my great grandma Lizzie Baker.

Daddy explained to me that his mother, Lue Ella Baker had met and married a man by the name of Charlie Clark. His family was from Carroll County, Georgia. Today, many of them have settled in Breman, Georgia, others in Heflin, Alabama. Obviously, their union did not last, because daddy always told me that his father left him when he was four years old. She had several children by Charlie Clark: There was Elijah, Wilkie, Odell, Lelia, Elizabeth, and another sister they called "Punkin," and Beotis. Well, according to some of the older family members, after Charlie left her and all those children, her brother Jack Baker (Uncle Jack), went to Carrollton, Georgia and got her and brought her and the children back to Springfield, where she sharecropped and raised her children on farmland owned by Noel Foster and various others.

Daddy was also careful to tell me stories of his school days. Grades one through six were taught at "Pine Hill," a "church school" in the Wehadkee community, where the children all had to sit around a pot-bellied stove and have class with one teacher. Kids in grades seven through twelve had to come into town to go to school, and my daddy always told me that he wanted to go real bad, but couldn't go because he had to help his mother on that farm. He adored his mother, and hated to see her have to work so hard. Many times, recalling how hard she had to work, he would mournfully reflect: "I've seen times my mama would go and work all week long for white folks, cleaning their houses, and washing their clothes, cooking and taking care of their children; and all they'd give her would be a stack of old newspapers."

After he got up some size, though, he always told me he took $1.40 and came to town to Roanoke, Alabama, a farming town. He found work with Dr. G. W. Bonner who was a prominent white doctor. Daddy drove for Dr. Bonner, and chauffeured him every where he went. He also learned how to assist Dr. Bonner in caring for the sick. Once, while rambling through my large collection of daddy's things, I ran across his military separation record. On it was a statement of his occupation before enlistment in the army. It read:

"MAIN OCCUPATION: Chauffer.

Job Summary: Drove automobile for physician making routine and emergency calls on patients. Was responsible for attending to upkeep of car and saw to it that vehicle was always in shape for ready travel. Held state and municipal driving permits."

From everything I ever heard, Dr. Bonner really loved my daddy. And all over town, people called him "Dr. Bonner's Boy." Daddy really wore this as a "badge of honor" and was very proud to be known as "Dr Bonner's Boy." According to those who remembered those times, nobody ever bothered daddy either, because he was "Dr. Bonner's Boy." He could go flying through town in Dr. Bonner's car — nobody said a mumbling word, because that was Dr. Bonner's "boy" driving Dr. Bonner's car. But, in due time, daddy was rescued from Dr. Bonner. By the time the U.S. was fully engaged in World War II, with only a 7th grade education, daddy was drafted in the Army, and his life took on a new direction. I would imagine that at the time, he probably didn't see it as being rescued. But, that is precisely what it was.

In conversing, Daddy would frequently revisit his military years. He hailed these years as the best years of his life. Recalling how young he was when he was drafted into the army, he would often reflect: "...I was 21 years, 2 months, and 2 days old, when I got drafted into the army — young, ignorant and stupid ....hadn't never been out of Randolph County...I was a big Randolph County fool!"

During many of our father-daughter conversations, daddy would delve deeply into reminiscing with me about how deprived he was made to feel upon enlistment in the Army. Having come from a sharecropping family and being deprived of educational opportunity, he didn't know how to do anything. He recalled that upon induction in the Army, there were numerous opportunities for those who had skills and talents. He recalled his Master Sergeant querying the enlisted men:

"Is there anybody here who can blow a bugle? You don't have to be all that good, if you can just blow one note, I have a job for you!"

"I couldn't do that."

"Is there anybody here who can type? You don't have to be able to type fast, if you can do any typing at all, I have a job for you!"

"I couldn't do that."

"Is there anybody here who can read music — just a few notes— we'll train you to do what we need you to do for Uncle Sam!"

"I couldn't do that."

"Anybody here ever cooked in a café; in a lunchroom?"

"I hadn't done that either. I wanted to be something so bad, but I didn't have no education. So, there was nothing I could do but just stand there and look like a big Randolph County fool!"

Since his only work experience had been picking cotton, farming, working the land, and working a little while as Dr. Bonner's chauffeur, he was assigned to the medical detachment. There he learned how to assist in caring for the wounded soldiers and learned how to be a surgical technician. This was the closest he had ever come to being formally educated. It was here that daddy probably developed his true appreciation for education. So, he took advantage of every opportunity to learn in the military, and achieved the rank of Medical Technician 3rd grade.

In a matter of only three years, his army qualifications changed to read as follows:

"SUMMARY OF MILITARY OCCUPA-
TION AND CIVILIAN CONVERSIONS: Was in
charge of Medical Aid Station serving 650 men
in Field Artillery Unit. As non-commissioned officer in charge, supervised and assigned duties to
5 technicians. Assisted Medical officer in surgery,
administering of medications, blood plasma and
the dressing of wounds. Gave immunization shots
and did routine vaccinations. Also administered
sulfa drugs, bismuth-arsenic and McPherson for-
mulas for veneral disease. Requisitioned drugs
and other supplies necessary to the operation of
aid station. Was responsible for maintenance and
use of all equipment."

Daddy took full advantage of his military status, sending money home to his mother, so she could buy a home, and get off the farm. He always said, "I got tired of seeing my mama moving around from house to house, and tearing up her furniture, and never being able to stay anywhere. I bought her a house. I told her to go find her a house that she liked, and buy it. I sent money home every month to pay for the house." I suppose that daddy learned many other lessons by being in the military. He learned that life had more to offer black people than just a meager existence comprised of living and working on somebody else's land. He also learned to resent the legalized mistreatment of Blacks in the south, after having gone overseas to risk his life defending a country that persisted in treating blacks like second class citizens. It is my contention that this is when he began to be convicted in his heart about getting involved in the movement to end racial discrimination.

He often shared with me, many of the war stories from his Army days, many which I don't recall. But, I know he had a vivid memory of the comrades he served with.

In July of 1945 at age 25 daddy was discharged from the Army. He returned home to a sick bedridden mother, Lue Ella Baker Clark Holiday, having re-married a gentleman named Ed Holliday. Being the compassionate young man that he was, he sat by her bedside, tended to her, giving medicines, baths, and trying to do the best he could. Without a doubt, all of his medical expertise was an asset in providing the best care he could for his mother. But, soon— very soon after his return from service, she died, and somehow, her passing had such a profound impact on him that it left an indelible imprint on his heart and mind placing in him a desire to become an undertaker.

Now, as I understand it, Dr. Bonner really wanted daddy to come back to work for him. I guess he thought daddy would just pick up right where he had left off—as his chauffeur and errand boy. But, having experienced life outside Randolph County and the United States Of America, daddy had a greater vision, now. He just wanted better. He had learned that there was something better to be desired for blacks, foremost among these, respectability and dignity. So, his first priority was to complete his high school education.

I don't pretend to know what circumstances drove him to want to enter the mortuary field. But, when one revisits the setting and the racial climate of the times, it could have been any number of things: the conditions of his mother's burial; perhaps the absence of decent burial services for blacks in Roanoke at that time. Who knows? It is very likely also, that, given the times, it might have had a lot to do with the fact that the only black people who seemed to get any degree of respect were just that: preachers, teachers and undertakers.

After release from the army, he learned of the opportunity to use his GI benefits to finish high school. So he moved to Anniston, Alabama, and attended Cobb Avenue High School, where he earned his high school diploma. He believed himself to have laid a good foundation for going into the undertaking business.

At that time, his good friend was Roy Minnifield of Wedowee, Alabama. He asked Roy to be his partner and help him start a black funeral home in Roanoke. But at a time when the world was terribly unfriendly to blacks, Roy being worried about the risks of two black men trying to go in a business, just wasn't too receptive to that idea. Because his friend opted out on his idea, Wilkie Clark's desire to become an undertaker was postponed by 25 years.

In the meantime, somewhere along the way, he met a young teacher, named Miss Peters. She was a few years older than he was. But, they fell in love and married in 1948. I guess is was during this time period he also started work for the Atlantic Coast Line Railroad Company. They were childless for several years, but eventually, their union was fruitful and I was born in 1953. They were wonderful parents. My childhood memory serves me quite well as I think back to the many Saturday morning road trips with them. Usually, our travels took us to Anniston, Alabama. This was my mama's home. She had an uncle Ulysses Peters, living there, and her mother Mary Will Peters. So, they were always traveling back and forth to Anniston, Alabama to see about the elders. Mama also had cousins there whom she loved very dearly. Her cousins were Moses and Doshie Barrow, and Ruby Birdsong. Every time we went to Anniston, I got to spend time with mama's family.

On these road trips, mama would always have the car supplied with towels, cloths, and toilet tissue. Daddy would sometime have to find a dirt drive and pull off the road, and travel a piece down into the woods. Sometime puzzled about why we had to do this, I'd observe as he'd get out of the car, and walk back up toward the road to look out. Mama would get out of the car, and walk further into the woods, and squat down on the ground to urinate. When she finished, she'd clean herself good, and return to the car. Then daddy would return to the car, and back out into the highway and we'd resume traveling. I always considered it so demeaning that mama and daddy had to use the bathroom in the woods. But, where else could they go? In my own immature mind, I could never come up with an alternative, because I had never seen anything else. Daddy loved mama's family, and I never heard him complain about the frequent trips to Anniston.

I remember being very young, and being dropped off in Anniston, where I stayed the whole summer with mama's family. Daddy would have to go to Birmingham to work; mama was in school at Alabama State in Montgomery, and I was in Anniston. Every other Friday, though, he'd make a circle, picking me up in Anniston; picking mama up in Montgomery, and we'd spend the weekend together, and start all over again on Monday.

Now about the same time, under the strong influence of such local individuals as John Tommy Thompson and Ms. Attrie B. Stephens Henderson, he became enchanted with the NAACP, a national organization at that time lead by an army of aggressive black attorneys and politicians working through the judicial system and political action to improve social conditions for blacks.

By and by, when mama finished her schooling at Alabama State, they started traveling a different direction. They would go to Birmingham regularly to NAACP meetings on Saturdays. They really enjoyed these meetings. Being young and impressionable, daddy was captivated by the NAACP. There would be so much stuff to bring back home. All kinds of books, pamphlets, and placards. There was all kinds of material about voting, and the bill of rights. All the way home, they'd talk with excitement about what was said and done in the meeting.

By his very compassionate nature, my daddy's heart was touched by the deplorable plight of black folks during those times. He had a genuine love for people and was unselfish and giving. In addition to having witnessed a lot of the inequitable treatment of blacks, he also experienced much of it firsthand. He grew in his loyalty and support of this organization, Subsequently, he became the local NAACP President, and through these activities, began to grow in his understanding of the deeply rooted racial problems that African Americans faced in achieving their goals. He was growing so passionate in his desire to be a catalyst for social change in his hometown, that I believe God suffused him with a unique anointing to minister to the social, civic and humanitarian needs of African-Americans in Randolph County in a way that garnered much love and respect for him. He was SO dedicated to this work that he devoted the better part of his life in a personal quest to perfect himself as a champion for people in his community. Also a staunch Methodist, and an enthusiastic bible scholar, he somehow learned to blend all these roles in an almost mystical magical way that enabled him to help people all over the county and beyond in countless ways.

As daddy's civil rights involvements intensified, he began to embrace the mainline philosophy being touted by the NAACP, black institutions of higher education and all the major players in the civil rights movement. The NAACP was not only concerned for the education and political rights of blacks, but the economic advancement of blacks also. They espoused the philosophy that civil rights was also tied to economic liberation. This meant that true progress in civil rights for blacks particularly in rural communities would NEVER be maximized without the progress and support of a black middle class business community and so this further fueled his desire to join the ranks of other local black businessmen. In our community, there were several other pioneers who had somehow ventured out and managed to go into their own businesses, like the late John Tommy and Linnie Thompson, Jesse A. Terry, H.T. Rosser, Booker T. Williams. Daddy had a strong desire to strengthen that population by becoming a part of it. Needless to say, the racial climate of the times made it next to impossible for a black person to enter the business world.

On the way to his dream of owning and operating his own funeral home, at various times, he tried several other business ventures. Some, he abandoned—probably with good cause. He went into the "scrap-iron" business. During this time, he had a big old truck that he outfitted; and he went around collecting scrap metal. I have no idea how this business worked, but it was short-lived. And if my memory doesn't fail me, I believe it was because someone he had helping him out, wrecked the truck. So, he junked it, and abandoned the business.

At another time that I'm unable to pinpoint, my daddy went into the "Septic Tank" cleaning business. For those who don't understand what this is about, very few African Americans in our community had indoor bathrooms. But slowly, as times got a little bit better, people started to build bathrooms inside their houses.

Despite indoor bathrooms, there were no provisions for the waste water. So, people had to install septic tanks. A septic tank was a big concrete or steel receptacle built like a huge box, buried underground to catch all the waste water from the house. It caught the sink water, bathtub water, and whatever was flushed down the toilet. Well, these tanks could only hold so much, so this established a need for people to periodically have their septic tanks cleaned. You could always tell when somebody's septic tank needed cleaning, because often, you could see the waste bubbling up on the ground. And, if you lived close by, the scent of an septic tank in need of cleaning, could run you clean out of the neighborhood. Can you believe, Daddy got himself a big truck and outfitted it, and for a while he was going around cleaning septic tanks and coming home every day smelling just like shit? Although I cannot recall the exact reason why, that business was very short-lived too — but I'd be willing to bet it had something to do with the scent; he couldn't stand any kind of offensive odors. The minute it hit his nostrils, he'd lose his stomach. But, he obviously didn't give up on his dream of being in his own business.

Even later, he hooked up with an outfit out of Gadsden, Alabama, and for once, he really got a taste of what it felt like to be "white collar." Daddy was well-acquainted with a gentleman from Gadsden named Q. D. Adams. They were co-laborers in the NAACP, the voter's leagues, and many other statewide groups. Q. D. Adams was selling insurance, and securities, and several other products and was able to use his influence to get Daddy a position as a securities salesman, with a company called Diversified Financial Corporation. I never shall forget how enthusiastic he was about this new job. This company manufactured a product called "Mr. Chill." Mr. Chill was going to become the next great money-maker and Daddy's job was to get people to invest in the company. The sales training he got from this company, is probably the first time he really got his feet wet in terms of business and marketing. He was a natural-born salesman, and his memory was so phenomenal until he could rattle every word of his sales presentation off like a well-rehearsed stage performance. Many times, I would be riding along with him, as he traveled throughout the county showing people "Mr. Chill," and explaining how investments worked. There were very few black people around, who after hearing Daddy's dramatic sales pitch, didn't invest in "Mr. Chill." Daddy used this opportunity to expand his knowledge of investing, and whenever he visited people to talk to them about investing, he would teach them as best he could about the direction in which black folk needed to move to improve their economic status. It is obvious that even then, black people — everybody — was looking for a way to escape the poor economic conditions they found themselves in. The idea of investing held promise for them to get out of poverty. But Diversified turned out not to be a good company to invest in. Unfortunately, the company did not do well. Even though I was very young at the time, I can remember my mama and many of her friends discussing Diversified. They kept talking about a "reverse split." Whatever the case, some of the investers were able to retrieve their investments; however many other investors, including Daddy lost their money. After this turn of events, Daddy quickly disassociated himself with Diversified. I know in my heart, that daddy thought by getting people to invest in Diversified stock, he was doing a good thing that would be ultimately benefit black people. And even though the company turned out to be a disappointment, the experience was invaluable. For the first time in his life, Daddy had gotten a chance to experience a new level of "respectability;" to work on a job where he could don a suit and tie. His white colleagues at Diversified had let him in on a previously well-kept secret. They had educated and trained him well. At last, he had had his orientation to the ways of corporate America, and I suppose he just couldn't get it out of his system.

Again compelled to revisit the idea of going into business for himself, this time from the vantage point of a civil rights leader, he continued to view business ownership as a necessary vehicle through which to help his community in the struggle for social justice; a way to make himself "accessible" to the people in the community; as an NAACP leader and often openly controversial figure, he couldn't afford to be "bound & gagged" by the threat of racial or economic reprisals from a hostile employer. Often challenging the oppressive and racially inequitable conditions within the City and County, he now had even stronger and more compelling reasons to go into business for himself. The 1960's saw the creation of new laws that were slowly opening doors and providing economic access to blacks. And all over the nation, black leaders were being prompted to test these new opportunities by applying for business loans, seeking equal housing opportunities, and enrolling in public schools that had been forced to desegregate. Finally, in 1968 and 1969 a work-related injury forced daddy to leave his job with the

Atlantic Coastline Railroad. So, unable to continue working for the railroad, he had the perfect opportunity to work toward the establishment of Clark Funeral Home.

During this era, many funeral homes were set up in houses or similar structures — thus the term funeral "home." He asked my mother if he could use her property which had a vacant rent house on it on what at that time was Riley Street (Now Wilkie Clark Drive). She agreed, and he enthusiastically started remodeling the place. He completed a lot of the projects with his own hands. He pulled old plaster off the walls; put up new sheet-rock and painted; cleaned up around the place; formed and poured the prettiest little concrete porches all around the place. The finishing touch was beautiful snow-white paint on the wooden clapboard siding. It was a very attractive wood-framed Antebellum, bungalow styled house, much like a little cottage — very dainty and classy-looking. It really fit the neighborhood. After spending quite a sum on labor and material, some where in the midst of the process, the city advised him that he would have to petition for the re-zoning of the area for business; this also meant that the neighbors would have to agree for his property to be re-zoned for a funeral home business before he could open it. Now, in retrospect, this could be considered one of the mistakes that might have been avoided, if he had addressed the zoning issue BEFORE investing all that money trying to fix up the old house.

But you must remember, I told you earlier, daddy was an optimist. He was a positive thinker by nature, And he saw the good in everybody and everything. And, because of his optimistic nature, he often neglected to see the very thing he reminded me of — the world waiting with outstretched arms — a hammer in each hand — waiting to knock the hell out of you!

That Stubborn Crab Mentality

Being an optimist, he just knew all of his neighbors would graciously agree to re-zone the property. But, again, to his dismay and disappointment, many of them (now deceased) congregated at City Hall with a petition to protest the re-zoning. Again, very hurt and disappointed, because many of his opponents were also his fellow churchmen and women. He could not believe that Christian people would withhold their favor the way they did. It was at this point that for the first time in my life, I saw my father, almost reduced to tears. He almost broke down in the City Council meeting; I could see him trembling — I don't know if he was trembling in fear or in anger; but in that moment, I secretly prayed for him and in my spirit, I could feel him fighting to hold himself together.

In retrospect, I can't help but to consider the racial aspect of this issue — because certainly there was one — no matter what the situation, there ALWAYS was. First of all, at the opposite end of our street, Riley Street, there was a white-owned funeral home owned by the Quattlebaum's. In all my life, I had never heard anybody complain about them being there. They had never been considered a nuisance and even if they had been, I wonder would ANYBODY have cared how we (the black residents on Riley Street) felt about it? Now, ironically, we all know Quattlebaum's faced Riley street, but never used a Riley Street address; rather, they used the College Street address— clearly distancing themselves from any connection with the black neighborhood; because College Street was a white street. Moreover, for years, we had lived right under the constant threat of an explosive gas fire because there was the Standard Oil Company, right across the street from our house. It was like a big gasoline distribution center; it was a big commercial place where all the Standard Oil trucks would come in and out all times of the day and night to re-fuel; and I guess they went around re-filling all the service station gas tanks. In addition to underground gasoline tanks; there were three huge tanks that sat up on block pillars above the ground. It was a very busy place — owned and operated by the Hodges family. It sat in the heart of our neighborhood. Nobody had ever complained about them. Aside from that, consider the fact that all around that part of the street, there was A Masonic Lodge Hall, boot-leggers, juke joints; another run-down and dilapidated Funeral Home, and everything else you could name. Saturday nights, young people were all in the streets walking to the "Shing-lar" where they partied way into the wee hours of the morning; and you could hear the jukebox thumping all over East Roanoke. Less than a block away was "Tiny Whaley's Store and a another noise-maker, Tiny Whaley's Skating Rink, not to mention at the southerly end of the street, the "Blue Bird" Cafe. As far as I can recall, nobody — not even the city, had ever raised an issue about zoning.

I have very often wondered how my daddy's civil rights activities might have figured into this complicated equation. When had the City of Roanoke ever even cared about what was put in the black neighborhood? They just didn't care. Why now, did they care so much? But, now, all of a sudden, there arose a zoning issue. I don't even know if my daddy ever considered any of these factors at that time. He was probably so upset and confused by the commotion caused by his petition. I think he was just trying to get it done in a non-adversarial way. But, he learned, there were going to be adversaries every step of the way. I believe that under other circumstances, he probably would have fought this action more aggressively. But he had already invested so much, and he was so hurt by the mere fact that these were his own people, black people, protesting what he was trying to do. There was ONLY ONE person who stood up for him at that time, Mrs. Susie Rosser, my godmother, and our very good neighbor and long-time friend. She and her husband "Lightening Rosser" had worked hard and set up a very nice, first class Nursing Home (Rosser's Nursing Home) on the other side of town that we called "Hill City." For a black facility, it was quite impressive. She stood up in the City Council meeting, and in essence, she rebuked the group of protesters — She put her hands on her big round hips, and pointed her fingers, and told all the protesters, "You all ought to be ashamed of yourselves — down here protesting trying to keep somebody down; this is a low-down, dirty, shame!" She was strong and forthright in her comments. I know without a shred of doubt that her strong presence, and her strong words, is the only thing that gave my daddy strength in that hour and allowed him to hold his head up.

Now, about the protesters petition, I just have to go a little deeper into this story and give you my take on the petition. I now find it so very ironic! At that time, many (if not most) blacks in our community were extremely naive about civic matters — as a matter of fact, did everything they could to avoid these issues. But, because my daddy was so eager and energetic in participating in the NAACP, he had learned a lot about how the system works; and through his association with NAACP, had learned about the "Right to Petition." He is probably even the one who introduced this strategy to that group of protesters.

Several years earlier daddy had started to appeal to the city council to pave our streets. They began to lobby the neighbors to get on board and help push for pavement on our street. Every black street in town was dirt, except for maybe one. So, even though none of them really knew what to do, the neighbors had begun to gradually agree to help. So, my mama and daddy were the very ones who

read and dug through their vast collection of civil rights information, which could be found in every nook and cranny in our house;
and figured out how to draw up the petition, and present it to the
city council. I recall so many occasions when daddy would appear
before the city council, and remind them that he had seen asphalt
taken up in the white communities and replaced with new asphalt.
On many occasions, I heard him tell Mayor J. P. Phillips, "I'd be
happy if you'd just take some of that old pavement you took up in
the white neighborhood, and bring it to my street and put down."
So, they continued the effort to present a petition for pavement.
And how my daddy marveled the day he drove home, and saw the
big yellow caterpillars moving up and down our street, making it
ready for pavement! He lit up like the sunshine! Everybody was
so excited that it became a daily entertainment to sit outside and
watch the work progress.

After much work, talking, pleading, and a lengthy wait,
their petition was successful, and not only did the street get paved,
but we got sewerage lines installed as well as beautiful curbs.

Everybody in the neighborhood had learned from this
experience, and it caught on, so one by one, other blacks in their
neighborhoods began to petition for their streets to be paved. It's
ironic that Daddy having been the one who taught these crows the
power of the petition, now had to become the object and a casualty
of his own teaching! This, to me was just a dam sad commentary
on how people will take a weapon from you and then turn around
and try to knock the hell out of you with your own dam weapon.
Quite naturally, he was very despondent for quite some time after
that.

Amazingly, over time Daddy bounced back from this major set-back. I remember so well, during those times, relationships
became quite strained at our church as he continued to try to go to
Bethel every Sunday, and face these Judases whom he had to sit in
church with and worship with. I recall so well how daddy would
reflect back on how he'd meet some of them on the street and they'd
try to go the other way; drop their heads, or otherwise avoid him.
He'd run right up to them and just smile and shake their hands and
greet them so enthusiastically — he'd reach in his pocket, take out
one of those strong camel cigarettes, light up, prop his foot up and
start a conversation. The way he'd be carrying on, you'd never
have known anything had happened. And I would just look at
him and shake my head in disbelief. I remember so well, there

were people in our church who were so mean and nasty toward my daddy. He was always aggressive and outgoing, and loved to get up and talk in church. It seemed like every time he would get up in church to speak, or comment on anything, the very woman who had led the protest against his re-zoning petition, would start to mumble and grumble under her breath — loudly enough so she could be heard. It was as if she wanted people to know how much she despised him. But, in his "preachy" kind of way, daddy would always say, "they can't stop me....they wish so bad that they could stop me, but I ain't going to let nobody run me away from my church." And this is when, at a very young age, I started to take a critical look at religion and church folks. The human side of me would have made me distance myself from Bethel -- as far away as I could get. I probably would have permanently dis-associated myself from THAT particular church. But, there were others in our church family who wholeheartedly supported daddy in his effort, and encouraged him and resented the nay-sayers. Through this experience, daddy taught me a very profound lesson, that has come more into focus only in the later years of my life. You don't give up; you don't back down. You don't shy away from your enemy. You confront him — head on. And that is what daddy did every time he entered the church doors. He never missed a beat; never missed a Sunday — continued to meet and greet those people with love — and totally ignored their nastiness. This whole ordeal became a "hot topic" at home for quite some time — years even. But, he always would end the discussion with "father forgive them, for they know not what they do!" Mama and I were incensed over this; but daddy would continually talk about "love conquering all..." Mama was so mad until she almost quit going to church. She loved Bethel, and continued to support the church financially but she never looked at Bethel the same. She would tell you quick just whatever was on her mind. And she didn't bite her tongue. She would always say, "I ain't no hypocrite, and I'm not going out there to that church pretending to like it, and trying to be with them hypocrites after what they've tried to do to Wilkie. Oh, she was upset! I absolutely do not understand for the life of me, how he did it. But, certainly it was at this time in my life, that I learned some very humbling spiritual lessons, that have remained with me throughout life. But, there also arose within me a totally new level of respect, admiration and awe for my daddy.

Now thwarted by yet another obstacle, one would think

that he was about ready to give up; but I guess daddy was thinking and strategizing, while others were sleeping.

As my memory serves me, I think they all thought they had him defeated. Maybe, for a while, he felt that way too. But, somehow, he was made aware of the possibility of picking up the house, and moving it to another location. So, he started working on that. Unfortunately, he was forced to dismantle all the pretty construction work that had been done; bust up those beautiful concrete porches (stoops, he called them) that he had poured; and split the vacant house in half, and move it to it's present location on LaFayette Highway.

Personally, I felt it was a blessing in disguise. Because, we lived on a lovely place. Our home was situated on the north end of Riley Street, right across the street from the Standard Oil Company. Our place was huge. We had four lawns. The property on the back side of our house ran all the way down to Old LaFayette Highway, (then U.S. highway 431) which at that time was a main route through the city. But, it was rough, hilly, all overgrown and unlevel.

When the building was moved to LaFayette Highway, it was set there in the middle of that over-grown field behind our house. Again, daddy had a lot of work to do. By that time, daddy could only afford just enough grading to allow one to drive up to the funeral home. He was also faced with the task of putting the place back together, and setting it on a new foundation. His cousin by marriage, King George Thornton had been going to Tuskegee Institute, where he took a brick laying course. So, daddy bought a few blocks, and King George helped him underpin the place. The move had taken a terrible toll on the place. Because of the move, the integrity of the structure was permanently breached; at that time, house-moving was not as well understood as it is today; and we probably didn't have as much know-how as we do now, about re-assembly. So, because of that, our building had walls that were out of plumb, floors that were unlevel, and all sorts of structural issues. But, I like to think that over the years, these have added to the character of the place, and are subtle reminders of my father's struggles. But, he got it put back together; and pressed on. Same house, new location! Boy, were those protesters mad now! After that, it became crystal clear that their mission wasn't just about zoning; it was about that "crab mentality" that black folks have always been renowned for — it was about keeping a good man down. But,

134

you just can't do that: keep a good man down, I mean. Well, it was on to the next project. Getting the doors open.

The Battle With S.B.A.

I recall during those years how hard my daddy worked and struggled to get the money to finance his business.

Being "daddy's girl" I was often his companion on his 2-hour trips to Birmingham or to Atlanta, to talk to this one or that one about getting a business loan. He would tell me, "I want you to go with me, so you'll learn about business." I want you to be exposed to things I was never exposed to. You won't learn if you are not there to hear what is said and see what is done." He often said that was one of the reasons why blacks couldn't progress because they didn't train their children or expose them and often made them leave the room when business was being discussed. Not my daddy! He wanted me to hear everything that was said. It was almost like he needed a 2nd pair of eyes and ears for verification and interpretation of whatever was discussed. Even as a child, he acted as though he trusted my interpretations of whatever we heard and saw.

And thus began my business education at age 14. The racial barriers made it hard. No financial institution was about to loan daddy the money to start a business — despite his sterling credit, (I know because my mama helped him keep it that way). There were times, when I could see how persecuted he felt. There were even times when I saw him cry. Seeing a man cry — not because he's NOT strong; but because he IS strong yet forced to suppress that strength because of his race — well, that was hard for me to witness. When it's your daddy and he's your super-hero, to see him clearly so defeated by circumstances that he can't control — that hurts. It even hurts today, when I remember those times, times permanently imprinted on my mind and in my heart. He literally begged Small Business Administration for a direct loan to help him get started.

I think the first few times he met with them, they told him he didn't have sense enough to run a business. He was treated disdainfully, almost as if he didn't have any business there to request assistance. Essentially, what he had to do was apply and be turned down by three banks. Well, we can all guess that part probably wasn't difficult. It was very humiliating and intimidating. It was also ironic, that having borrowed money for all kinds of reasons, prior to that, he was not qualified for any kind of business loan from any bank.

Then, they started to intimidate him about his limited education and ability. They sent him to all kinds of workshops, and so forth to prepare him for running a business. I remember him going to places like Tuskegee, Opelika, and other places to workshops and seminars. It's not that he couldn't have benefitted from this training. But, what made it humiliating was to think they thought NOTHING, of any other knowledge he might have derived from any other sources. If they were black, that meant they were automatically considered inadequate and unacceptable.

My daddy knew all kinds of people; professionals from all walks of life. His connections with the NAACP had placed him in contact with some of the greatest business and legal minds in the State of Alabama; black attorneys who had graduated from the prestigious Howard University School of Law and other schools that were turning out aggressive black lawyers like attorney David Hood, Arthur Shores, Demetrius Newton, Solomon Seay, Fred Gray, and Oscar Adams. Through these individuals who befriended him, he had a lot of expert help laying out his business plans, but despite his best efforts, elaborate business plans, mandatory business counseling sessions; and expert assistance preparing his loan proposal, and everything else they had either recommended or required him to do, SBA made every excuse in the world to decline his loan application. But, my daddy never quit. Many days, he was up before the sun rose, getting ready to go. I'll bet he made 40 trips to Birmingham. Often, when he'd arrive at the SBA office, he'd have to sit and wait for hours. It seemed that they would deliberately prolong the waiting before anybody would see him.

I think one day, daddy just got so mad, and so fed up with being turned down, that he "unloaded" on his loan counselor— a Mr. Barksdale. He got up early one morning, and I heard him tell mama, "Hattie Lee, I'm fixin to go to Birmingham. I'm fed up with this shit, and and I'm going to raise hell today; they can let me have the money or not...I'm raisin hell. I dun gone there all dressed up, and smellin good; suit and tie; I am goin just like I am today." I don't know what happened that fateful day. I have often prayed in my heart that daddy wasn't too hard on Mr. Barksdale. Because, I don't think anybody (other than me or mama) could take one of his cussin-outs. Finally, confronted, I guess SBA ran out of reasons for denying him the loan, and they finally granted it and loaned him a measly $13,500.00, which was only enough to tie him up in knots and not nearly enough to enable him to be competitive in the funeral market; but just barely enough to buy the 2nd hand equipment he needed to get the doors open. During those times, I recall daddy telling me, "we can't give up... and we are not going to give up. People don't think that a black man is entitled to have an office; we are not supposed to have sense enough to run our own businesses.... we are supposed to be sweeping floors, digging ditches, swinging off the back of a garbage truck, or cleaning somebody else's shit. But, we have to do this to put ourselves in position to help our people. That's where the real freedom lies."

A Long-Awaited Day Arrives at Last

Despite all setbacks, on February 18, 1970, at age 49, Wilkie Clark opened the doors of "Clark Funeral Parlor," and they've been open every since. Two days later on February 20, 1970, we received our first request for service on February 20, 1970 for the family of the late Mr. Emzix Stegall.

From that point forward our family's life changed forever. Everything revolved around the funeral home. We ate, slept, and lived it. The beginning of our life as a funeral home family was the end of family outings together, family vacations, long afternoon car trips, and leisure outings and family trips to the grocery store. As a family, we committed to be near our telephone at all times to ensure that we were available when needed. As a family, we did all our going in shifts.

When I think back now, I still have a very hard time imagining how it was that he was able to get up before day in the morning— EVERY MORNING. In the beginning, it was so muddy around the building especially on rainy days, until every day, with mop-in-hand and bucket a-swinging; he would meticulously wax the beautiful hardwood floors of the parlor. He'd mop them until you could see yourself in those floors.

Sometimes, we'd have to wax the floors several times a day, but daddy made sure the parlor was clean whenever anybody walked in.

He took so much pride in keeping the little place clean. He was fanatical about keeping the funeral home clean —spotless! Often, he would be mopping and preaching about cleanliness being next to Godliness. It was almost as if he was intentionally trying to hype himself up — sort of like a self-motivational "pep-talk." But, I'd be standing nearby listening and watching. Usually, I'd hear him before I saw him, because the talking is what would get my attention; so, I would move toward the voice because I wanted to try to see who in the world he was talking to! Lo and behold, he'd be taking to himself!! He'd be sort of fussing in a "preachy" way —but actually, he was teaching; and, the secondary benefit was that as I watched his behavior, I was absorbing everything he said and did. "...Don't nobody want to come in no nasty place. You want to do business — all you have to do is keep yo place clean; treat folks nice; smile at 'em; say nice things to 'em; talk nice." Because daddy couldn't afford to pay anybody to work full-time, we took on many of the tasks as a family, and just got the work done.

I remember being fifteen years old, and going to summer school. One summer, our school offered the first typing course in summer school. My daddy had a fit for me to take typing. He told me, I want you to go to summer school and take typing. "I want you to master that typing," he would say. "You are going to be my little secretary." We had one of those old ancient Royal manual typewriters — but it worked. It had the letters on it, but you could put the blinders on it for learning. I was passionate about learning how to type, and became one of the fastest in my class. Today, I still can type better than 92 words per minute, just from taking that one typing course. After I learned the home keys, and the fundamentals, I worked hard to improve my speed; then my writing skills; learned how to write letters in various forms like the block, modified block, and so forth. Soon, I was handling all my daddy's written correspondence. Amazingly, Daddy wasn't a whiz with writing, but ironically, he was verbally very eloquent and articulate. So, he'd dictate to me, what he wanted to say, and I could literally type it word for word as he spoke. Afterward, I'd sort of "clean it up" grammatically, and add a few "howevers," and "wherefores," and when I'd finished, he would read what I had written, and with those big hard rail-road hands of his he'd ball up his fist and gesture as if he was taking a punch at me! I'd have to dodge his licks because daddy was what you'd call "cock strong," and didn't know his own strength. Sometime he'd hit me on the shoulder or the arm and exclaim, "Gal! You are brilliant! You just like ya ma! You know you can write yo ass off!" He would often say of mama's writing, "You don't ever want to get caught up in the point of Hattie Lee's pen... she can tangle you up, and you'll never get loose." Even though I loved the compliments, I'd hurt for days, after one of his love licks. But, from that, I learned the importance of communicating with my clients in writing. Daddy taught me that letter-writing was the most professional way to communicate because it made people respect you, and was an excellent way to get people's attention, because if it is important enough for someone to sit down and write a letter, then it must be serious business; it serves as documentation.

That very next school year, he encouraged me to take book-keeping. I did the same thing. Wanting to help my daddy, I de-voured everything I could about bookkeeping. As time passed, we learned together the things we needed to learn to run the business. Anytime he needed something typed or written, I was the one who did it.

It truly was a "family business," because daddy enlisted the help of his favorite cousin, Lillie Mae Thornton, who had gone to school for cosmetology; and she would style all the ladies' hair. She was another live wire. We called her "cousin Lillie Mae." She was always fun to be around. Even though she was there to fix hair, she often would end up staying around to help do whatever else needed to be done. She was a hard-working woman, who had seen hard times, and knew about hard work. She had ten children, and didn't look a day older than her oldest child. She was always will-ing to stay around until everything got done.

When times got a little bit better, another friend of the fam-ily, Mamie Smedley Higgins worked with him for a number of years. Mamie would be there everyday at 8:00 O'clock. She'd bring her knitting, her needles, and her TV and all she had to do was answer the telephone, and be nice to the people who came in. This allowed Daddy time to get out in the community and fellowship (which he loved doing), go to meetings out of town, and just to oc-casionally be free from the business.

Often it was hard. Because we all had to wear several hats and perform a variety of duties and still do a good job, in addition to whatever else we were doing. Sometimes, that meant getting up earlier and dressing grungy to do all the dirty work in the back-room or outside; then running home to shower and dress for the public before visiting hours. But, we pulled together and did it. Mama was like a rock. Sometimes as in all families, she and daddy would argue. I would try to take sides. I'd be mad with him too, and vow not to go to the funeral home and help him — but mama demanded that I go. She would say "Charlotte, I don't care what Wilkie has done to me; he's your daddy and you'd better get up off you're a - - and go help him. He's good to you. I can cover the ground I stand on, and you don't need to get involved in our fight." And that was that. I had to go. She never allowed me to cop out on daddy. I call her that Virtuous Woman described in Proverbs 31.

Daddy Comes Into His Own

The next 20 years of daddy's life was filled with activity — a constant adventure in self-perfection as a practicing mortician, community leader, and spirit-filled humanitarian. Although these early years were anything but easy, daddy was extremely happy and fulfilled doing it. Daddy's life as a funeral director was marked by countless personal sacrifices aimed at helping others. Wearing all these and other hats, he did everything in his power to secure social and economic justice for African-Americans throughout the area. His many humanitarian acts and kind deeds added a special flavor that attracted many friends and followers. He earned the respect of others because everybody knew him to be an unselfish, kind, generous man; and because before the doors of Clark Funeral Home ever opened his reputation for "servant-hood" had preceded him. The Funeral Home merely gave him another vehicle through which to serve. He garnered the support of his family who bolstered him in his efforts — or at least most of them. There were times when he even went to the bank and borrowed money to help people, or co-signed with them to borrow money; and although mama and I didn't necessarily support that — we thought he was out of his mind! But he did it anyway! He couldn't stand to see anybody suffer. He was so passionate about it until he would often try to assume the burdens of others. We often had to talk real hard to him and tell him that he couldn't do that, because it just wasn't good business. But, in that regard he was determined. He would take risks with people that he hardly knew. Often there were women in the community who did not have husbands with any measure of fortitude. They would bring their wives to daddy to see if he could help them with their dilemmas. Some of them just didn't know how to speak up for themselves. They lacked the confidence to confront and address many of the issues of everyday life. Didn't know how things worked; Didn't understand legal processes and procedures. Daddy was an expert at this, and could explain things to people in a way that they could understand. Seems like there was always some mama who's son had gotten into some kind of trouble and had gotten locked up. Daddy would go to jail and sign the bonds — get them out of jail., help them find lawyers, tell them what to say when they got to court — a lot of the time he'd even take off and go with them. When children got into trouble with the principal at school, instead of their own daddies going, my daddy was the one who went to the school to meet with the principal to discuss and attempt to resolve the matter. He went all out for anybody who needed him, who could convince him that the need was genuine. I am sure the archives of the Roanoke Leader and Randolph Leader bear record of his many visits to the City Council, the County Commission, the Randolph County Board of Education in the interest of some issue affecting the African-American community. Daddy adopted the slogan "Where Courtesy Dwells and Service Excels!" and was well-known for swiftly answering his door with a warm smile and lively conversation for every visitor; often greeting the ladies with a hug and a kiss. Often misinterpreting his outgoing personality and friendly gestures for being "fresh" he was sometimes talked about, but we knew him best; and we knew that he was just a man who had a genuine love for people and he demonstrated that in the way he treated and greeted them. Most of his days he came home exhausted; but his favorite boast was "I'm the Chief Cook & Bottle-Washer, so I have to do whatever I have to do to command that post."

We knew that meant that HE was the boss; the CEO. He would say, nobody had to make me get up to go to the Railroad. Nobody has to make me go to my own business.

At a time when our county and municipalities should have had in place, some kind of indigent burial fund, often being the "Good Samaritan," and at great personal sacrifice and financial loss to himself and the business, he would provide countless funerals to individuals who couldn't afford to bury their dead. But, regardless of financial circumstances, no one was denied his service or his compassion.

Not knowing or caring about what happened in the African American communities, NOT ONCE were we ever acknowledged by our city or county— they didn't care how black folks got buried. They didn't concern themselves with preserving anybody's dignity but their own. There was no form of compensation, no tax breaks of any kind; not even a pat on the back.

During the early years of our operation, he lost a lot of money. Many of the families we served, had not made adequate provisions for their deaths. They were too busy struggling to live. Times were hard for everybody but particularly hard for blacks in Randolph County, Alabama. We still have the record books of the many individuals whom he buried – often with NO compensation. He probably could have pursued payment. In the first place, 100% of our clientele was black.

We were all poor. We were the underclass. So, what would it have profited him to pursue payment? Instead of resentment, he had so much compassion for others until he would often take a loss rather than to demand payment for his service. As I got older and matured, mama and I would sometimes speak very harshly of those who availed themselves of daddy's services and neglected to pay him. But, he would come back with "Don't dog 'em..... if they had it, they'd pay it....just don't dog 'em."

Whenever we wanted to be annoying, mama and I would tease him by saying that he had two wives; mama and the funeral home. He would get so mad! In retrospect, however, I realize that he was not married to the business; he acted the way he did out of necessity. And if married to anything other than my mama, he was married to his commitment to succeed at doing what he did best. Running Clark's.

Daddy's professional tenure was remarkable. Despite meager resources, he absorbed everything available related to the death care industry and implemented every available service that was appropriate for our community. He joined and attended every professional association, seminar, or training that was scheduled. He joined the Alabama Funeral Directors and Mortician's Association, and was loyal in attending annually; but I believe a time came when he eventually outgrew this organization and therefore, had nowhere else to go. During his active years with AFDMA, he tried to encourage the Association to adopt plans whereby its members could buy cooperatively in bulk quantities to secure better pricing for their inventory items. This certainly made a lot of sense. But, nobody wanted to hear that at the time. He often said that African American funeral directors were too selfish and untrusting to leverage our buying power; and that we would always suffer as business people until we learned to trust each other, and really ban together to make our businesses better. I think he had a great idea; but he was ahead of his time.

The only thing that prevented him from participating in his conventions or other meetings was a request to provide his service. He was loyal to his clients and in 20 years — never — not even once, missed attending a funeral service that the company was conducting. Today, we continue to embrace the professional example he set. He got up earlier; worked harder; longer days and hours; studied constantly; checked, doubled-checked and re-checked to make sure that he provided perfect care to his client-families and subjects. He often said he worked harder in his own business than he had ever worked his hardest day on the railroad; but that was what made it rewarding!

Over the years, Clark's evolved into a "hub" for the African-American community. When it came to information, resources, and know-how, people trusted daddy implicitly; and he worked hard to maintain that trust. People would travel from near and far to seek out daddy's knowledge, not just about death, funeral service, and dying; but amazingly, they consulted his wisdom about how to manage their lives; he became their unofficial life-management consultant; and it was extraordinary how they trusted his advice and wisdom. And he freely shared it. Most of the time, people brought their problems to him. Usually it involved some form of racial mistreatment or injustice; sometimes it was only perceived mistreatment; nevertheless he would take out his time, and talk with people, giving the best advice he could; most of the time interrupting his own work to take up their concerns. Often, it was just a matter of naivete; many of them just didn't have a clue about how to handle their problems. Sometimes they would involve problems of a personal nature. He always took the time and gave them his best he had. There are times when I just think people just loved him and loved his spirit so much until they created reasons to come around. Some days, he would have numerous visits of this nature all day long, day after day in succession; his whole day consumed, he would then stay up half the night trying to catch up on his work. I remember him waking me in the middle of the night to help him get things done, so we could make sure we met our mortuary obligations before the morning. As he aged, my mother and I worried about him because it seemed that people expected so much of him — sometimes, we felt, too much; and he seemingly tried to take all of their burdens on himself. One of the most important things he did for our community was amass a great amount of knowledge and resources on civil rights issues which he was always ready to share. If he was needed for any humanitarian purpose, he would cheerfully stop whatever he was doing to take care of others. He became widely known, loved and admired for his personal attributes, more so than as a businessman. We know in our hearts that it was his personal attributes of unselfishness, compassion and loyalty to his community that helped him to succeed as a businessman.

Despite all of his effort — our efforts as a family in business, we still continued to experience what I considered to be instances of racial prejudice from a lot of the die-hards that remained. Often, these incidents affected our ability to operate effectively. How well do I recall how Daddy would frequently stop in the midst of his own personal or business concerns, just to do battle with the City Of Roanoke. It seems that we were always at war in one sense or another. I never shall forget how (it seemed to me) that the city was always trying to pick a fight with him. But, he would cheerfully don his boxing regalia and do battle. Some years after the funeral home opened, daddy was finally in a position to install a concrete driveway entering the funeral home grounds. The driveway was on an incline, and tapered down to the highway. There had always been a trench that spanned the front of our business property along old LaFayette Highway. Because of the poor drainage facilities the city had always provided in the black neighborhoods, the ditch would often fill with water, and has been known to cause people to have terrible accidents. It became a breeding ground for mosquitoes, and all kinds of bugs, and was very unsightly. One time, during one of those overflow incidences, the city, through its attorney Lewis H. Hamner tried their best to start a fight with daddy accusing him of installing an "illegal driveway." As I recall, he received a letter written on behalf of the City Of Roanoke, inquiring as to what he planned to do about the "illegal driveway" he had installed. Again, I think my daddy probably christened Attorney Hamner's ears with a few of his "choice words," and the issue was dropped. Ultimately, they became friends, but I don't recall exactly when.

I felt my mother and father were fairly secure financially. My mother retired from being a public school teacher. My dad had gotten his railroad retirement; and I was teaching school. For several years, daddy had earned a 30% disability from VA. So, he had other sources of income. They had banked at our local bank for at least 40 years. Had established both personal and business checking accounts with them. My daddy had excellent credit; he could borrow money anywhere for almost any reason. He could go anywhere and buy anything because my mother was meticulous in managing his and her money; and her credit was also perfect. She had every credit card in the book; and paid on every one of them on time, and kept her accounts in perfect standing. As a matter of fact, she probably killed herself, laboring and pouring over the bills and juggling the books for our house and the funeral home — because that is what she did every day of her retirement. As late as the 1980's, after our business was well-established (we thought) the bank where my family had conducted all their business would not consider loaning us the money to buy an updated funeral coach (hearse). I could not believe that. Daddy and I went in together and talked to the bank about a loan. The officer, a Mr. Hester, told my daddy, "Wilkie, it's not that we don't want to loan you the money, but who would we sell it to if you lost it?" I was incensed, mostly by the very fire my daddy had placed in me. I was on fire that day! And despite the fact that daddy put this fire in me, it always seemed as if he was constantly having to douse water on it to cool me off!

It was as if he didn't even consider my daddy's record, or his accomplishments; OR the potential for repayment. All he saw was the possibility that the bank would lose if it had to repossess the vehicle. I couldn't help but to feel that daddy was so resented and hated by a lot of the power-brokers in town, because he took some very radical and controversial stands. I wanted to immediately close and move our bank account — but he would not allow me to do it. He just said in his humbling sort of way, "you can't treat everybody the way they treat you... you have to be bigger than they are; the best way to whip his ass is make him look you in the face every time you get a chance; every time he has to look you in the face and drop his head, he'll actually see himself, for who he really is." When we told our sales representative that our local bank would not finance the vehicle, he immediately got on the telephone and called Union Bank and Trust Company in Montgomery, Alabama; and sight unseen, we were financed within a matter of minutes. From that day to this, I vowed that as long as my family and I continued to operate Clark Memorial, I would never seek any form of financial assistance from anybody in my town. Such experiences make you cynical and untrusting– and that has nothing to do with my being African-American. But it has everything to do

145

with my being HUMAN.   Since its beginnings, Clark Memorial has performed close to 2000 services in and around the perimeter of our community. Over that period of time, we have performed services as far away as Lanett, Alabama, Franklin, Georgia, Decatur, Georgia, and Tuscaloosa, Alabama. We have maintained archives and records of every service performed and we are the guardians of nearly 2000 life histories, among which are some of our communities' most outstanding citizens. We have often served as a resource for individuals in other parts of the country, seeking geneological information on deceased family members.

Because our cultural heritage and history remind us of the devastating effect slavery had on African Americans resulting in numerous cases of non-existence of any records of numerous ancestral births and deaths, to the best of our ability we have persisted in encouraging our families to be meticulous in preparing and wording their obituaries in such a way that they provide a detailed record of the lives of the deceased, which ultimately becomes a historical document or geneological record.

When I was 15 years old, and in the 10th grade at Handley High School, I knew that I would one day be a Licensed Funeral Director, and that I would be operating Clark Funeral Home, because I witnessed my father's determination to be a successful businessman; he declared that I would own a business — regardless of any other directions my life took; I would either own and pay someone else to manage or I would manage Clark Funeral Home. It wasn't necessarily about trying to get rich. It was about setting an example of creating new generations of black business-owners as a vehicle for social justice and racial progress. It was about racial pride. It was about proving to society that blacks didn't need a white overseer to crack a whip to make us work; that we had within us the discipline to work hard for ourselves; it was about being self-directed; self-controlled; and self-sufficient; it was about developing our own work ethic, and dismantling the rumor-mill generated by the overwhelming majority of whites about our being lazy, dumb, inept, ignorant, and clowns.

Time To Lay Down His Sword & Shield
To Study War No More

Daddy always expressed an awareness of death as a necessary part of life. He was quite realistic about it. I suppose we had seen and worked with such a large number of our people who were just in no way prepared for their deaths. No wills, no advance funeral plans, and very often no life insurance. He often commented about how poorly African-Americans prepared for death. He would say that we act like we are going to live forever. He let me know how important it was to him that something be left behind as a reminder to his posterity that he had done something significant while here.

In 1979, when my son, Wilkie Sherard Frieson was born, he knew that he would one day be a Funeral Director and that he would own Clark Funeral Home because his grandfather constantly told him he would; in honor of his birth, his grandfather closed a loan on the property I described earlier, known as the "Old Standard Oil" company on Wilkie Clark Drive, (then Riley Street), and planted fruit trees in honor of his grandson's birth. I remember him saying "when Sherard is 15, this property will be paid for. I didn't have a china-man's chance.... I can't look back on my life and say I had ANYBODY to help me. I want my grandson to be able to say, "this is what my grandpa left for me." It gave him immense satisfaction knowing that he was able to do something for his grandchildren that nobody could do for him. He saw this as forward movement for African-Americans. He saw this as a way to break the generational curse of lack and poverty often shared by underprivileged cultures of people in a land of plenty.

Later in 1982, when Je'Lynn Mikele Frieson was born, she also knew that she would one day be a Funeral Director, and that she would own Clark Funeral Home, because from the day she was born, her grandfather indoctrinated her with the idea. Prior to his death, he made it so, through his Last Will and Testament.

So, he started preparing me for his death very early. He would talk to me about it. He would say "ain't no need of whooping and hollering over me when I die...I'm going to die....we can't get out of this world without dying." Often, when he would talk this way, I would cry. And he would tell me to hush....because he was making sure that my mama and me would be taken care of when he died. He would jokingly say, "You and Hattie Lee will be better off when I'm dead than you are with me alive." But, despite what he said, I would well up with tears. He would tell me that he wanted the funeral home to continue to operate. He would talk to me about the things I needed to do to ensure a smooth transition. And I believe he did all he could to facilitate that by allowing me the autonomy to manage the business while he was alive, so he could satisfy himself that I was capable of doing so. He also facilitated the transition by letting his client base know that I was there and could help them handle their business. So, his client base learned to trust me, just as well as they did him. In my effort to not let him down, I did everything in my power to earn and maintain their trust. If you ask me, he was a very intelligent man. He didn't wait until he died, to plan for his death. But no matter how well-laid the plans, I could never have been prepared for it.

A Divine Appointment

Contrary to the way daddy had planned it, mama passed away on February 23, 1989. Only five months afterward, my daddy died very tragically, during the early morning hours of Saturday, July 29, 1989, when our family home burned. In retrospect, I can only say that it was predestined by God, to happen that way. How do I know that? Now, I want to tell you something that I have only shared with my very closest friends and I probably worried my late husband to death in the days leading up to my daddy's tragic and troubling death. Although it's been more than 15 years, I remember it as vividly as if it was yesterday. One night during that week, I had been awakened in the night by a terrible nightmare. I woke up sweating, and screaming, and choking. I hadn't been sleeping well at all, because my mother's death was still fresh. On this particular night, I had drempt that I was trapped in my own burning house. In the dream, I stood in my bedroom, and looked out of the west window to my right. There was a white cloud of smoke, rising and billowing seemingly from one of the houses on the next street over, which was "Avenue A." In my dream, I was brought back into my own bedroom, and as I turned and looked around my own house, it suddenly was engulfed in smoke. As I continued to visualize the events in the dream, I saw myself crawling toward my front door. I was gasping for breath, and never made it, because it was at that time that I was so frightened by the event that I woke up screaming; as I sat up in bed, I could feel my own hands around my neck, literally choking myself and cutting off my air. This dream was so troubling until I could not rest. It worried me to the point that I started looking for books to help me interpret it. It just so happened that this particular week, Oprah Winfrey was going to host a show about dream interpretation, and because I had been so vexed and troubled by the dream, I had reminded my husband multiple times, telling him not to let me forget to watch that episode of Oprah. I did get a chance to watch the show, but unfortunately, the show was no comfort or help to me. So, as the week passed, I continued to wrestle within myself as to what this foreboding dream meant. It was not until the night of daddy's death, that I was finally able to piece it together....my dream could only have been been a divine forewarning of what was to come, and the moment those little boys knocked on my front door, I knew — as a matter of fact, the first words out of my mouth were, "Oh Lord, My God, please don't let this be the end of my dream!" Regrettably, though it was just that.

On that day, in addition to losing my very special friend and comrade, I was ever so hurt over the loss of my beloved home, because of the warm and fond memories of growing up there in Wilkie and Hattie Lee Clark's house. For me, they had made our home a respite — a place where I always felt I could go and feel the safety and security of their presence, and their love. Now, in the twinkling of an eye, over the course of several horrifying, dark and dreadful hours....it, too was gone. Reportedly, the fire had started from the stove and smoldered in the attic, ultimately consuming the structure and my dad. Upon learning of the death, the entire community was in shock, disbelief, and dismay over his passing. Because daddy had been such a controversial figure down through the years, people started raising all kinds of suspicions about the tragic event.

Although, I too was in shock, I found it quite believable. Daddy was 69 years old, and I know he was exhausted from years of helping others. And he had started to "slip." People were urging me to demand an investigation into his death. And although daddy had been very controversial and could be extremely oppositional and adversarial about his issues, I just did not and still do not believe anybody who really knew him could have had a hand in the fire or his death.

Totally insensitive to what I was going through, the County Coroner, Don Benefield could only add insult to injury by mentioning his concern that my daddy was known to be a drinker and thought his death might have been attributable to intoxication. I felt he was totally out of his place, because he didn't know a dam thing about my daddy other than what he had heard from other white folks, whose only motive was to discredit him. Many people didn't even realize that I knew it, because I never discussed it, but there was so much speculation about my daddy's death that even I was under suspicion. Judging from prior conversations with others, the Roanoke police department and Fire Marshall secretly questioned other people about me, and my relationship with my father. Reportedly, some individuals had indicated that I could have even been responsible for my father's death. But, I really didn't care what they thought. The only thing I cared about at that time was the fact that I had lost someone very dear and precious to me. And I didn't know how I could go on living. There was just no need for all that drama. There had been countless occasions at home, when he would come in dog-tired, put something on the stove and fall asleep; and we'd all be awakened in the night with the smell of something smoldering. I had lived in the house with them up through 1987 and was in no hurry to get out. Then, much to my dismay, my mama somehow started trying to push me out. As I observed them aging, I became so protective of them until my husband and I had constructed our home a rock-throw from theirs, on our old church property. I remember one night, after Clarence and I had finally moved to our house, mama called me on the phone very upset, in the middle of the night and wanted me to come to the house. It was about 2 or 3 a.m. I got to the house, and there was daddy laying very quietly and solemnly on the living room couch. I sensed something very foreboding. I looked to the left into the beautiful room where he slept, only to be shocked by the still-smoldering charred room and its contents. The vinyl mini-blinds were melted on the windows; my mother's beautiful chiffon draperies were just fragments hanging there on the double windows; the carpet was charred. The only place in that room that had sustained no evidence of fire was a narrow area in the middle of the bed, where daddy had been laying there smoking a cigarette. The entire bed, around its perimeter, the sheets, mattress and everything was charred. How he walked out of that bedroom alive, could only have been an act of God. Mama said, "Charlotte, that's why I don't want you sleeping in this house. Wilkie is going to burn both of us up in here. He needs to stop coming in putting stuff on the stove and going to sleep. He went to bed smoking a cigarette, and burned up my bedroom. I just had that bedroom redone." Mama was so upset that night until she couldn't even remember if she had paid the fire insurance on the house, and was worried about how the damage would be repaired. Knowing mama as I did, I should have known not to worry. She was meticulous about things like that. But, she was in her mature years, and her memory was sometimes shaky. Ultimately, the damage was repaired and life continued for a little while. Oddly enough, in retrospect, I believe that the earlier event had been an omen of what was to come that fateful night in July.

So, I know daddy was tired. People who didn't live in the house with us had no way of knowing, but mama and I realized that he couldn't have lasted much longer and kept up the same pace — which he was still trying to do for the sake of appearances. He had been continuously on the go — almost non-stop for 30 years. And yes, people often tried to make light of his drinking— tried to use it to diminish or shade his character. But, they couldn't. As he moved into the mature years of his life, he did enjoy taking a drink. "White Label Scotch" was what he loved. The black folks in Randolph County often drove him so hard until we knew he probably needed that drink just to get himself to relax and fall asleep at night and sometimes just to get through the days. But, my mother had never permitted me to let that thought diminish my impressions of my father. She would say, "Charlotte, don't you pay any attention to what these Negroes say about your daddy... he's a better man drunk, than a whole lot of other men sober...you could put five or six of these black men together and all of 'em put together still wouldn't make one good man." When mama would say those words to me, I felt so empowered! She reminded me that everybody had some faults. But, she helped me to realize that despite any faults he may have had, his greatness transcended his faults. And, regardless to how much Scotch he may have drunk, when black folks got in trouble or needed help, they still knew how to find my daddy. And usually, he would never turn anybody down, if he felt he could help them. Up and down the dangerous highways; running here and there; going to meetings in town and out of town; going at every beck and call. He was tired. He was also still grieving over my mother's death. And he was being fiercely pursued by insensitive women who saw mama's death as an opportunity. Daddy was exhausted. Reportedly, he had been out to dinner with a lady friend of his, and he had then come home, and put a pot of some description on the stove. It has always been an enigma to me why he would go out to eat, and then come home and cook. But, that's what has been concluded. He probably sat back in his recliner and fell asleep. He was awakened by the stove fire, and probably tried to put it out, which was a grave mistake. Earlier that Friday evening, I had driven by the house twice on my way to and back from the post office, to mail some letters. I don't know why I didn't see the obvious. The house was pitch dark — which was very unusual. That should have alerted me that something was wrong. But, daddy and I had been sort of fussing because I being the jealous daughter, was resentful of all the women who were visiting and calling him. I felt he needed time alone, to reconcile himself to my mama's death. Mama hadn't been dead a good four months. Daddy was trying to act like everything was fine, but I knew better. I felt it was my place to demand that others leave him alone and give him his personal time to grieve and give him space. So, we had fussed about this. I was mad at him, and didn't stop by that night. To further dramatize his anger with me, earlier that week, he had taken my house keys, so I didn't have access to the house. That particular night, as I drove by slowly, I longed to catch a glimpse of him, and usually he'd be sitting in the living room, lights on, curtains all sprawled open, and I could look straight through the house, but not tonight. Yet, in the calm of the night, it never occurred to me that anything might be wrong. I went home, and undressed and went to bed, and probably an hour later, several little boys who had been out playing near Old LaFayette Highway had looked up toward the house and noticed flames coming out the back. They knocked on my door, and not completely asleep, I got up and went to the door. The little boys stood on my front porch, and I stood there with my front door gapped open as I talked to them. Hardly before they could get the words out of their mouths my husband seemingly sprang out of bed and ran right past me, and in what felt like a single leap he was on daddy's front porch. In an attempt to compose myself, and maintain my mental clarity, I immediately ran to my phone and called the fire department, who informed me that they had already gotton a call about it. Then I swiftly joined my husband at Daddy's house. Unable to open the doors, Clarence kicked the front door in, and my husband was met with a smoldering stifling cloud of black smoke. He ran to the hose in the front yard, and wet his shirt, and put it over his face, got down on his belly, and crawled through the house, feeling atop the beds, and chairs, but could not locate daddy. Finally, after the arrival of the local Fire Department and what seemed like hours, he was found — laying face down under the dining room table, apparently overcome by smoke inhalation. I was totally shocked, but many family friends comforted me by saying that was the way he would have wanted to go — "out with a bang." He was a lively and exciting person. His exit certainly created an aura of excitement. But, it took me years to come to terms with it. The one thing I do know is that my daddy died happy and fulfilled having accomplished his dream and goal to own and operate his own business, and that completed his life.

Although I had always perceived my dad's importance in our community, I don't think I ever realized the magnitude of it until he died. Black undertakers came from near and far to assist with the difficult preparation of his remains. One of my main worries was that he would not be viewable, and I would never have a chance to lay my eyes on his precious face again to say a final farewell. This was so important to me in light of our weeks of estrangement prior to his passing. But, they labored night and day to make the viewing possible. For that, I was and will be eternally grateful. On the day of daddy's funeral, the church simply could not hold all the people who came — from near and far — they came. Everybody, who was anybody was at the funeral. Mr. Earl T. Shinhoster, the Regional NAACP Director was there; the Honorable Thomas Reed, State NAACP president was there; local officials, our Mayor Henry V. "Speck" Bonner.; friends came from all over the United States. They were in the church as many as it could hold— in the streets — standing all over the church grounds, and beyond— sitting on the front porches at neighboring homes. I was overwhelmed by the vehicles that covered the entire community. As I was ushered through each moment of the event, it appeared to be a gigantic ant hill crawling with ants. People had to park and walk from neighboring streets, to get to the church. I was so inundated by all of it until it seemed as if I were in an out of body experience. I knew that my daddy was a beloved member of our community, so I wasn't surprised at all. But, I was engulfed by the grief, and my disbelief that all of this was even happening.

Now, I regret having chided my parents for "condemming me" to a difficult life; because I knew eventually they would die, and leave me alone, with the enormous responsibility of trying to single-handedly manage a Mortuary Business and the few pieces of property they had acquired. Even way back then I knew, that I would never forsake my heritage. My mother gently reminded me that during their child-bearing years, life had always been so uncertain for black families, they just didn't want to have a house full of children that they couldn't feed.

According to Erich March, Vice President of March Funeral Homes in Baltimore, Maryland, "From ancient Egypt to the modern day practice of mortuary science, black people have played a major role in caring for the dead and rendering services to bereaved families. In the African-American community, the profession of funeral service has always been a respected cornerstone of black-owned businesses. The black funeral director has always had a history of providing extraordinary service to accommodate his or her community.

Four institutions in the African-American community have survived the desegregation of American society and remain as uniquely owned and patronized by the black community. They are the black church, the black barber shop or beauty salon, the black cocktail lounge, and the black funeral home, which was usually operated as a family business and passed on from one generation to the next. The African American funeral director has always been a trusted and admired member of black society, respected for their compassionate service and leadership qualities. In addition to operating funeral businesses, many have gone on to hold political office and provide a wide range of economic benefits to their community." (1997)

I vividly recall one year during the late 1990's when the Alabama Funeral Directors & Mortician's Convention convened in Birmingham. Mayor Larry Langford of Bessemer was there to open the morning session with a welcome from the Birmingham-Bessemer area. The most provocative statement he made had to do with the duty incumbent upon every black business owner to lead the way in the continued liberation of African American People. He stressed that we cannot prosper in our businesses, if black people the people we depend upon for our livelihoods, are not prosperous. In essence, he said that we (African-American Funeral Directors) cannot afford to sink into a comfort zone, as long as our people are suffering outside the comfort zone. Once an African-American businessman or woman has elevated himself to the level of an successful entrepreneur, they have an obligation and a duty to work for the betterment and the benefit of the entire African-American community. I do believe that my daddy arose and fulfilled that obligation with everything in him. And to this very day, we remain steadfast in our obligation to support those who support us and make our success possible.

154

I am reminded of an event that drew national attention to my community in 1994. I was serving as the only black member of the school board in my county, a position that my father along with many other black heroes of my community, had fought for and won through a Federal Court Decision. The principal of one the largest high schools in Randolph County made a public announcement in a school assembly that in essence would preclude students from bringing a date of another race to the high school prom. When a young bi-racial student by the name of Revonda Bowen questioned the principal regarding whom she was going to bring to the prom, he allegedly told her in an open, public assembly that her mother and father had made a mistake (by producing a mixed child). Without question, our entire community was outraged over this; and as the issue escalated, the nation learned of the travesty, and became outraged too! I felt a duty and obligation not only to the children of my community, but to the children of time past who had come under this man's abrasive methods of dealing with black children, to take a stand against his racist conduct. There was a lot of publicity surrounding the issue, and the white component of our community was vicious persecuting me and accusing me of instigating all of the media coverage. In the midst of all of this, I vividly recall a conversation with Jim Vice, owner of our local radio station, who queried me: "Now, Charlotte, what are you going to do, are you going to be a funeral home director, or a civil rights leader?" It then became obvious to me that white people were not of the same mindset that blacks are. If you are a mortician, then you are not a political person. The two don't mix. I was so gotten off with by his question, until I don't even remember how I answered him. But, I never will forget the question. Regardless to how I may have answered him at that time, I'm going to answer it for everybody reading this: I'm going to do both. For as long as God allows the breath of life to move through this 51-year-old body of mine. I'm going to be a Funeral Home Director, and I will forever be dedicated to the civil rights movement. Because, right here in Randolph County, Alabama fifty years after the Brown decision of 1954, black people still are not free!

Although we may not advertise it, it is understood within the black communities that their funeral directors are natural born problem-solvers; and often, that relates to civil rights. They depend on their funeral directors' business savvy, political and sometimes legal connections, to stay in position to help them when they need help. And this, too is a part of the persona of the black funeral director.

I am grateful that my father taught me well, the importance of my duty to uplift my race. Mainly because entrepreneurism puts me in a better position to do just that and because my prosperity is based upon the black funeral market, and not dependent upon how well white folks like me, I can afford to be a mouthpiece for my people.

Up until the day he died, daddy held fast to the honorable and dignified role of the African-American Funeral Director. Up until the day he died, daddy remained positive, enthusiastic and energetic about his profession. Oh, I have no doubt that he had some downs. But, he took great pride in his accomplishments, in his work, and in everything he was involved in. He met every new day with a positive attitude and outlook.

In retrospect, I have, since his passing come to realize that daddy's greatness transcended any levels that Clark Funeral Home could have elevated him to. Many individuals enter into business enterprises, and without expending any energy at all, they expect their businesses to dignify them. But, daddy dignified Clark Funeral Home. Every time he entered the doors, something magical and mystical happened. It was as though his very presence breathed the breath of life into it. He was just that kind of man. In the 15 years that have followed, we have feebly attempted to embrace those same qualities that elevated him to the level of greatness he achieved. And every day, we honor him and remember him with all our love, reverence and respect.

Every now and then, I walk through the funeral home, and I see daddy and feel his spirit all over me. I often get very misty, because I remember how things used to be versus how they are now. I remember how hard we worked because we couldn't afford to pay extra help. In these 15 years, I have educated my son in the mortuary science field; I have also mentored another young man in the mortuary profession, Gabriel Carr who is like part of our family in the mortuary field; and my daughter now takes a very active role as administrative assistant. They are so proficient and well-trained in the business until my role is now minimal. I am back in the classroom and working toward retirement. I remember how daddy and I had to struggle sometimes with heavy men and women on the old time "gurneys." Now, we have high tech devices that makes it insultingly easy for one-man OR WOMAN to handle a remains. I remember the days of the old manual typewriter, daddy sitting at his desk hunting and pecking; it took days to process a funeral. Now, we have five computer systems automating all aspects of the business operation. Second-hand equipment has been replaced with new more up-to-date technical equipment to help us work faster and more efficiently. We've tried to give our place a cozier, classier more business-like feel. I look around and see all of it; and wish he could be here to enjoy it; or at least that he could see it. And my heart breaks because some his dream has actually come to fruition. Because of him and the man he was, we are living better than he did. We do have it easier than he did. But, in my spirit, he is still the "Chief Cook & Bottle-Washer."

The Stigma Of Being The Daughter Of A Civil Rights Leader

I can not close this chapter of daddy's life without amplifying the impact that being his daughter had on my own life. As soon as daddy died, in my spirit I began to discern how I would probably spend the rest of my life, being constantly tried and convicted as a result of having been his daughter, and so closely identified with him and his civil rights activities. Everybody in town knew that I supported him, and stood firmly with him on most if not all of his endeavors. My trials began just as soon as he was dead, not even a week after his burial. Over the years, our family had banked with the Commercial Bank of Roanoke. I guess it was owned by the Schuessler family in Roanoke.

They were a very prominent and wealthy family. Of course, there was another family associated with it, the Hester family. Though I am not sure and don't really claim to know specifically, the Landers apparently had a part in it too. Often times, people would come to Daddy when they got down on their luck and needed money. Sometimes, if he had the money, he'd just go in his pocket and lend it to them— for many of them, it ultimately became a gift, because in an overwhelming number of cases, he was never paid back. But, he never worried about it (or at least that's how it seemed). Down through the years, daddy would help various people out by co-signing with them at the bank to borrow small sums of money. I don't think he ever cosigned a loan for more than three or four hundred dollars. But, there might have been about four or five loans that were never paid back. I even recall daddy sharing with me how, at one time or another, one of the loan officers of the bank maybe Mr. Schuessler or Mr. Hester had even called him in and had a discussion with him about it. In essence, they told him that they understood that he wanted to help his people, and that they could require him to pay back these loans, but they didn't want to see his credit all messed up that way. They told him that the reason he could come into their bank and borrow any amount he needed was because he had always paid them back. But, they advised him to stop co-signing with people to borrow money, because if they had decent credit, they could get the money themselves, and wouldn't need a co-signer. Now, at some point in time, many many years prior to this, daddy had borrowed for himself, in the neighborhood of $3,000.00 to buy the "Smedley" property which was right next door to us. To secure this loan, he had pledged the accumulated cash value of one of his life insurances as collateral. The face value of this policy was in the neighborhood of $10,000.00. And daddy had made every payment on time, and satisfied the loan, and had had a renter on the property for probably 20 to 25 years. Immediately after daddy's death, I now found myself with a mountain of expenses from his funeral, enormous expenses in connection with operating the funeral home; everybody had started to hound me about the bills owed both for himself and the funeral home. I was overwhelmed. I wanted to take care of the bills, but, I felt that everybody in this God-forsaken town knew what I had just been through. What kind of people were they?

I found myself thinking: "Is there absolutely no sensitivity to my need to grieve for the loss of my father?"

I had already begun the process of probating my daddy's will. So, in the midst of all of this financial chaos, I called the probate judge, who told me, not to let anybody worry me. He told me that every one of the creditors was at my mercy, and to take my time, because I had six months at minimum to settle my daddy's estate. I had a double dose of financial chaos, because all my mother's affairs had not even been settled either. So, my mom's and daddy's training came in right on time. I sat down, and started writing letters. In my spirit, I thanked my mother for teaching me "the power of the pen." A letter to every creditor, letting them know that I was the executrix of my daddy's will, and that I was not about to be hounded about my parents' debts. Every creditor had a right to file against the estate, and that was the route I advised them to take.

In my letters, I even scolded them in anger for being so insensitive in light of all that I had just gone through. In my heart, I felt that every one of them knew what they were doing, and this was just a case of them wanting to twist the knife that had already pierced my bleeding heart. During that time, I would have to just steal away to be alone, almost every day, so I could cry, gather my thoughts and reflect. Just having lost both my parents, and trying to hold on to every shred of hope, I knew I needed to make sure that the Funeral Home could continue operations until I could clear my head and make some decisions about how I wanted to proceed. I filed an insurance claim on my daddy's $10,000.00 policy because I knew I could collect these funds, and they would help me keep the business running along for a little while.

Lo and behold, when I heard back from Liberty National Life Insurance Company, they informed me that they could not pay the benefits, because Commercial Bank of Roanoke had a lien against the proceeds. I couldn't imagine what in the world they would be holding my daddy's insurance for. I questioned Ed Drummond, the agent who serviced the policy, about it. And he told me he couldn't discuss it with me, that I needed to check with Commercial Bank. Somehow, I sensed that Ed knew all into this matter, and that perhaps he even had something to do with it. So, I immediately went to the bank to discuss this matter. Once I got there, I was met by Mr. John Landers, who presented me with a document, that showed a list of unpaid loans, that daddy had cosigned with other folks to borrow money from the bank. I sat very quietly and subdued in Mr. Landers' office at the bank, and I thoroughly examined the document that he gave me. He told me that when daddy signed over his life insurance, that covered any other (subsequent) obligations that he entered into with the bank, and that they had a perfect right to put a lien on the policy! Suddenly, the light came on in my head. Now, I was getting it. It suddenly dawned on me that Commercial Bank had kept my daddy's life insurance all that time — long after he had satisfied his own loan, which he had originally secured with that policy. They had held on to it for probably for 20 years or more — waiting for him TO DIE, so they could get their money. They probably knew he would not stand for it. They didn't even dare approach him with it. But, now that he was out of the way, they figured they could bluff me! They knew I'd be caught off guard, and probably in a moment of emotional weakness, wanting to do the right thing, I would succumb.

As I sat and read, and closely examined all the loans they had listed on their document, I realized that some of the loans went back further than the Alabama Statute of Limitations allowed — as far back as 8 to 10 years. If they have ever had the intention of collecting, they had every right to do it within the time allowed by law. Now, they were trying to collect on out-dated debts — debts they had no right to collect on. But, everything about this matter, smelled F-O-U-L! I began to feel my blood boil, and I believe that in that very moment, the spirit of Wilkie Clark rose up in me, and I went back in time to the rail road track, talking to ole Mr. Shannon.

Very emotionally, I then said to John Landers, "You don't have the right to hold my daddy's life insurance!! My daddy used this policy to secure his own personal loan which he paid off years ago, and whenever he paid that loan off, you had an obligation to release this policy!! You are completely out of line. You are free to file a claim against his estate, but you can't claim my daddy's insurance proceeds. Who do you think you are, to by-pass me, to confiscate my daddy's life insurance? And keep me from getting paid? What do you think gives you the right to put a hold on my daddy's life insurance? Every dam one of these loans is outdated, and the only way I will even consider paying any of these, is when you to follow the proper procedure and file a claim against his estate at which time I will give consideration to your claim."

Twenty years in the funeral business had taught me that life insurance was one of the most precious and protected assets that an individual can own, and nobody can force you to use your benefits in a way you don't approve of; nobody can claim your benefits other than you. And since I was the beneficiary, I knew that I was in control. I told Mr. Landers, I would see him in court and left the bank. I was probably so mad, until I forgot I even had a car parked in the bank parking lot. I immediately walked across the street to Attorney Lewis Hamner's office and when I got myself quieted and composed enough, I blurted out what had happened. Seeing how dam mad I was, Mr. Hamner took a look at the documents that John Landers had presented to me and picked up the telephone. My visit with Mr. Hamner left me in a state of utter disbelief. But, it gave me a new level of respect for the same man who several years earlier, as the City Attorney had written my daddy a letter threatening to prosecute him for building an illegal driveway at the Funeral Home.

Mr. Hamner spoke to John Landers on the telephone and he wasn't nice either. He told him that every dam loan on that document was outside the statute of limitations, and he had no right to do this. He demanded that he release my policy immediately or he would send me to an out of town attorney and I'd own Commercial Bank. I still vividly recall his words: "John, you're wrong– you're just wrong." He even threatened to resign as the banks attorney. Still in a state of shock, at this white man who for once, I believed did right by me, again, tears welled up in my throat, and nearly choking from anger, hurt, and humiliation, I wept. He admonished me: "Alright Charlotte, now, I got that all worked out for you. Go on back over there and get your policy. Now, I dun took care of it for you. Now, don't you go running off nowhere else now, and try to do anything else!"

I guess he was asking me not to go get another lawyer, and try to sue the bank. I never wanted to sue them anyway. All I wanted was what was rightfully mine. But I wept profusely because I was so hurt and I realized that the world would still be plagued by all the things my daddy had struggled and fought so hard against. As I left the bank with my paperwork, releasing daddy's policy I continued to cry because I realized that in many ways, my fighting days would not be over. This was only a beginning.

My father's impact on my life had been so far-reaching, until there are no words that I could either write or utter to adequately convey the love, reverent respect and admiration I have for him. He shaped my attitudes and beliefs, and laid a strong, firm foundation on which I could build my life. He shaped my attitudes and beliefs about racism. Witnessing his intestinal fortitude and forthright manner gave me a rational framework within which to cope with the life-long "racist moments" that have bombarded me in the years prior to and since he passed off the scene of time. He instilled in me a passionate hatred, and righteous indignation and intolerance for any degree of racism, prejudice and bigotry. Although his blood, and his influence still flows through my veins, I am nowhere near the person he was. I am nowhere near the woman I want or need to be. My attitudes are different. Whereas he could make a joke and laugh some things off just to bring calm into a heated moment, I take it to heart; and I get mad, mean, contrary, even willful and vicious when I encounter racial mistreatment. My acquaintance with him has spawned in me an almost magical kind of knowledge and wisdom that emerged from some mysterious place within me, according me a much clearer understanding of the issues that truly matter most in my life. With that understanding, in every situation that comes my way I now know how to cling to faith—a faith that daddy alone imparted to me — as the real —the only stronghold on my life.

If I could somehow meet that Mr. Barksdale, who was his SBA loan counselor, the one thing I would have him know is that I remember how hard he tried to make it for my daddy. But, that my daddy, though he is dead, is triumphant and victorious through me and my children. If I could meet the bankers who turned him down repeatedly for loans to purchase his funeral cars; I'd let them know that we did get a loan — and in the years since, we've bought several and paid for every one of them. This entire journey has been a long walk of faith — but it has led us to such a satisfied ending; because it proves that the word of God is true; that you can speak to your mountain and command it to be removed, and it will move; that mustard-seed faith still brings forth fruit; that truth pressed to earth will rise again.

In the case of Wilkie Clark, his ultimate success as an entre-preneur won't ever be measured in terms of how much money he made in business;   but in the final analysis, it will be measured by the level of hope he instilled — in me and my mother; and an entire neighborhood. This, he accomplished not by power, not by might. But he did it by the grace of God.

So, how do you summarize a lifetime of good works in as few words as possible? You don't. You just stop writing.

Wilkie Clark

REMEMBERED

An Anthology Of Praise

EXCELLENCE

"Show me someone content with mediocrity

and I'll show you someone destined for failure."

—Johnetta Cole

A Brother Reflects
Beotis Clark

Youngest Brother Of Wilkie Clark and "baby" of the family

Photo: Courtesy Of Mr. and Mrs.
Beotis and Belle Clark

I am Wilkie Clark's baby brother. During our boyhood, Wilkie shielded and protected me, and kept me with him until I was old enough and able to take care of myself. He taught me so many things about life that help me to survive today. Wilkie was my third oldest brother. He carried me with him to play, to school, to church and to clean and rake the yards for neighbors to make money for our personal needs.

My brother Wilkie was very strong in faith, knowledge, wisdom and understanding. His faith gave him hope and love. Our family was comprised of very strong people. We were raised by our mother, Lue Ella Baker Clark (later Holliday) and our grandmother, Lizzie Baker who was a "midwife." Our mother was the only girl out of a large family of boys. Our father left home while we were very young. But we had some very good uncles that trained us to be men. Uncle John was a disabled veteran from World War I. He was always there for guidance. Uncle Morgan, was very humble. He was a farmer. Uncle Jack was a very powerful force in the community; Uncle Vest was a carpenter. He did not get a single lesson in architecture, but he was blessed by God with a gift for building houses. These men were our mother's helpers. She could count on them, for they were there to tell us right from wrong. And we listened to them. They did not spare the rod. If you did wrong, you were punished in love with pulling down the strong holt "the belt."

166

Wilkie liked to play baseball. On Saturday evenings, we played ball in the corn pasture. All the community would come out to the game to see the Clarks and Bakers and neighbors play off.

Wilkie learned many skills from our Uncle Jack Baker. Uncle Jack would make our toys from old broken wagon wheels. Once the toys were made, Wilkie kept them moving. He could run around the house. He loved to race on foot and 99% of the time, Wilkie won the race.

Our Uncles taught us to cut wood for heat, milk cows, help our mother wash the clothes, build a fire around a black wash pot, to wash clothes in warm water. Our mother went into town and washed clothes for white families for a living. Wilkie would go with her and help her with this hard job, washing the clothes on a rub board. There was no washing machines. This job gave mama money for all our clothes and other things we needed.

Wilkie was surrounded by strong people who knew how to take a little and make a lot. They believed that God would provide and that "if you make one step, he will make two."

Our family planted and grew all of our food, raised hogs, cows, vegetables, peach and apple trees. Wilkie was taught how to save the vegetables for the winter. They would partially cook the food and then placed it in tightly capped jars. This is called canning. They cooked fruits, preserves and jellies. We had good food all year long.

Wilkie helped my mother milk the cows. In summer, the milk and butter was placed in a jar and sealed tightly, tied on a rope and let down in the well to keep the milk cool. There was no refrigerators.

In the winter, usually in January, we killed the hogs and cows. And Wilkie learned how to treat the meat so it would stay good to eat all year long. Hog-killing was on Saturday. All the men came together to help with this great activity. The ladies would clean the chitterlings, and make the seasoned sausages. It was very cold. Wilkie learned to grind cane for syrup. This was a fun time when the boys would drink the juice. If you drank too much, you could get very light headed.

As a young boy, Wilkie accepted Christ as his Savior at Hunter's Chapel A.M.E. Church, and also worshiped with his cousins at Wehadkee Baptist Church. His religious faith taught him to "...love the Lord thy God with all thy heart and soul, and love thy neighbor as thyself." On these two commandments, hangs all the law of prosperity. Wilkie learned to reach out and touch someone and make this world a better place. He believed that God Is. "I can do all things through Christ Jesus who strengthens me." This gave Wilkie courage to lift up the broken hearted and to love his family. He knew God requires us to walk humble before Him. Give God all the honor and the glory; and God will supply all your needs. This made my brother Wilkie a very strong and loving man. This was my brother Wilkie.

Written with all my love.
Beotis Milton Clark

COLLECTIVE WORK
AND RESPONSIBILITY

"No matter what accomplishment you make,
somebody helps you."

—*Althea Gibson*

Retrospective:
The Impact Of A Great Man
By Reverend R.L. Heflin:
Beloved Pastor Of Pastors, Small in Stature,
But a Giant of a Man, Beloved and Respected By All

Photo: Courtesy Of
Rev. R. L. Heflin

Brother Wilkie Clark was a great man. The most times we don't realize the greatness of a person until they have passed on. He was a man that was concerned about his people.... very much in the image of God, who said "if my people who are called my my name would get the right attitude, then he would do the job." So, Brother Wilkie was a man who went about trying to encourage the people to get the right attitude so they could free themselves from their oppressed conditions, and get about the business of freedom, justice and equality. He was a man that hungered and thirsted after righteousness. And he didn't give up on nothing that he started. Sometimes, we didn't think he could do it, and maybe we didn't give him the support that we should have given him, but that didn't discourage him. He kept pressing on. And I confess, that many things he said, I didn't think he could do them, but he proved me to be wrong. I hope I don't have to give an account at the judgment.

We went to Dr. King's funeral together — he, and brother Jesse Terry and I. We were riding along, and Brother Wilkie got so excited, until I had to call him down. He said "you know in the judgement, when Dr. King gets up he's gonna be equal to Jesus Christ..." I exclaimed "...don't say that brother Wilkie!..."

Whatever he went at, he put his whole heart and soul in it. But, whatever he said he was going to do, he did it. A lot of times, I thought he wasn't going to be able to do it. When I see him again I'm gonna have to apologize.

We all were worried about him, because he was SO outspoken. We were always afraid that the white folks were going to do something bad to him. But he didn't seem to worry about it. He just kept right on going.

He was a brave man. And I confess, most black folks around here were looking for him to be killed. He was talked about; mistreated; a lot of people called him "crazy." A heap of black folks in Randolph County was afraid to let white folks know they even associated with him, but you can believe one thing, when they got in trouble, they ALL knew how to find brother Wilkie. But, he didn't seem to mind putting his life on the altar, not for himself but for others.

I believe he wanted to see judgement roll down like water and righteousness like a mighty stream. I don't believe there will ever be another Wilkie Clark in this area. He still lives. We cherish his memory, and we give God the praise. One time after the assassination of Dr. Martin Luther King, Jr., we were at a meeting in Montgomery, Alabama, and and Dr. Martin Luther King, Sr. was the speaker, and he used these words: "... anyone who says Martin Luther King, Jr. is dead, they are out of their minds... he still lives, because the word says 'blessed are the dead who die in the Lord, henceforth yea says the spirit, that they may rest from their labor, and their works do follow,' So, I say, brother Wilkie Clark is not dead for his works do follow. So, I say, "goodnight my friend," I'll see you in the morning.

THANATOPSIS

So live, that when thy summons comes to join

The innumerable caravan which moves

To that mysterious realm, where each shall take

His chamber in the silent halls of death,

Thou go not, like the quarry-slave at night,

Scourged to his dungeon,

but, sustained and soothed

By an unfaltering trust,

approach thy grave

Like one who wraps the drapery of his couch About him,

and lies down to pleasant dreams.

(William Cullen Bryant 1794--1878)

Favors Remembered
By Tommy Bridges
Owner, Southeastern Casket Company,
Sylacauga, Alabama

Wilkie Clark was a man of character and love. The first time I met Mr. Wilkie was at a very crucial time in the development of his business. He had just opened up Clark Funeral Home, in Roanoke and was trying to get his funeral home inventoried.

My daddy was Eugene Phelps "Slick" Bridges. Everybody called him "Slick." He ran Southern Casket Company in Goodwater, Alabama. And I was just a young boy, helping my daddy to manufacture the caskets. My uncle and cousins actually owned Southern Casket Company, and a bank and golf course. Daddy merely killed himself running the plant for them.

Southern was one of the biggest independently owned casket manufacturers in the southeast. They sold in twelve states.

My daddy and Mr. Wilkie formed a very deep, life-long friendship stemming from his need to have caskets in his inventory. We built and sold the caskets at a time when no casket suppliers were extending credit to black funeral homes. At that time, mostly all the casket companies had strict policies about not extending credit to the black funeral homes. Many of the big name prestigious suppliers still follow that same practice to this day.

My daddy would often put his job on the line, to help the black funeral directors keep their funeral homes inventoried. One way he accomplished this was by building a few caskets on the side under his own name and that is how he was able to help the black funeral directors. My daddy helped Mr. Wilkie with caskets whenever he needed them, and they remained friends until daddy died. My father worked about 48 years in the casket business. He worked very hard, and gave his life to the Casket business to make it successful for my cousins and my uncle. But, when daddy died, he had only seven or eight hundred dollars in the bank. But, he had helped a lot of people in his lifetime. And, if you talk to any of the older black funeral home owners, especially in the State of Alabama, they will tell you, that "Slick" Bridges helped them when no one else would.

I remember the time I was down on my luck and needed money to pay my power bill. I called Mr. Wilkie and asked if he could loan me some $300.00 to pay the bill. Without hesitation, he told me to meet him at the Funeral Home. I had to drive from Sylacauga, Alabama which was more than an hour away. When I got there, it was late at night, but he was there waiting for me. With a smile on his face, he handed me the money. When he handed me that $300.00, I don't believe he saw what color I was. He just saw a friend in need. I told him I would pay him back when I got on my feet again, and his reply was for me not to worry that everybody got down sometimes and needed help. He told me that $300.00 was very little in comparison to what my daddy had done for him and other black undertakers.

Mr. Wilkie was a true friend who loved others for who and what they were, not for what color they were. I believe he would have fought just as hard for me, as he fought for any of the black people he helped in Randolph County, Alabama.

Mr. Wilkie Clark will always have a place in my heart. God bless Wilkie Clark, and may he rest in peace.

Tommy Bridges, Owner
Southeastern Casket Company, Sylacauga, Alabama

Retrospective Of Lillian V. Shealey
Retired Educator, Beloved Family Friend

Mr. Clark was a very simple man with strong compassion for helping the children and the adults of our community. One thing I can truly say about Wilkie is that he was always a perfect gentleman. He worked hard for the poorest and unknowledgeable people. He was a motivator, a speaker, a helper, and often a financial resource for many of us.

God gave each of us a life and He asked us to be Christ-like

Photo: Courtesy Of Mrs. Lillian V. Shealey

in our efforts to maintain a good & peaceful life. Whatever good we do in this life will show how we appreciate, love and honor God. There is a scripture that says: "so as a man thinketh in his heart, so is he." Wilkie's thoughts were always centered on helping someone in this life. These were the thoughts he most often expressed. He was adamant and outspoken in his belief that the degree to which we helped others in this life; on this side of Jordan's River, would have a direct impact on where we would spend eternity.

His compassion reflected many of the episodes and events in his life and in the history of the world during that time, that stood out strong and clearly. He was very deeply influenced by Jesus Christ and he had a very high respect and admiration for Dr. Martin Luther King, Jr. and his life reflected the influence both of those figures had on him. In many ways, Wilkie was a lot like Dr. King, except when it came to the manner in which he did things. The comparison between the two is a lot like the comparison between "Dr. Jeckyll and "Mr. Hyde." Martin was the "doctor" and Wilkie was more like "Mr. Hyde." Wilkie would often talk big and flamboyant about helping someone find his way. Sometimes he would be mad because somebody had been mistreated; so he wouldn't come across as being as "polished" and eloquent like Dr. King was. But, he always had the greater good at heart.

We all learn our values early in life, beginning with our mothers and fathers. Wilkie often spoke of his life as a young man; how he helped his mother when she was old and sickly. That was one experience that followed him and had a lasting impression throughout his life. He told me of his experiences he enjoyed as he grew up working long and hard with Doctor G. W. Bonner. He learned much about how to help the helpless & poor when he was at home with his mommy, and from that doctor. He felt that he could always help his fellow man— black or white. He worked hard with our community sometimes with help but most of the times without it. He would stand tall many times all alone. But if he felt he was right about anything, he stood anyway. The most trouble he ever got into in his life, was on account of trying to do something good to help somebody else. But, that was his quest.

He told me of his experiences with the U.S. army in his later years. He thought it was a high privilege to work with the medical division. He had no medical training; he did maintain a great mind that he acquired from mommy at home and that doctor that he could and would work well with the U.S. Army taking care of the soldiers, and he did. He returned home with honor from the U.S. Army medical division and lived his life as a great inspiration and asset to our community. He wasn't a saint with a halo and angels wings — none of us are. But, he did a lot of good things for people everywhere. He was beautiful person.

I loved and adored his wife. We all called her "Pete." She was one of my dearest friends. Wilkie loved "Pete" and he loved Charlotte. He would often times talk harshly about them but in the final analysis, he would turn the world upside down for either one of them. That was "Wilkie's way" he showed his love for his wife and daughter.

A Conversation With Addie Sue Wilson
"A Friend In Need"

One busy afternoon, I happened to be in the post office when I bumped into an elderly lady I hadn't seen for quite some time. Her name is Addie Sue Wilson. Seems like I have known Ms. Addie Sue all of my life. Somewhat surprised but delighted to see that she was still up and about, I remembered her from many previous encounters, all of which had been pleasant ones. I fondly recalled the year 1978, while I was pregnant with my first child.

Photo: Courtesy Of
Mrs. Addie Sue Wilson

Ms. Addie Sue would visit my parents' home regularly. During those visits, she would tease me about being pregnant, telling me she could predict whether my baby was going to be a girl or a boy, and she told me emphatically that I was going to have a boy (which by the way, I did). We would talk about old fashioned beliefs and folkways, and how black babies used to have to be delivered by mid-wives because "colored folks couldn't go to the hospital back then." While her visits back then would be pleasant, I still sensed that there was something else going on in the background, because, every time she came by to visit, she would always end up getting up and sort of sliding over to where my mother was, and slipping something into her hand as if acting secretly. Although I never saw what that something was, I assumed it was money.

I remembered Addie Sue because she had always, even after daddy's death, remained a great fan and admirer of our family and made a point to tell me so. Not only was she an admirer of me, but everytime she saw me, she made it her business to admire daddy, and to talk about what a good man he was. She would always add "your mama too... they was some good people; I never will forget them." Her strong endearing remarks always left me wondering and curious, knowing that there was a story somewhere in the background. So, on this particular afternoon at the post office, she spoke to me, again commenting on daddy's kindness and generosity.

Responding, I said to her, "Ms. Addie Sue, I'm writing a book about my father. You have always spoken so highly of him and my mother; would you mind sitting down and having a conversation with me about it; perhaps you can tell me something I can write in my book."

Without a moment's hesitation, she exclaimed, "Why sho I will! There ain't nothing I wouldn't do for you, or Mr. Clark, or Mrs. Clark. They was some good people, yo mama and daddy.... I'll come over to yo house and talk to you and tell you a lot of good things about your daddy for you to put in yo book."

Ms. Addie Sue, now, 81 years old, made good on her promise to talk to me. We had a wonderful conversation. Recalling our meeting, she was seemingly so happy and content in her reflective state of mind.

She began: "I'm 81 years old, born March 31, 1922."

I said, "Ms. Addie Sue, you are just two years younger than my daddy would have been if he had lived. He was born March 8, 1920." "Right....seems like I known your daddy all my life, as far back as I can remember. Where is your Aunt Lelia?"

I reported, "Auntie Lelia passed away about four years ago, Ms. Addie Sue."

"Yo daddy's sister Lelia was one of my best friends. I used to visit her a lot at her house —just like a sister; we was good friends.... real good friends." She continued...

"Hun, your daddy and your mama went all out they way to help folks. If you wanted to go anywhere, Mr. Clark was the one who would carry you. He always kept a good car to drive, and he was a smart man; he knew how to get around in the world. Could carry you anywhere you wanted to go. Folks back then didn't know how to go nowhere. But, he'd put you in his car and carry you where you needed to go. I remember one time, I needed to get to Atlanta to get a car that was broke down. Mr. Clark took me to see about my car. Oh how I miss 'em — both of 'em!"

"Hun, I tell you the truth, if it hadn't been for your daddy, I'd 'a lost this here house I got right here. I borrowed $4,500.00 from the bank to build a room on my house. I was working at Traylor Nursing Home for seven years, but I had my mama. Mama was sick with kidney poison. I had to take care of my mama. So, I told mama I might as well quit trying to work, and stay at home and look after her. Well, I quit working to look after mama, and messed around and got behind on my house payment. The bank was fittin to take my house. Hun, I walked the floor all night long, pullin' my hair out wonderin' what was I gon do.

I needed a thousand dollars within a certain length of time, or I was gonna lose my house. I thought about Mr. Clark, and I decided I was gon go and see him and see if he'd let me have the money. I went on to the Funeral Home to see him, and I told him I was bout to lose my house. You know how he'd talk to you; he said, "What you owe 'em honey?" I said, "I owe 'em a thousand dollars." He said, you know white folks don't want to see us with nothing no how. I'm going to see to you not losing your house. You go up there to my house, and you tell Mrs. Clark that I said to let you have that thousand dollars." Mr. Wilkie Clark let me have that thousand dollars, and I paid 'em fifty dollars a month until I got it paid. I would'a lost my house — now hun, you tell me where could I go to now? I don't know nobody in Roanoke I could go to and they let me have a thousand dollars. I'll never forget you daddy or your mama."

Now, I left that encounter with a deeper understanding about why Ms. Addie Sue was the way she was about us. I couldn't help but to ask her one final question.

"Ms. Addie Sue, people have told me so many good things about my daddy. Have you ever heard anything bad about my daddy?"

"Hun, all I ever knew about Mr. Clark or Mrs. Clark was good. I don't know nothing bad about 'em. If it was any bad it come from folks talking on the street — just gossip from people who didn't know your daddy and your mama. They was just some good people. They would help anybody, any way they could."

It was a perfect way to end my day. Before I left, I had to promise Ms. Addie Sue a large photo of my mother and my father. I'll have to keep my promise to her, just as she kept hers to me.

178

HOPE

"We never lost hope despite the segregated world of this rural town because we had adults who gave us a sense of a future and black folk had an extra lot of problems, and we were taught that we could struggle and change them."

—*Marian Wright Edelman*

A Tribute To Roy Terry
By Charlotte A. Clark-Frieson

Roy Terry (right) is pictured here with brother Rudolph, and mother, Mrs. Velma Terry. Photo: Courtesy of Roy and Cotina Terry.

This portion of the book is a placeholder, for what would have been a "Retrospective" written by Mr. Roy Terry. Mr. Terry's contribution to this book is missing, due to circumstances beyond his or my or anyone else's control. But, in spite of his unavailability to do so at this time, and of necessity, I am compelled to insert something herein anyway, for knowing of my father's profound love, admiration and respect both for him and his family, I fear he would not rest in his grave if I were negligent in my treatment of this subject. Daddy couldn't have loved Roy and Rudolph more if they had been his own sons.

For that reason, I have opted to reserve this section of the book to pay a special tribute to an African American family of entrepreneurs that we know as the Terry family.

So because I, the daughter of a civil rights leader and entrepreneur, was privileged to witness the incredible journey of this mighty family, I am writing in their stead, in hopes that they will find in their hearts to accept and acknowledge this writing, not as an exaltation of my father, but rather an exaltation of an African-American family that by all definitions earned their right to a place of respect, not just in the history of this local community, but the world.

Right here in little Roanoke, Randolph County, Alabama amid all the bigotry and racism that earned the State of Alabama so much notariety, in the 1960's their father and mother, the late Jesse A. and Velma G. (Heard) Terry started a manufacturing

180

enterprise that in its finest hour, emerged as one of the foremost black businesses in the nation, spanning four generations. Their specialty was upholstery, and garment manufacturing. They had four sons, one of whom passed away as a youngster. There was Jesse, Jr., Roy, Rudolph, and William. All the Terry boys were bright, intelligent youngsters, entitling bragging rights to every teacher and administrator at the Randolph County Training School. My mother was probably at the top of the bragging list. They sprang forth at a time when everyone in our little community placed hope in those who would one day grow up and leave this seemingly God-forsaken locale, broaden their knowledge and return home to contribute their new insights to help move our people forward in time. They received encouragement from all directions: home, school, church and community. All of them were blessed to attend Morehouse College in Atlanta, Georgia, where they all majored in various aspects of business and business administration, and returned home to join their parents in moving Terry Manufacturing Company, Inc., to an unthinkable level of greatness. They brought back with them, fresh, new ideas and alternative strategies for ushering African-Americans toward new and higher expectations and standards.

To their credit, we can cruise through our community today, and point to numerous tangible places, and objects that stand as earthly monuments to their work in this vineyard.

In their hay-day they were hailed as one of the most outstanding black businesses not merely in the State of Alabama, but in the nation. They exceeded all imaginable expectations, when they landed contracts to manufacture the athletic garments for the 1996 Olympics hosted in Atlanta, Georgia.

At the urgence and insistence of my father, who mentored them in Civil Rights, they, too became drum majors for justice throughout Randolph County and the State of Alabama, marching to the seemingly never-ending, stubborn beat of mistreatment, injustice and inequitable treatment of others in and around our community. Once committed, they fought to break down racial barriers on every playing field, and on every level. Having allied themselves with the biggest, baddest and boldest of civil rights advocacy groups and organizations and with the addition of Reverend R. L. Heflin, who complimented this team, they formed an impenetrable coalition that could not be severed, broken, infiltrated or corrupted.

There is no way, without generating another extensive, and in-depth writing, that I can adequately or appropriately chronicle all that this extraordinary family has done to lift the level of consciousness in our community. But, I reserve this moment to revere, honor and elevate them to their rightful place in the history of this our grateful neighborhood.

As this family, a great pillar upon which our neighborhood has rested, continues on their pilgrimage through crisis, it is my humble prayer that God will embrace them, and that they will emerge whole again, ready to rejoin our community in the continuing struggle to have our rightful place in the archives of time.

Mr and Mrs. Terry are pictured at Terry Manufacturing Company with sons Roy, Rudolph and William Terry at ages 20, 22, and 24. Below, family poses for photo following "Jesse Terry Day," honoring the achievements of Jesse A. Terry.

SELF-HELP

"If the white man gives you anything, just remember,
when he gets ready he will take it right back."

Fannie Lou Hamer

Douglas M. Heard Reflects
On His Concern For Equal
Employment Opportunities
Randolph County Schools Transportation Supervisor

Photo: Courtesy Of Douglas M. Heard

I knew Wilkie Clark all of my life. Having grown up in the same neighborhood where he lived, there are probably a lot of interesting or extraordinary things that I could share about Mr. Clark, but the most outstanding memory I have of him is how he took me to my present position as Transportation Supervisor for the Randolph County Board Of Education. When I say that he "took me," I mean that he literally took me to the job. Let me tell you about it....

As a young man, I had enlisted in the army, and made a career in the military. Young black men were just wanting a better life than Roanoke, Alabama could afford them. What did Roanoke, Alabama have to offer a young ambitious black man? Nothing but Handley Textile Mills and Wehadkee Yarn Mills. Textile industries were just about the biggest industries...the only industries in town. You could look around, and what did you see black people doing? Those who had been lucky enough to land jobs as mill hands had just about worn themselves down in the mills; some of them farmed; a lot of them were still domestic workers working in and around the homes of affluent whites. I just wanted better. So, I went off to the military, and put in 20 years. But, after all those years in the military, I came back home to Roanoke, and very little had changed. So, I decided that I wanted to go to school and further my education. After my return home, I would occasionally hear about or read in the newspaper about the controversy between blacks and the public schools. Desegregation definitely was not working out as well as expected, at least not for blacks. And I know that is what led to my employment.

I had always known of the rumblings of controversy between blacks in Randolph County and the County Board Of Education. But, since I wasn't close to any of the issues, I probably didn't pay much attention to them at that time. But, I knew that Wilkie was involved in all or most of the discussions that had been taking place. Disgruntled parents were always talking to him about the way their children were being treated in the schools, and there had always been talk of concerns among the black leaders because the County School System had so few, and in many cases NO blacks working. For that reason, Mr. Clark was always into it with Randolph County Schools...not a single black principal; not a single black clerical worker or secretary; not a single black coach; there were a scant few black teachers; but what was sure enough astonishing is the fact that in a system with five schools, no black could qualify to even be a janitor, and perhaps one was qualified to cook, or work in the school lunchroom. They were always making excuses by saying they couldn't find any qualified blacks to hire.

Well, one day, Wilkie personally carried me to the county seat in Wedowee to meet the Superintendent of Education. At that time, our school superintendent was Mr. James "Jimmy" Holmes.

We walked in and he said to Superintendent Holmes:

"I got a man here that is qualified... this is Douglas McArthur "Mack" Heard."

So, Mr. Jimmy Holmes, asked me to show him my credentials. I had all my credentials with me, so I showed them. So, after he looked at all my credentials, he told me I was probably over qualified. He continued,

"The man I have in charge now, only has a ninth or tenth grade education."

Jeff Langley, who was the assistant superintendent at that time, commented, "You probably wouldn't want that job, because you were a Master Sergeant in the Army and you probably had a desk and everything; this job is only fixing tires."

Why he made that comment, I will never know, but I figure he was trying to discourage me. Nevertheless, disregarding Langley's comment, Mr. Holmes called to the school bus shop, and asked Clayton Johnson who was the school bus shop supervisor at that time, to come down to meet me in the superintendent's office.

Clayton Johnson walked into Mr. Holmes' office bragging,

"I can show you, or tell you how to do any kind of repair work on a school bus."

I countered, "I'm familiar with school buses..."

He then challenged, "I got one up there, that I can't get to running....been sittin' two months; reckon you can do anything with it?" So, I was assigned that task; that was my first task. I repaired the bus according to the transportation super's instructions, but after following his instructions to the letter, the bus still wouldn't run.

So, with persistence, I said,

"Let me troubleshoot the bus."

After a few minutes, I found the problem. He had insisted on having me replace the fuel pump in the tank, and in the course of troubleshooting I had discovered that it was only a blown fuse. So, I believe that this is when I won their confidence. I have been an employee for the Randolph County Board Of Education ever since. I continued to work there as a mechanic under Clayton Johnson.

Eventually, Clayton Johnson died. It was rumored that he committed suicide. Some people even tried to say that he did it because of me...cause he was scared I'd get his job. After his death, there was a lot of speculation about who would become shop supervisor. There were others on the job who had been there longer, but had nowhere near the qualifications that I did. I had brought twenty years from the U.S. Army as an auto technician with me, plus three years at Opelika State Technical College Auto Repair and Refinishing Program. I felt that I was the most qualified person for the job. But we were all fearful....and watchful, because we knew that this school system had a long history of racial exclusion. Although everybody felt that I was the best qualified and should be promoted, we didn't expect it.

Surprisingly, I was promoted to transportation supervisor for the Randolph County Board Of Education. As a result, I became the first black individual to hold a supervisory position for the Randolph County Board of Education (since court-ordered desegregation). Up until I was hired, no black had ever worked as a professional mechanic in the county school bus shop.

Well, just as sure as I was promoted to supervisor, the devil got busy trying to bring me down. Shortly after I was promoted to Transportation Supervisor, one white employee, Laymon Wilson, approached me and said: "Everybody's kin to each other around here, 'cept you."

I took it he was letting me know in no uncertain terms, that he was probably a Klan sympathizer, and in no way keen on working under the supervision of a black man. I certainly knew intimidation when I saw it. I told him it didn't make any difference. But, they (all three of the mechanics working in the shop) went to a certain school bus driver's house and told him that they were not gonna to work for no nigger. Quite naturally, word got back to me and I knew that I was going to really have to beef up my act, and keep my ducks in a row. So, after that, I started assigning them jobs individually, so I could document everything that went on. I immediately implemented an evaluation procedure. I assigned Mr. Wilson to do a brake job on a small bus. He could take it apart but he couldn't put it back together.

So, he came into my office, and told me, "You just as well go ahead and fire me, because I can't put this back together."

Yet he had been on this job for more than twenty years, and couldn't do any repair work on school buses. So, I recommended to Mr. Jimmy Holmes that we send him to trade school or mechanic school in the afternoon.

Mr. Holmes, concluded, "He only has a year before he retires, so we'll just let it slide for that year, then he'll be retired."

So, Wilson hung around another year and, mind you, he was the highest paid man in the bus shop— He was even making more money that anybody else, including me! Some time passed before this matter was finally addressed and corrected by the school, because there were still other men working in the school bus shop, with less education and training or experience who were making more money than I was.

Despite many obstacles and bad experiences, I have remained on this job as transportation supervisor but it has not been easy. There is still occasional resistance from whites to working under the supervision of a black man. Even though I'm very aware of this at all times, I try to keep it in the back of my mind, rather than in the front. But, as a result, I have gone through a mountain of unnecessary job-related difficulties that just simply would never have become an issue if I had been a white supervisor. In one such instance, very recently, the present school superintendent of education suspended me from my job, and wrote me up for sexual harassment, just because I was doing my job. This happened all because one resentful white bus-driver lied on me, accusing me of sexually harassing her because I caught her on one of the buses with a man whom it was rumored that she was dating, when she should have been in the classroom doing her duties as an aide. I reported this to the school principal, and because I reported it, the young woman, and her friend both engaged our school superintendent and other employees in an evil conspiracy to cause me enough trouble to last me a lifetime. A sexual harassment charge can follow a person for the remainder of their lifetime. Even though they supposedly investigated the matter, and found no evidence to support her claim of sexual harassment, there is still a written reprimand in my file today as a result of that incident. The potential for these kinds of crazy unimaginable episodes to pop up always makes it impossible for a black man to work on a job with any peace of mind.

I know in my heart, that if I were not a black man, I would probably be hailed as one of the best supervisors the school bus shop has ever seen. But, that's why you have to know who you are and who's you are. I know I'm good at what I do. I know the Randolph County School Bus Shop probably runs better than it ever has. I know that we have better transportation service for our children than we've ever had. I know that I'm probably the best qualified man they've ever had in the history of the school; and I know that in all the years I've been in this world, all the places, I've been, all the jobs I've worked on, that I am not a sexual harasser. But, there are some situations where I just have to be the bigger man, take things in stride, consider the source, and pray for the lesser men and women. And that is what I try to do.

Thanks to a man by the name of Wilkie Clark, I know and understand the importance of standing up for my rights, and not letting anybody make a floor mat out of me. I know that racism doesn't have to conquer or subdue me. I understand how to demand justice and equal treatment for myself. Because of Wilkie Clark I know that we have to vigorously pursue justice through every means available to us, including the United States Justice Department and the Federal Courts. And for those issues that can't be resolved through the courts, we just have to pray for our oppressors and leave them in the hands of the Lord.

Thanks to my friendship with Wilkie, I had the opportunity to prove myself and secure employment on the basis of my ability, training and qualifications. I regret he is gone, because I know that he would still be vigilant in watching the actions of the school system, to make sure that fairness and justice prevailed in Randolph County in all matters.

Douglas M. Heard now resides in Newnan, Georgia, and continues to serve the Randolph County School District as its Transportation Supervisor.

Robert Joiner, Jr.
Deeds Remembered
Deacon of Peace & Goodwill Baptist Church
Vice-President of the Randolph County Branch, NAACP

Photography:
Charlotte A. Clark-Frieson

That man would give you the clothes off his back. "Lightening" Rosser always said he would never have anything, because if he ever did get ahold of anything, he would give it away. He just believed in seeing other people happy. The man tried to help everybody.

Most of the years that Wilkie served as President of the NAACP, I served as his Vice-President. We had many joyous times together, and then we had some scary times together. A lot of times, trying to get things done, it would just be him and me. Sometimes, he had it all by himself.

At times, he was quite funny. He walked on his heels. We'd go to the City Council meeting or School Board meeting, and his shoes would be clacking, because his heels hit the floor before the rest of his foot. I'd pick at him about the way he walked.

But I could always sense the tension whenever there was a meeting between the races. Trying to work with the N.A.A.C.P. was no laughing matter. But, we had to do something to keep up our nerves. So, we talked trash, and gave people something to laugh about. He was often despondent about how apathetic black people were about the idea of bettering themselves. Many just plain didn't have any interest in local affairs. Many never read the newspaper, or tried to understand what was going on in the community. He would often say: "If you want to hide something from a Negro, put it on the front page of the paper."

190

As they got older, Mrs. Clark would often comment, "We've retired from having sex."

Wilkie would laughingly say, "Hell, you have, but I ain't."

When Wilkie wasn't busy burying people, I often enjoyed going to the funeral home, just sitting around and listening to him talk about civil rights. He'd tell something funny, then he'd start to talk serious about civil rights and black folks, and how far behind time we were. That was his favorite subject. He spent all of his time, running and ripping up and down the road trying to help people.

Way back in the 70's we had an incident to happen to a young black boy named David Pickard. David was a young boy from Wedowee, Alabama. He was driving from Georgia to Alabama, when a Georgia State Trooper began to pursue him. Probably in fear, David Pickard tried to outrun the trooper, and finally the chase ended with David pulling off the road, and running toward the back of someone's house. The Trooper shot David in the back, and killed him as he was trying to flee from the officer. According to all accounts, that boy, David Pickard was literally running for his life.

Wilkie Clark gave the boy a funeral. Brought in civil rights lawyers, and speakers to bring this travesty to the attention of the entire community. At his insistence, the black community started the "David Pickard" fund to aid the family in seeing that justice would be served in his case. Quite naturally, there were no consequences for the Trooper. Killing a black man at that time only meant that was one less black man to have to see. That was all.

His memory was extraordinary. He could go off to NAACP meetings in New York, come on back to Alabama; and then go to another big meeting in Birmingham, then come back home and tell everything that happened at all three meetings word for word. There is no way I could hold everything that went on in all them meetings in my head. He could quote the law, and famous court decisions verbatim. He had an extraordinary head on him.

Every once in awhile, he'd take a drink. I used to wonder why. After running with him for a while, and seeing the kinds of things he had to go through, I began to see why he drank. Time you think you had one problem solved, then here come somebody else with another one. He would go from Wedowee to Montgomery at his own expense, running to meetings trying to get the information he needed to help black people in Randolph County, Alabama…. wearing out cars and tires.

Mrs. Clark would often say, "Wilkie has worn out every car we ever bought, going to meetings, and trying to help these people, and they don't care a hill of beans about him."

I remember one time, we went to the city council. Local police officers were going buck wild in Roanoke….running renegade! One officer had sped down Riley Street (now Wilkie Clark Drive) in pursuit of someone, and shot into a family's home in the black neighborhood. This family had little children in the home. Luckily, no one was injured, but the issue raised concerns. Quite naturally, nothing had been done about it. So a delegation of blacks from different organizations decided to go to the city council to ask that the officer be relieved of his duties. Well, several meetings and a lot of discussion took place, and still no action was taken. But, eventually, at one of the city council meetings, it was inadvertently disclosed that the officer had been released after making the mistake of grabbing Mayor Bonner in the collar.

Infuriated by this news, Mr. Clark disdainfully retorted,

"Yaw'll ought to be made to keep him! Long as he was shooting in black folks houses, he was a good officer; but when he grabbed "Speck" in the collar, he was no longer a good officer… You ought to be made to put up with his ass from now on!"

Robert Joiner, Jr. has been a loyal member and officer of the Randolph County Branch, NAACP since the 1960's. Following the death of Wilkie Clark, he assumed leadership and served as President of the local branch until 1992. He continues to live in Randolph County, and to raise concerns about issues affecting the people of the community.

ACCOMPLISHMENT

"People will know you're serious when you produce."

—*Muhammad Ali*

Reflections On
A Long and Loving Friendship
"Exaltation For A Great Warrior"
By Bishop Lathonia J. Wright
Founding Pastor, New Life Worship Center,
Roanoke, Alabama

Photo: Courtesy Of
Randolph County Commission

For any reader to comprehend the magnitude of the impact that Wilkie Clark exerted on my life, one would need to have a general idea about my beginnings. I grew up in East Roanoke during the 50's, 60's and 70's, somewhat isolated from the general population in that I was raised in the Pentecostal faith, and all of my young life I was soaked, like a human sponge, in the firm doctrines of Holiness, which at times restricted my participation in certain activities, and placed firm and rigid boundaries on my associations with certain people outside my own circle. Having been widowed during our childhood years, my mother the late Mrs. Annie Lois Wright, was raising both me and my younger brother, Danny as a single parent. Perhaps the one stable influence in her life was her association with the Pentecostal faith. Under the ministerial direction of the late Elder Wade Wright, Sr., and later on his son, the late Bishop Wade Wright, Jr., I received a thorough knowledge and understanding of scriptural things, and was raised to behave according to the instruction I received while a student of religion at East Roanoke Pure Holiness Church of God. There was a scripture to address every aspect and avenue of my life. Having been reared in this environment, I was very opinionated, quite rigid in the way I approached people and life in general, and quite unyielding in my belief that no one outside my circle of faith either studied or understood scriptural things to the extent that we did. Perhaps we were all quite adamant about that.... until I came to know Wilkie.

194

Great warrior that he was — on countless occasions, he took me on scripturally, and many times, won the battle! To him, "holiness" had everything to do with how we treated our fellow man, and addressed the issues of life.

As far back in time as my memory can carry me, I had this mysterious awareness that there was an unusual man in my community by the name of Mr. Wilkie Clark. This is probably how everyone knew him and there was no one who didn't know of him or hadn't heard about him. He had a reputation that preceded him in that he was quite extraordinary, and was such a natural part of the setting here in Randolph County, Alabama until ironically, I don't even think I can pinpoint our first meeting. But, like a mighty Oak Tree whose root is firmly grounded inside the earth that envelops it; whose branches reach forward and hover over those who depend on it for shade, he was just always an integral part of our community in East Roanoke, Alabama. He was a natural part of the scenery, and for that reason, I don't think anybody could ever imagine a Roanoke, Randolph County Alabama without him in it. As a mere consequence of his being here, at some level, perhaps not intellectual, but more on a spiritual level, he made a colossal impression on me. Young and impressionable man that I was, and desiring to better myself, I had watched him, and was attracted to him; desired to emulate him. Fifteen years after his passing, he is just as vivid in my mind as he was then. Fifteen years after his passing, the strong and passionate influence he exerted on me is still a firmly fixed part of my persona. He exerted a strong influence on my life. His wit and wisdom was priceless. He exuded a matchless aura.

The forcefulness with which he operated in our community and the impact he had on our community have been unequaled by anyone who has come on the scene since his debut. It is my honor to exalt him for the great works he wrought while here.

Reflecting on my long and intimate friendship with Wilkie Clark, I am reminded how, in theology, we frequently talk about oral tradition, which is reflected in the Ministry of Jesus. Whenever Jesus would minister on earth, His disciples would write as a means of recording everything that was said. Then afterward, they would reflect on what was said, and what was done. I said all that to say this: At the time we were walking and talking together, we were so caught up in living life, and doing what we were doing; and we assumed that he would always be around. How disastrous it is that nobody thought about writing or recording Wilkie's profound and penetrating words or chronicling his amazing works in preparation for this day?

Sometime during the early 1970's, I developed an interest in the funeral home. So, I decided to go by and talk to Wilkie about helping out at the funeral home. Being the warm hearted, approachable man that he was, he embraced my desire to learn about and work in the funeral business; and from that visit until the day I laid him to rest on a hot day in August of 1989, we engaged in an impenetrable friendship that I shall never forget.

Outside of his own family, I probably spent more time with Wilkie Clark, than anyone else I knew. But, I dare say that time was well spent...never wasted, because of the caliber of man that he was and because what grew out of that relationship was a new emerging black man, re-shaped and re-molded by his influence... that man was me. For that reason, I could probably tell enough stories to fill another whole book.

Wilkie Clark was such a multi-dimensional person until he is almost indescribable. He was like a multifaceted diamond, that was constantly being polished on every facet... extremely passionate on every facet of life. He was the kind of man who would literally take the shirt off his back and give it to you if he thought you needed it. Wilkie Clark is the one who got me into the civil rights movement. He was unique. He had an unusual way of expressing himself as no one else could. He could not be intimidated by any man. It did not matter who you were. You could be the emperor, the governor, the president; he'd cuss you out, if he needed to. He'd ask you to forgive him and then go on about his business.

The one thing I recall most clearly about him is how much fun we had working together at the funeral home. He was a funny fellow. He was witty and humorous. But, in the same vein, he was serious. He could make you laugh until tears rolled. He could and would cuss you out, and then apologize and then have you laugh about getting cussed out. You couldn't get mad at him.

He was passionate about his work. He loved the funeral business like nothing else, and made that love contagious. At times it seemed he wanted everybody else to love it just as much as he

196

did. He would get a bit annoyed if you didn't love it as much as he did. And I think that for him, being in his own business meant more to him than anything else. But, it allowed him the freedom and the time to deal with the major issues of racism and oppression in his community. I observed him as he wrestled with these issues. He was always studying, reading, talking to others — submerged in trying to understand the hows, whys, and wherefores of racism.... and fighting it with everything he had in him. Being in his company and presence as much as I was, it wasn't long before I realized that I could not continue to associate myself with him and merely sit back and be an innocent bystander, or an observer. I, too became just as convicted in my heart about these same issues, as he daily spoon-fed me with understanding of the spiritual, economic, and political impact of racial oppression.

Although he was passionate about and consumed with civil and human rights, he could swap lies with the best of them.... And he'd have everybody just rolling in laughter. But, when it was time to get serious, you'd better believe no one was more serious than he about what we were doing. When I consider the caliber and nature of man that he was, he was so elevated and lifted up by his anointing yet so humble and human. Wilkie Clark was a man who worked on himself to the extent that his life became a never ending quest to smooth out all the rough edges; he had refined what had once been crude. He perfected himself as a speaker, a businessman, and a Christian. He could have fraternized with great statesmen, and college professors, the educated and the elite, but he elected to find himself an humble place among his own people in his own home town and be a friend to mankind.

Without question, my association with him changed my life; though it never changed the person I was, it certainly impacted the way I approached life, and situations, met obstacles. I don't think Wilkie ever compelled me to change the person that I was. But, what he did ask of me, was to refine my understanding of spiritual things; to elongate my view of life; expand my outreach; dig deeper into the meaning of the issues of life; love my people; and if I wanted to be a pastor, learn how to shepherd my people. He believed in the "Social Gospel."

In reminiscing with his daughter, I learned that over the

years, she had laughingly described our relationship as similar to that of "Batman and Robin." For me, we were more like "The Lone Ranger and Tonto." For the whole of 20 years more or less, Wilkie and I were constant companions. Subsequently, we became co-laborers in the vineyard of our neighborhood; co-warriors on this battlefield of racism and oppression and comrades in just trying to live and shape our identity as black men in the oppressive State of Alabama.

I would come by every day and we would devote hours just locked up in the little place we recall as Clark Funeral Home. Amazingly, we could stay closed up in that little Funeral Home for hours, just the two of us. Frequently, the house would fill up with men, just dropping by as the day progressed. Sometimes with bibles in hand, we would debate the scriptures. We would talk about everything from the Bible to Politics. He was generous enough to share with me a lot of his beliefs...about God, the family, the church, everything. He was a dedicated African American. And although his early roots were in the AME church, he had developed a deep love for the United Methodist Church, but had problems with the church not taking a stand with regards to racial matters. He had a problem with preachers not taking leadership role in matters of race. I recall one time Wilkie shared with me, a religious article that appeared in U.S. News & World Report. This article had a very profound effect on my view of the ministry. I recall him telling me about one time when he had tried to show the same article to another preacher and get him to read it; He recalled, "That Negro said he didn't have time to read." He said, "I told him he had time to be a fool!"

His next priority was the NAACP. This was an organization he had an almost worshipful reverence and respect for. He believed strongly that the NAACP was the 20th century "Moses" that would elevate blacks and lift them out of the oppressive conditions under which they had to live. He supported it with his whole heart, soul, spirit, and with his money. As long as he lived, he took personal responsibility for maintaining an active NAACP branch in Randolph County. Many people were afraid to join the NAACP. But, he continued to forge ahead, speaking out boldly against injustices — sometimes, all alone. Until I personally encountered him, I had never before seen any such manner of black man as him.

In much the same way Jesus did, Wilkie used stories, and humor, to get his point across. Wilkie was a wonderful story-teller. And as he pulled you into his story, you would hang on his every word. He was very dramatic and entertaining as he narrated. He always kept a bottle of liniment in his desk drawer. He had this unusual belief about liniment being the cure for headache.

He would often say, "Why would you put something in your stomach, when it's your head that's hurting?" He would dramatize this by taking liniment and applying it to his head when he had the headache. He reasoned that, "It ain't your stomach that's hurting… it's your head." When you take an aspirin, it's got to get in the stomach, before it can go to the head." When you delve more deeply into this, I suppose this accounted for his philosophy of "direct action" when confronted with issues of racism. I suppose his humor was a stroke of genius; because at that time, black people were scared to death. Many of them didn't understand how to talk about or face the issues that were preventing forward movement and progression in our community. They couldn't stand to have their shortcomings pointed out. They would get mad if they felt you were insulting their conditions, or their pastors, or their understanding of their oppressive state of existence. He could effectively use humor to lighten things, and yet make a strong point that helped black people see things in a different light. He could make you laugh, then he'd say something that could motivate you to go out and change the whole world, or at least to think that you could.

He would often tell a funny story about the preacher who was up preaching from Genesis 2:7 about when God first made man. The preacher started reading…. "And the Lord God formed man of the dust of the ground, and breathed into his nostrils the breath of life; and the man became a living soul…" Then suddenly a wind blew and turned the page over to Genesis 6:15, and the preacher, unaware that the wind had turned his page, continued to preach…, "He made him 300 cubits long, fifty cubits wide, and 30 cubits high….." Wilkie concluded "folks said, "What in the hell kind of man was that?"

During his young manhood, Wilkie went to live in Anniston, Alabama for a short while. It might have been during his post-war years, when he was trying to finish high school on the GI Bill.

Wilkie told plenty of lies about a neighborhood lunatic by the name of "TyCob," in Anniston, Alabama. We never really knew if "TyCob" was a real person or somebody he made up. But, his "TyCob" stories were hilarious.

He would often talk about the years when Mr. J. P. Phillips was the Mayor of Roanoke, and how he'd go to the City Council meting and talk so hard, yet not be heard. He often recalled how he'd beat on the desk; and whenever he finished, Mayor Phillips would say, "Thank you for coming, Wilkie." On one of those City Council adventures, Wilkie said Mayor J. P. Phillips asked him, "Wilkie, what do yaw'll want?" Wilkie said he replied, "I want everything yaw'll white folks got, including syphilis.....If you got syphilis, I want that too."

One time, in a conversation with the Chevrolet dealer, Wilkie said, the car dealer said, "you just can't get none of these colored folks to do nothing. You can't get nobody to help you in the yard, or put up fence posts; these coloreds just don't want to work nowadays..." Wilkie said he asked him, "Have you tried to get one to manage your car dealership?"

Wilkie Clark always acknowledged that on a basic level everybody is a racist. White folks would look at him in disbelief when he would make that statement in public! We understood that he'd make those kinds of statements to try to shock them into facing their own prejudices. In support of this declaration, he would say, "You are racist, too." Look at who you married. Look where you go to church. I married a black woman; I attend a black church; I live in a black neighborhood." Can't you see, we are all racists? But, we knew that he was not a racist in the sense that he was hate-ridden. But, he understood that only by getting them to admit and face their racism could we begin to thrash out and eventually overcome its effects on all of us.

In the early years, the funeral home operated an Ambulance service. Early one Monday morning, I never shall forget, Wilkie called me in the middle of the night to go with him.

Mama said, "Where are you going?"

"I got to go pick up a body."

We had to go pick up an old white man. He lived on Springfield Road; he was having a heart attack and for reasons unknown, Quattlebaum could not, or would not pick him up. So, they called us. We picked him up, and I got in the back with the man, and Wilkie went speeding on down the road toward LaGrange, Georgia. As we crossed the Chattahoochie River Bridge going into LaGrange, Wilkie said "Old Klu-Kluk, ought to stop and throw 'em in the river." We knew he would never have done it... and if he had really hated the white man, he would never have gone and picked him up in the first place. But it was just another funny script, I suppose just to lighten the moment.

Then, he'd get serious and start to talk about when he was overseas in Japan, during World War II, fighting for his country; he would talk about how scared he was, as he walked through the jungles of Japan, an M-16 rifle in one hand, and everything he owned in the world in the other, and how he could visualize "home" so well, longing to be back in the United States. Then in sharp contrast, finally returning home how, he had to return and face the grim conditions of racism, bigotry and discrimination.

Aside from the tremendous influence he had on me, I know that he impressed many other youngsters in our town. There was one kid, in particular on whom he made such a tremendous impression until the young man did something that almost cost him his Funeral Director's licenses. There was a young man growing up in Roanoke, by the name of Allen Lee Hines. Allen idolized Wilkie. When I was a young man in my 20's, helping out around the funeral home, "Twinkie" as he was known all over town, was just a very young chap, probably no more than 12 or 13 years old. But, he adored Wilkie Clark so much until he could often be seen just standing off a distance, and watching his every movement. Somehow, Twinkie made himself acquainted with Wilkie, and started to hang around at the funeral home. It was obvious that Twinkie wanted to be part of the funeral home crew, but he was so young. Occasionally, Wilkie would let him come around and help wash the cars. And Twinkie got where he'd just sit around and listen to Wilkie talk with the other men. He would watch him like a hawk. He'd try to talk like him; walk like him; drive like him. He literally tried to do everything that Wilkie did. Well, this one time, when Wilkie and I had to go to Camden, South Carolina to pick up a remains, the Alabama state inspector, Warren Higgins had paid us a visit. When we returned, there was a report on Wilkie's desk that read: "I've been up to inspect your business, and found you to be out of compliance with the Alabama Funeral Service codes. A minor was left in charge." Undoubtedly, Twinkie had let Mr. Higgins in to the funeral home, and taken him on a tour, giving the impression that he had been left in charge of the place. I'm sure you don't have to be a rocket scientist to figure out that upon Wilkie's return from Camden, South Carolina, Twinkie Hines got one of the worst of Wilkie Clark's cussin outs. He never told Twinkie not to come back. But he cussed him out BUT good and let him know that "you almost got my business closed, don't do that anymore." Well, I don't have to tell you that Twinkie and Wilkie became life-long buddies. Twinkie Hines grew up hanging around Wilkie, and to this day, continues to mark his way of talking and his mannerisms. Does that not speak volumes about how much power the "men about town" have in shaping the future direction of the African American community? For many of us, Wilkie Clark was the one we chose to be like. There was something about him that introduced a new level of hope into our spirits throughout the community. He was a lighthouse, a strong tower in our community....trying to lead the way.

Together, we traveled far and near. I can't count the days and nights we traveled together, and the conversations we had. He believed that because "God Is" that no matter how much earthly power other men might have in various situations and circumstances, God would always have the last say-so in history. He was adamant, that man could never override our outcome in history. So, he made every day a new adventure. We literally "nurse-maided" the people in our community. And every day there would be new cases cropping up. Amazingly, we were the unofficial "therapists" for the black neighborhood. Mothers who couldn't handle their children, came to him; disenfranchised voters came to him; those intimidated by the oppressive system of racism, came to him; those seeking redress of grievances came to him; those who were just plain naïve and disoriented, came to him; and he ministered in his unique way. And gradually, day by day, healing evolved.

He was somewhat like the Queen, Esther — ordained for such a time. There had to be a "Wilkie Clark" who could literally be controversial, yet at the same time be humble enough to sit down at the table of negotiation, yet stand firmly on his convictions.

He could look city officials in the eye, and tell them: "Every last one of you is gonna die and go to hell on account of the way you have treated black people!"

I cannot begin to count the confrontations during the 1980's. There were numerous confrontations with our former, and current Mayor, Henry V "Speck" Bonner. I think that these were perhaps some of the worst of times, because we all were pushing hard for change, and change was coming, but not without resistence. Often in fits of anger Wilkie would say: "If I get to heaven and "Speck " Bonner is there, I'm going to turn around and go back." Everybody would fall out with laughter! ..... He wouldn't crack a smile.

There is probably not a soul who doesn't recall the great "Radio Debate" that Wilkie and Mayor "Speck" Bonner had regarding redistricting in Roanoke. There had been for quite some time, a fierce debate over redistricting in Roanoke, Alabama. There had also been a federal court case; so, pursuant to winning this battle, the black leaders in the city had formed a strong alliance, and were fighting with all the force they could muster, because a victory would cinch the future election of blacks to public office. The City Of Roanoke had been enjoined from conducting a city election until the redistricting plan was implemented, however, Mayor Henry V. "Speck" Bonner, in disregard of the federal court order, was insisting that the city elections would go forward. These two gentlemen debated until it became downright humorous.

Wilkie declared, "You won't have an election until you do it."

Speck retorted "Oh yes we will!"

Wilkie would come right back, "I bet you won't."

This literally went on for the duration of the program. It was great entertainment for the African American community, and left them bubbling with community pride. I do believe that before it was all over, Mayor Bonner and he eventually developed a mutual regard for each other that was timeless.

If Wilkie Clark thought he was on the side of right and righteousness about an issue he would fight you to the death. Not only would he fight; For him it would become a mission in struggle. I recall a time when during the Primary Election there arose some problems with Republicans crossing over into the Democratic Party, and then, crossing back over after election. In response to this, the

Supreme Court had made a ruling that you had to identify your party preference in order to vote in the Democratic Party. Wilkie didn't agree with that, and went to great lengths to dramatize his opposition.

On the day he went down to cast his vote, he was asked, "What is your party preference?"

In his typical flamboyant way, he replied "That's none of your business, I don't have to tell you that!"

After repeated back and forth altercation with the election officials, he told them, "I have a constitutional right to cast my vote on the basis of my conviction without having to disclose any information to you about my vote. It's none of your business!"

Finally, not succeeding in getting admitted to the ballot box, he said, "I'll tell you what, I'll be back."

He came back to the Funeral Home and called all the way to Montgomery to the Alabama State Attorney General's office, to inquire about having to disclose this information before he could cast his ballot. They informed him of the law that had been passed. Once, proven incorrect, he'd humbly concede defeat, and move on to the next challenge. So, in that instance, he had to succumb, and returning to the polling place, he reluctantly disclosed his party preference.

One of the last things that Wilkie Clark did to catalyze change in our community, was to help facilitate litigation against the Randolph County Commission to convert to single member voting districts. As a result of the ultimate success of this effort, I now sit as a Randolph County Commissioner, serving my 4th term.

It was the pinnacle of his pride to be able to say "I run a funeral home in Roanoke, Alabama." His favorite expression was, "I'm the Chief Cook & Bottle-Washer....if you want to know who has the last say here, I do." At an innate level understand what that means to a black man. That he really is the man. So, to satisfy his need to be the man, Wilkie Clark literally created the environment wherein he could fulfill his role as leader. Think about it: where else could a black man be in charge? In his own business; in his family; in his own home; with his wife and child and in his community. He understood his role, he knew it and he lived it.

He was a successful business man, who had such business

savvy, because of his understanding of simple basic economics. He said, "every dollar you earn is not yours to keep." In this country, we have lost our sense of economic direction. We could probably run this country, and balance our budget, if we simply applied his basic economic philosophy.

For me, Wilkie Clark was a 20th Century "Maverick — a pioneer who dared to go where precious few other black men had gone before in our local community. He dared to challenge the system if he felt like the system was unjust. He was not afraid of anything. And he always proclaimed that regardless of what powers were brought to bear on our race, God and *He ONLY,* would have the final say in our outcome. Wilkie was passionate; and his passion came from his conviction. He had a stern...firm faith in God. I won't say he was religious, but he had a stern firm faith in God. His conviction stemmed from his passion about people and from his religious conviction. He loved people.

I called him "Boss Man." That was my favorite way to address him. He'd also call me "Boss." I suppose that was our way of acknowledging each other as men. Observing him in the process of living life, you saw courage at work; rooted an unfaltering faith; anchored in love for his fellow man; buttressed by his conviction that God is not a liar, and will make good on his word. I loved Wilkie...in much the same way that a son loves a father. I miss him so much. Our community misses him. Rest in Peace. Brave warrior, you have earned your reward.

Bishop Lathonia J. Wright is the founding pastor of the New Life Worship Center, located on Handley Avenue in Roanoke, Alabama. He has pastored extensively throughout the Missionary Baptist Churches in Randolph County, Chambers and Coosa County, Alabama. He currently serves as an elected official in Randolph County, Alabama as a member of the Randolph County Commission. He is Licensed as a Funeral Director in the State of Alabama, and continues to work in Funeral Service. He devoted more than 20 years of his life as a co-laborer with Wilkie Clark and others, to open up more opportunities for African American progress in Randolph County, Alabama.

SELF-DETERMINATION

"Stand on your own two Black feet

and fight like hell for your place in the world."

—*Amy Jacques Garvey*

Jerome A. Gray Reflects On An Evening Spent In the Company Of Wilkie Clark

Photo: Courtesy Of Jerome A. Gray

More than twenty years ago in the late 1970s, I had the opportunity to meet a most remarkable man—the affable and unflappable Wilkie Clark of Randolph County. At the time, I was wearing two hats, serving as state field director of the Alabama Democratic Conference and state secretary of the NAACP State Conference. Although I can't recall the first time that I met Wilkie Clark, I'm sure it was at a meeting of the Democratic Conference or the NAACP. From the outset, I was impressed by Wilkie Clark. I liked his manner of speech, his animated style, and his expressive face. When he talked to you, he often got real close, as if he planned to whisper some secret or share some great confidence with you.

The great confidences that he often shared during these close encounters usually involved some graphic account of how "low-down" some white people were, especially those who sought to thwart black folks' progress. It was always a special treat to be in Wilkie Clark's company, because he was a masterful linguist when it came to using black speech and robust profanity to indict white folks for their many racist misdeeds and injustices.

One night, in the 1980s at an NAACP State Convention in Huntsville, Wilkie Clark and I stayed up almost all night, expounding and recapitulating on what it's like being a black man in America. For the most part, I was the great listener and learner; Mr. Clark was the great talker and teacher. He was in rare form that evening. After a few drinks, he became an east Alabama griot, sharing with me the rich and troublesome history of his struggle to be a strong, stand-up black man in Randolph County. His liquor

207

was talking good. It told old truths, boldly, about one man's courage and determination to be a giant and not a gnat, in his community. I learned so much from Mr. Clark that night. And I gained so much respect for him as well. The evening went so well and so long, until we ended up at Waffle House, where we continued our dialogue, almost till dawn. He was in his element. And I was in hog heaven. Mr. Clark was chain smoking, and sweating and drinking coffee, non-stop. As he spoke of his life, his family, and the burdens he'd had to bear, his expressive face would sometimes go from a broad smile to a deep dimpled scowl. Indeed, he let me know that at this point in his life, he "ain't taking no shit from anyone." From the tone of his conversation, I was totally convinced that Wilkie Clark was a man on a mission.

What I particularly liked about Wilkie Clark was his commitment to justice. From his conversation it didn't take me long to learn that he admired black men who had the guts to stand up to white men, and to fight for justice and equality. Therefore, that explains why he was so fond of my boss, Dr. Joe L. Reed, the chairman of the Alabama Democratic Conference. On one occasion Wilkie Clark told me: "Jerome, I just love Joe Reed, because these white folks are as scared of him as a rattlesnake."

On another occasion, he was proud of me, too, when ADC sued the Randolph County Commission, the Randolph County School Board, and the City of Roanoke, challenging their at-large election systems in the mid-1980s. I took the initiative to draw the redistricting plan for the Commission, that created a majority black commission district for the first time.

Alas, on the night that I and my ADC office assistant, Darryl Sinkfield, traveled to Randolph County to present our proposed redistricting plan to the Commission, Wilkie Clark met us outside the county courthouse in Wedowee. He was beaming with pride. His body language and his words communicated excitement for what we were about to accomplish. He told me: "Jerome, ADC's got these white folks scared to death. And don't you lighten up on them when you go in there." I didn't.

The meeting room was packed with whites and blacks. Periodically, during my presentation, I would look in Wilkie Clark's direction. His face was aglow, as if to say "Now is my time to get justice after all these years."

We had a successful evening. The Randolph County Commission agreed later to adopt our proposed plan, with some modifications. In 1988, Reverend Lathonia Wright became the first black to be elected to the Randolph County Commission. However, perhaps the best outcome of all, was to see Wilkie Clark's daughter, Charlotte Clark-Frieson, succeed in becoming the first black elected to the Randolph County Board of Education, as a result of the redistricting lawsuit, coupled with the pioneering courage and audacity of her dad for so many years. As William Shakespeare might say about all this: "All's Well that Ends Well."

Jerome A. Gray hails from Evergreen, Alabama. He is the full-time State Field Director of the Montgomery based Alabama Democratic Conference, which is the state's oldest, and largest, and most influential Black Political Caucus in the State of Alabama.

FULFILLMENT

"I don't think there's anything in the world I can't do. ...
In my creative source, whatever that is, I don't see why I can't
sculpt. Why shouldn't I? Human beings sculpt.
I'm a human being."

—*Maya Angelou*

Chronology of A Black History Maker
He Stood Up, He Spoke Out, and Made A Difference!!

By no means does the chronology provided below represent the full spectrum of humanitarian work that Wilkie Clark did in Randolph County. But, perhaps it will provide you with some precept of the manner of man he was, and the concern he evidenced for the betterment of his community. It is my vision to prepare and publish a comprehensive summary of his life's work that does justice to his memoir.

March 8, 1920
Wilkie Clark was born in Carrollton, Carroll County, Georgia to the parentage of Charlie Clark and Lue Ella (Baker) Clark

1920's and 1930's
Attended a one-room school called "Pine Hill" at Wehadkee

Early 1940's
Came to Roanoke, Alabama, probably seeking work. Worked as a Chauffeur for Dr. G. W. Bonner

May 8, 1942
Drafted into the United States Army, served during World War II in the Asiatic-Pacific Theatre. (Documentation: U.S. Army Enlisted Record)

July 4, 1945
Honorably Discharged from the United States Army
(U. S. Army Separation/Qualification Record)

Late 1940's

Lived in Anniston, Alabama, there he completed his high school education under the GI Bill at Cobb Avenue High School (Documentation: High School Diploma From Cobb Avenue High School)

Worked at Bynum

May 1, 1948

Married the former Hattie Lee Peters who was a young school teacher, working in Randolph County

Worked for the Atlantic Coastline Railroad

Early 1950's

Became acquainted with the NAACP

August 20, 1951

He became a registered voter (Voting Record Issued by Randolph County, Alabama Board of Registrars.)
(Documentation: Delayed Certificate Of Birth)

September 11, 1953

Became the proud father of Charlotte A. Clark-Frieson, who was his only child. (Documentation: Birth Certificate Of Charlotte A. Clark-Frieson)

May 17, 1954

Brown vs Board Of Education decision was won by the NAACP in the United States Court Of Appeals. This was a great victory for civil rights movement. Civil Rights leaders began to push toward enforcement of Court Decisions.

1960's

Began to Petition the City Of Roanoke, for the pavement of his own street; later assisted others in doing the same.

August, 1966

As a means of gradually achieving de-segregation of the public schools, the local system began to implement a plan that came to be called "freedom of choice," wherein parents could "choose" to send their children to predominantly white schools, or allow them to remain in the black schools. It was this year that daddy decided that I should be one of the seven black children "carefully selected" to go to Handley High School. He insisted that I go. The only way I escaped going in 1965 (the first year of "freedom of choice") was because I had been ill that summer, and mama wanted to keep me at the black school so she could look after me. He insisted on taking me to the school to meet my 8th grade homeroom teacher, Ms. Jimmy Jenkins. And he insisted on taking me to class the first day of school.

1968-1970

Wilkie Clark worked toward the establishment of Clark Funeral Home (Personal Papers)

Late 1960's

Wilkie Clark began to petition the City of Roanoke and the Randolph County Sheriff's office to hire black police officers.

He also appealed to Alabama State Representative Richard Laird and others for the appointment of blacks to work on the polls on election day. (Letter From State Representative Richard Laird)

February 18, 1970

Clark Funeral Home Officially Opens in Roanoke, Alabama

Summer, 1970

A Federal Court Decision closes the Randolph County Training School, and all black children are dispersed throughout the county to predominantly white schools

1970's and 1980's After School Desegregation

There were numerous grievances brought to his attention, regarding the mistreatment of black students by then Principal

213

Hulond Humphries. During these years, every complaint and case was carefully documented and investigated.

School Term 1972- 1973
A student named Tommy O'Neal was repeatedly sent home by the Randolph County High School principal, because his parents refused to allow him to shave the "peach fuzz" on his face, that school administrators interpreted as wearing a "beard." This incident gave rise to a chain of subsequent incidents that became racially charged, and resulted in nearly 20 years of controversy between the Randolph County High School Principal Hulond Humphries, and the African-American communities throughout Randolph County. In perhaps 99% of all the cases, Wilkie Clark was sought by parents of students attending RCHS to assist them in addressing their grievances either with Principal Humphries, or the Randolph County Board of Education. This proved to be one of the most difficult and engaging of confrontations in the history of race relations in Randolph County.

March, 1976
Wilkie Clark announced his candidacy for a seat on the Randolph County Board Of Education. He became the first African-American to qualify for and seek an elected office in Randolph County (Documentation: Randolph Leader Archives)

April 22, 1976
The African-American community sponsored a well-attended campaign banquet at the Men's Haven Sportsman's Club in Roanoke, for Wilkie Clark, wherein Ross Dunn was featured keynote speaker. Mr. Dunn was an outstanding black activist from the nearby "Valley" (Chambers County) area who was also serving as NAACP president during that time.

Monday, February 28, 1978
Organized and lead a protest movement wherein a large group of local citizens congregated at the Roanoke City Hall, in protest of the re-assignment of Roanoke's first black city councilman, George Poole. (Documentation: Randolph Leader Archives)

October, 1979
Supported the organization and participated in the first major march to take place in Randolph County, aimed at protesting police brutality in Roanoke. The March was held on Saturday, October 12, 1979.

February, 1980
Intervened in the expulsion of Mary F. Joiner from Opelika State Technical School (Documentation: Personal Papers)

March, 1980
Intervened in the expulsion of Vickie Jordan from Randolph County High School (Documentation: Personal Papers, Letters, etc.)

January, 1981
A vigorous protest march was staged in front of the old Roanoke Leader building, in response to an editorial published by Edgar Stevens, former editor of the defunct Randolph Press Newspaper. Stevens had written an editorial which he entitled "Y A W N" characterized by his flamboyant and blatant expression of his distaste for the late Dr. Martin Luther King, Jr. In his editorial comment, Stevens expressed his indignation over the commemorative observances that would be forthcoming to honor the life of the slain martyr. (Documentation: Wilkie Clark is pictured as he prepares to speak to protesters, in the January 28, 1981 Issue of the Roanoke Leader).

June, 1983
Confronted Roanoke City Council about closing of swimming facilities in the High School Gymnasium (Documentation: Copy Of Petition; Randolph Leader Archives)

September, 1983
Helped to lead the movement to institute Deputy Voter Registrars in Randolph County

September, 1983:

With the help of James Davenport, one of his loyal Vice-Presidents, and Lawrence O'Neal, discriminatory practices in the Wedowee Key Club Exposed

October, 1983

Led Protest of a proposed Klan March and Rally downtown Roanoke, Alabama

July 5, 1984

Recipient of NAACP 25 Years or more Service Diploma, in recognition of his distinguished career in Civil Rights. Name recorded in the archives of the NAACP. Given at Kansas City, Missouri.

August 6, 1985

On Behalf of the Wilkie Clark Community Center, $5,000.00 was paid to Ernest Heard, Jr., Secretary and Lonzell Moody, Senior Warden, Roanoke Beauty Lodge #139. The funds used to purchase this property consisted of money raised by the black community, to purchase this property for the future Wilkie Clark Community Center. Documentation: (Receipt issued by Ernest Heard, Jr.)

April 4, 1987

Reverend Lathonia J. Wright, President of Randolph-Chambers SCLC awards their first Dedicated Service Award to Wilkie Clark.

July, 1987

Traveled by bus to Washington, D.C. to participate in the first "Lizzie Baker" Memorial Family Reunion hosted by Dr. Thornton and his family. This was one of his most memorable family gatherings.

1988

Wilkie Clark named as one of three Plaintiffs in lawsuit filed by the Alabama Democratic Conference, against Randolph County Commission, to create single member voting district.

March, 1988

At the insistence of local NAACP Vice President, James Davenport, and Treasurer Lawrence O'Neal, an extensive investigation was made into Randolph County School practices. Charges were filed with The Office For Civil Rights, in Atlanta, Georgia.

Through all the years as a Civil Rights Leader

Daddy represented countless individuals before the Social Security Administration, to help them receive their benefits. He became so proficient in presenting their cases, until the Social Security Administration believed he was an Attorney specializing in that area of practice and would offer to pay for his services. Amazingly, once they discovered that he was not actually an attorney, they stopped trying to pay him. Of the countless individuals he represented before the SSA, he never charged one dime for his services in doing so).

Perhaps the greatest battleground was in the area of education, to which daddy devoted a large amount of his time and energies and resources. I respectfully reserve this discussion for a separate account of his activity, in which I will detail his many engagements on behalf of children in Randolph County Schools.

February 23, 1989

Wilkie Clark Suffers the loss of his beloved wife, Hattie Lee (Peters) Clark, his life long partner in the movement for black progress in Randolph County.

June, 1989

The first "Wilkie Clark Community Center" Summer Camp was held at Christian Memorial Baptist Church. This was a community initiative undertaken by several young African-American professional women who wanted to do something positive for children in the community. It was done in the name of Wilkie Clark. (Randolph Leader News Article appeared in June 28, 1989 issue).

July 29, 1989
Wilkie Clark died tragically during burning of his home in Roanoke, Randolph County, Alabama

November 2004
Wilkie Clark's Daughter publishes his biography entitled *"Chief Cook & Bottle-Washer," The Unconquerable Soul Of Wilkie Clark*

February 19, 2005
Clark and Frieson family observes the 36th Anniversary of Clark Memorial Funeral Service, and honor father with the debut of *"Chief Cook & Bottle-Washer," The Unconquerable Soul Of Wilkie Clark*

The Wilkie Clark Memorial Foundation is Officially Launched
Proclamations and Resolutions are Issued By:
The City of Roanoke, Alabama
The City of Five Points, Alabama
The Randolph County Commission

April 30, 2005
Wilkie Clark Memorial Foundation sponsors first Event at Chambers County Sportsman's Club, makes first public appeal for support. Dr. Barbara B. Boyd, State Legislator from Alabama's 32nd District is Keynote Speaker.

Wilkie Clark
March 8, 1920 – July 29, 1989
Photo: Courtesy of Charlotte A. Clark-Frieson

~ *Resolution* ~

Conclusion

In conclusion, I pray that this book has benefitted anyone who took the time to read it. If it made you weep; that's alright. It made me weep. If it stirred up your emotions, that's all right too! If it made you a little angry, so be it. It still makes me angry. If it serves as a testimony to anyone who may be in doubt about your capacity to make your dream come true, then, it did just as I intended for it to do. If it honors my father, then it helps me further my objective to keep the commandment, "honour thy father and thy mother that thy days may be long upon the land which the Lord thy God giveth thee." If it glorifies God, then to God be the glory!

I believe that the one individual who has truly benefitted the most from this writing — IS ME. First of all, it has made me whole and complete. It has allowed me to remember some of the most precious moments of my life. It has allowed me to bring closure to 15 years of grief over the tragic death of my father, whose sudden death, which was accidental and tragic, did not afford me the opportunity to say a proper goodbye. It has allowed me to fulfill my promise to my mother. It has opened the door for me to think through my purpose for being alive. As I have worked on this book, I have also been reading and studying The Purpose Driven Life by Dr. Rick Warren. Completing both projects simultaneously has been one of the most revealing spiritual journeys I have ever made.

I vividly recall the chapter in Warren's book that talks about how God pre-destined me; how he knew how many hairs I would have on my head; how he placed me with Wilkie Clark and Hattie Lee Peters Clark, because he was designing me with unique characteristics that I could develop ONLY BY THEIR motherly and fatherly influence. So, writing this piece has opened my eyes to MY own purpose in life, and I believe that God put me here to embrace and act upon my daddy's spirit of compassion for others. I truly believe that God has anointed me to do this; and for that reason,

I must conclude the internal battle that has from time to time consumed my spirit; every time I'd leave the business arena to re-enter the education field — when there would always arise within me this agonizing internal conflict. I am thoroughly fulfilled when I'm free to pursue this ministry. Wilkie Clark's Daughter is indeed a spiritual ministry that must be fulfilled, because every time I stray away from it, my spirit is vexed.

For the last 4 years, it has been my extreme honor and privilege to have taught in the private sector for an agency that I grew to love, respect and admire; and to work for and with one of the most purpose driven women I know, Etta Evonne Anderson Billingslea, my dear friend and colleague of many years and the Godmother of my children. There, at Ault Academy, we have also provided a very special and unique ministry to a population of troubled boys who are at-risk due to abuse and neglect — this too has been a divine calling. But, with the release of this book, and the launching of the Wilkie Clark's Daughter organization I know at some time I will be compelled to leave the agency; and regretfully, I anticipate my departure with ambivalence; and I do this with the utmost respect for the work done by educators in both the public and private sector. I also applaud and salute Mrs. Etta A. Billingslea for being one of the most inspirational educators for whom I've had the pleasure of teaching. While in her employ, teaching had to be more than just our job. Of necessity it had to be our calling. She often says, "we have to care."

But, spending 35 years of my life in the company of a dynamic duo like Wilkie and Hattie Lee Peters Clark taught me so many spiritual lessons that I will carry within me for the remainder of my life. I thank God for placing me in their competent care and I will forever be their daughter and love them throughout eternity for being the nurturing parents they were to me, up to my 35th birthday. I want to share with you just a few of the lessons I have learned both from my loving parents and from our 35 years in business. Some of these lessons came directly from daddy; some from mama; some are my own; and some just came from the school of hard knocks. I think they apply to ANY business you may consider operating.

1. To be successful in starting and maintaining a business, your primary goal need not be to make money. The emphasis has to

be upon meeting a need — not an imaginary need; but a substantive need. If your motivation is clear, pure, and humanitarian, the money will come. Sometimes, entrepreneurs allow the profit motive become the focus of their efforts. But, no matter what product or service we are peddling, we must never forget about "serving humanity." I have learned that being in business is not just an economic activity. It is very much a spiritual activity — sometimes, even a ministry.

2. Being in business means making tremendous PERSONAL sacrifices; time, money, and things—sometimes the simplest of things; it also means believing in YOURSELF, YOUR product AND the personal flavor that you add to YOUR service — whatever that may be. It often means being in competition with yourself. Sometimes, you'll work harder, longer hours, and for less pay than at any other job where you work for someone else; but the fruits of that are twice as rewarding. Once you commit to being in business for yourself; commit to becoming a MASTER of your product or service. Don't let anybody beat you doing it or delivering it! And always strive to outdo yourself. If you feel you've reached the top — your next goal should be to top that! My daddy used to always say: "I never saw anybody who did good work, who couldn't get work to do." If you do good, quality work, you will be in demand. But, if you just want to hurriedly complete a job, just to say I'm finished, I did it (regardless to how you did it), now give me my money! You're in trouble before you even get started.

3. You may not be able to get anyone else to believe in your dream; but as long as YOU BELIEVE in it, go after it!

4. As you cultivate your business, your product, your method of delivery, etc, you must also cultivate your customer, client, or buyer. In order for YOU to grow, you have to assume responsibility for the growth of your customer base. You have to constantly feed them with the knowledge they need that will enable them buy your product or service.

5. Over the years, we made many mistakes, errors and omissions; but "if you do what you've always done, you'll get what you've always gotten." Being in business means being flexible. You must be ready for change; and constantly review and renew; change; modify, revise; revert. Profit from your mistakes — fix things and move on. We were not successful because we did all things right. We are successful because we made mistakes — but

223

we learned from them; changed our approach and refuse to look back.

6. When you are in business, you cannot be corrupted by negative thinking, negative talking people, negative attitudes. Most people by their very nature are negative and cynical. This will get you in a rut. Get away from negative thinking folks— FAST! Hype yourself up every day — don't allow yourself to get in a rut. Ignore gossip; turn a deaf ear to it; Hear it and don't hear it; and keep moving forward. Remember, if people are talking about you, they're thinking about you. That's a good thing.

7. Be excited, enthusiastic and passionate about your business. You can't sell anybody else on your product if you yourself are not sold. If you don't have a product you believe in, you don't have a business.

8. You have to be ready to take risks — nothing ventured — nothing gained! And just accept the fact that you are going to lose some — Money I mean....THERE IS ABSOLUTELY NO WAY YOU ARE GOING TO GENERATE ANY AMOUNT OF MONEY AND BE ABLE TO HOLD ON TO ALL OF IT! YOU ARE GOING TO LOSE A LOT OF MONEY, before you truly learn how to make it.

9. Continue to dream and REACH for your dreams! Don't ever let the devil or anybody else steal your dreams. Taking the words of Chloe Brown, an educator and publisher, "Reach for the moon, and fall among the stars."

10. Time spent worrying about your competition is time wasted. Competing businesses don't set the standard for your profession. You set the standard for yourself–and make the standard high. Then, promote yourself.

11. Regardless to what kind of day you're having, always be kind! It don't cost anything. And the rewards are great!

12. My last recommendation is this: If you really have a desire to do something — a dream, perhaps of starting a business of your own, whatever your passion is.... first, look within yourself to be sure that you are wiling to give all that you may be required to give, to make it work. Then, look to the Almighty. If you don't know Him, I'd like to recommend that you get to know Him, and invite him into your life, and into your affairs; ask him for wisdom,

guidance and direction in moving toward your goals; take Him with you to every encounter along the way: every planning session; staff meeting; every consultation; every board meeting; every loan conference; every buying trip; when you sit down to write the checks to pay your bills and pay your help consult with Him. He WILL see you through. Now, all that having been said, I encourage you to revisit www.wcmf.citymax.com and join an organization committed to help set the stage for your success!

Let us help you set those dreams in concrete; let's make something happen; today; this week; this month; this year!

In the back of this book, is a list of individuals who have been intimately involved in the formation of the Wilkie Clark Memorial Foundation. But, I beg you, don't wait to be asked to help. You have gifts, talents, ideas, and value. Step on board! Volunteer! And step by step, let's make this journey.

I could list a million reasons why you should join; but I am not going to do that. Enough has been said. If Wilkie Clark could do it; You can do it. If Wilkie Clark's Daughter can do it; you can do it. With God's help we are all MORE THAN CONQUERERS.

SELF-RESPECT

" One cannot give to a person that which he already possesses."

—Toussaint L'Ouverture,
Proclamation, March 1, 1802

Epilogue

As I look back over my life, I would like to give God thanks and praise for placing me in the supportive, nurturing cradle of Wilkie and Hattie Lee Peters Clark. I couldn't have asked for better parents. Even as they sleep, I honor them for forming a dynamic progressive-thinking African-American partnership that helped shape the thinking and views of hundreds of people in our community; thus they had a big hand in shaping the events and history in the community where I now reside.

Unlike many cowardly people, they refused to flee to other parts of the country to seek refuge from the orders of the day; they refused to leave the home they worked so hard to build; rather they consciously chose to stay and fight so that my way would not be as difficult as the path they were forced to trod.

I thank God for a daddy who took me by the hand and walked up Riley Street to Sunday School every Sunday morning; and who went back every Sunday Afternoon at 5:00 o'clock to meet with the MYF; who took time to listen to me and be my friend; who took me and all my girlfriends joy-riding on many Saturday and Sunday afternoons; who spent every spare minute he had with me; who showed me how to own and run my own business; who lovingly relinquished possession of his only daughter, and gave my hand in marriage to the love of my life, the late Clarence Frieson, Jr.; who taught me how to be strong and tough; and to stand up and fight for what I believe in; and to press my way through difficult situations; how to "cover the ground I stand on."

Even though I wasted some of my years, playing around in school, I honor both of them for not giving up on me; even when I was playing hookie in Jr. College, goofing off (playing spades) and "doubling the cost" of my education; dropping in and dropping out all along the way. They never refused to help me if I showed the slightest indication that I ready to "get back up," dust myself off and try again. They were always ready to say, "If you want to go back to school, we'll help you." I want to thank God for every $10.00 bill my daddy gave me to drive to Auburn University from Roanoke every single day for a whole year — after I got serious and decided to quit playing around with my schooling and get my degree. Not once, did either of them ever turn their back on me. Because of them, I have cultivated an understanding of the concept of forgiving, unconditional love.

In conclusion, I would like to share with you some of the beloved scriptures that guided my daddy's life and governed his business dealings and all of his decisions. As I was growing up in his house, references were made daily to these scriptures.... they may not have always been quoted verbatim, but he alluded to them in making his point about whatever situation our family was facing. Subsequently, after his death, I began to delve deeper into the scriptures in an effort to discover why he relied so heavily upon them. Today, they continue to guide my life and undergird my decisions and directions; and I believe they govern all outcomes in my business and life affairs.

It has been almost 16 years since my father passed away. And with the passage of time, I have cultivated, I believe, that same kind of faith that helped my daddy to succeed as a business person. The road has not been easy. We have encountered many difficulties and hard times; but at every turn, the personal attributes of my daddy that I embraced met divine power, and because we KNOW there is a God, we have survived.

There have been numerous occasions and events related to running our business, when statistically, mathematically or numerically, or for any other RATIONAL reason, we should not have come through certain situations. But, by the Grace of God, we overcame! I can point to countless examples in which my Daddy's generosity has been a blessing to me and my children. In the years since Daddy died, there have been occasions when people would just blunder into my office unannounced and say: "Ain't you Mr. Wilkie Clark's Daughter? Your daddy buried my mama; and we never did pay him. But, we never forgot how good Mr. Clark was to us when our mama died. We came to pay off mama's funeral bill." Sometimes, I didn't even know or remember them; sometimes I did. But, I could go back into the records, and low and behold, there would be an unpaid open account still there showing the unpaid balance. Often times, they would come in knowing exactly how much they owed. If that isn't a good and perfect gift from God, you tell me what is!

If I had not been born to the parentage of Wilkie and Hattie Lee Peters Clark, would I have ventured into business on my own? Probably not. But, at the end of the day, I wouldn't take nothing for my journey.

Hebrew 11:1
"Now, faith is the substance of things hoped for the evidence of things not seen."

Exodus 20:12
"Honour thy father and thy mother: that thy days may be long upon the land which the Lord thy God giveth thee..."

Psalm 24:1
"The earth is the Lord's and the fullness thereof: the world, and they that dwell therein.

Psalm 37:1-3
Fret not thyself because of evildoers, neither be thou envious against the workers of iniquity. For they shall soon be cut down like the grass, and wither as the green herb. Trust in the Lord, and do good; so shalt thou dwell in the land, and verily thou shall be fed. Delight thyself also in the Lord; and he shall give thee the desires of thine heart. Commit thy way unto the Lord; trust also in him; and he shall bring it to pass.... "

Proverbs 23:7
"For as he thinketh in his heart, so is he...."

Psalm 37:25
"I have been young, and now am old; yet have I not seen the righteous forsaken, nor his seed begging bread."

Isaiah 40:31

"But they that wait upon the Lord shall renew their strength. They shall mount up with wings as eagles; they shall run, and not be weary; and they shall walk and not faint."

Mark 3:27
"No man can enter into a strong man's house, and spoil his goods, except he will first bind the strong man; and then he will spoil his house"

Romans 12:2
"And be not conformed to this world: but be ye transformed by the renewing of your mind, that ye may prove what is that good, and acceptable and perfect will of God."

Ephesians 6:12
"For we wrestle not against flesh and blood, but against principalities, against powers, against the rulers of the darkness of this world, against spiritual wickedness in high places."

Isaiah 40: 4 & 5
"Every valley shall be exalted, and every mountain and hill shall be made low: and the crooked shall be made straight, and the rough places plain: And the glory of the Lord shall be revealed, and all flesh shall see it together: for the mouth of the Lord hath spoken it."

Psalm 124 1-3
"Had it not been the LORD who was on our side," let Israel now say, "Had it not been the LORD who was on our side, when men rose up against us, then they would have swallowed us alive..."

HERITAGE

"What all achieving blacks successfully do is turn

the color of black into the color of victory."

—Audrey Edwards and Craig K. Polite, from
Children Of The Dream

The Value Of Organization
(A Final Appeal)

Ask yourself this question: Who else do you know — black, white, or polkadot — good, bad or indifferent — that would personally put himself on the line every day of his life, for the greater good of the people — individually and collectively — in his community? Can you think of any one man (OR WOMAN), in Randolph County, Alabama, any more dedicated to a community than the late Wilkie Clark was to his? — I know you can't. Because, most of us are inherently selfish, self-centered, egotistical scoundrels — by nature. But, compassion is a gift from God — compassion is the fruit of the spirit — the Holy Spirit.

Here's another question: Who else do you know, that would swiftly and unreservedly go to bat for any "underdog?" The only "dog" most of us want to be identified with is a BIG dog. But, who else do you know in Randolph County, Alabama, that would take the personal risks to help anybody who needed that kind of help? Who else do you know in Randolph County — or the world for that matter — that would personally guarantee personal loans for multiple individuals to whom he had no obligation or responsibility whatsoever, other than the mere understanding of the very nature and impact of the social and economic oppression that was brought on by racism and bigotry as it was exercised and practiced at that time — within the financial institutions, the corporate structure, the workplace and the education system?

You, reading this book, may not have been one of the ones on the receiving end, but let me assure you, there were a great many who were. Who do you know, that would risk his own personal credibility to stand up and be a mouthpiece — sometimes at the risk of losing his very life — to lobby the powers-that-be for an oppressed people? I'll answer that question for you. NOBODY! Nobody but a Wilkie Clark, who was both anointed and appointed by God for such times as those were, to do this work, in this vineyard. And all for nothing — not one dime did he get out of it — not one dollar— did he ever charge anybody for anything he did. His only reward, I pray, was a crown of life— a better life than he experienced while here.

Yet, out of all that he (and a few others) tried to do, even at this juncture of our history we as a people, regardless to whether we realize and acknowledge it or not, are still in a damaged state of existence. We HAVE NOT achieved the level of financial empowerment that is so desperately needed in order for our people to really be free, because there is one element still missing....that element is a sense of community that results only when people understand the need to organize their efforts.

As the news of the coming release of this book has spread throughout our community, I have been approached by various individuals who said, "I wish I had known you were writing a book about Wilkie...I remember thus-and-such!!" Well, cheer up my brothers and sisters, because I already see, there is another volume to be written. We owe it to his memory, to uphold the ideals he tried to teach us with his life, his interactions with his fellow-man, his bold deeds, and numerous earthly works. In the wake of my daddy, and other outstanding black men and women of our neighborhood, how can we afford to sit here and languish? If we allow their memory to fade away, we, too will fade away.

With his life, and the lives of the countless other great African-American men and women of our neighborhood, we must draw upon their exemplary lives, to teach on-coming generations of youngsters how to live in their communities— teach them about fellowship, black unity, community and neighborhood pride, compassion, human dignity, and initiative.

The Need To Organize

So, I honor my father with an organization because during his lifetime, he expressed a strong belief in organization as the most efficient and effective way particularly for oppressed people to achieve their goals. For as far back as I can remember, he expressed a belief in the strength of numbers. Thus, I learned the art of organizing.

For many years, he ran our local branch of a National

organization (The NAACP) in our community, through which he made numerous valuable contacts, connections and resources who were in a position to help himself (and others) meet their goals. All along the way, he was blessed to form relationships with those contacts, that somehow benefitted him either immediately or on down the road. In my mind, all of these benefits of organizing ones efforts, still ring true.

Some great entrepreneurial mind coined the phrase: "I'd rather have 1% of 100 people's effort, than 100% of my own effort." I think this one phrase captures the essence and power of organization. I firmly believe that when and if people learn to trust each other and organize their efforts, so much more can be accomplished. That applies to any goal one or more people set out to accomplish.

My mother used to say "association brings on assimilation." And, that's a good thing when the association's aims and objectives are noble. I've also heard the expression, "two heads are better than one." Well, in that same vein, what about ten or fifteen heads, or fifty or one hundred heads — all focused on one idea or objective? Without beating this horse to death, I hope you are getting my point. In light of the higher level of access to opportunities nowadays, we have no excuse for living under oppressive conditions. In light of greater access to education services, there is no excuse for ignorance and illiteracy. Through the art of organization, we have the vehicle for our continued advancement.

Simply put, an organization is defined as a group of people identified by shared interests or purpose, for example, a business; an association; a union; company, corporation or establishment.

My mission is to prove that my daddy was right. By simply organizing our efforts, we African Americans have a limitless potential to awaken and inspire our communities to achieve greater works than those who came before us.

As I drive through my own neighborhood, I see the deterioration, desolation, the depressive state of the neighborhood, and sense a sickening kind of neglect and lack of care or concern. There is a deep lack of inspiration and motivation among our people. And while integration has brought along with it, many opportunities, I now detect a sense of separation from all the cultural influences that made us a unique and great African-

American people. Things like a love for singing, dancing, the arts, entertainment, literature and other cultural influences that brought us out of darkness and into the light of intellectual pursuits and community pride.

Seemingly integration, despite its relative advantages, gradually stole our cultural identity and awareness of who and what we really are. It all leads me to wonder what has happened to the drive that our people once had? There was once a "buzz" that could be felt in every black neighborhood — a buzz of activity, movement, concern for the greater good and welfare of all, strong sense of initiative, and a restlessness that is no longer here. We now passively look to our churches to address many of these issues, failing to understand that the church does not form the economic base in a community. It is the ideal place to go worship, and energize our faith, but not to build an economy.

But, certainly we owe it to the memory of the "new black men" and women of the 20th century to reignite that flame that could once be seen from house to house, and neighborhood to neighborhood; rebuild the institutional cornerstones of black economic growth and prosperity that could once be heard on the weekends at the once thriving cafés and night spots.

There is something missing in our community due to the absence of the strong black men who sojourned here in time past. Missing because our neighborhood is devoid of some key economic elements necessary for every black community to thrive and survive: the pool hall, the game room, the "soul-food" restaurant, the nightclub, the dance hall, cultural entertainment center(s), rec centers, community swimming pool, and other wholesome outdoor places where our children can engage in "free play" and stretch their minds and develop their relationships.

So, I stand ready to meet the challenge of restoring our community to its former glory. I truly believe that organizing is the key. Through organization, we will demonstrate to our communities that we can overcome our economic oppression, we can change our depressive state of existence; we can prosper; black and in the South....because this is the land of the free and the home of the brave.

We will build archives to honor our great men and women;

we will build businesses and support our businesses to bring wealth into our own communities; we will clean up our neighborhoods; we will develop community pride; we will serve as role models for our youth; we will stand tall and strong in the wake of declining morality and reckless disregard for the virtues that have long held meaning for us. We will continue to embrace our historic institutions like the church, the school, the home, the Masonic Orders, the NAACP, and other great Civil Rights Organizations like it. We will accomplish these things by organizing our efforts.

Another Perspective Of Organization

In quite another sense, the word organization actually has to do with structure and arrangement. With organization, there is a sense of coordination, order and relationship. From the perspective of order, the opposite of organization is "chaos," which means a state of complete disorder and confusion.

It is my belief that the foundation for success in any endeavor is organization, whether by associating ourselves with a group, or by systematic arrangement of things or ideas.

So, I have established the Wilkie Clark Memorial Foundation, Inc. (aka Wilkie Clark's Daughter) Inc., as a vehicle through which to address critical elements of our African-American community's development. My prayer is that this organization will serve as a catalyst for transformation. This will be accomplished through pursuit of grants for the purpose of business development, community action and education. We will seek to bridge the digital divide. We will assist our community in taking advantage of new technologies. In the process of upgrading our collective status we will flatly refuse to allow any member of our community to suffer for any reason. It is absolutely essential that you commit and pledge to become a part of this exciting new network, in order to align your thinking so that it coincides with that of a new way of thinking, acting and believing!

I propose that in forming this alliance with Wilkie Clark's Daughter Org, we will together build a "New Black Community," equipped to move our posterity through this millennium. Here, we are going to nurture each other; support each other in our quest to change our lives and raise our standard of living; interact with each

236

other; inform ourselves; and help ourselves grow in the ways we think about and approach our goals for our individual selves and our communities.

Post Script

If reading this biography has blessed you, inspired you or perhaps raised your hopes, given you insight or helped you develop a perspective on the subject of the continuing economic struggles of African-Americans in the South, I respectfully and humbly request that you visit the following web sites, and post a review.

http://www.lulu.com/caclarkfrieson
http://www.wilkieclarksdaughter.net
http://www.lulu.com/caclarkfrieson
http://www.amazon.com
http://www.barnes&noble.com

THINKING SMART

"The issue is no longer where you sit on the bus or whether you can drive it; it's whether you can develop the capital to own the bus company"

—*William H. Gray III*

Last Will And Testament

In much the same way that many of us regard a funeral rite as a "final act" of love and remembrance for a beloved family member who has passed away, the "Last Will and Testament" can be regarded as the last act of love extending from one who comes to the end of life to those he will leave behind.

Wilkie Clark's love for his family and community was of such depth and dimension that I have often found myself wondering what kind of memorial bequests he might have left behind, given the chance to prepare his community ahead of time for his coming death.

If he had had such an opportunity, I believe that it would read something like this:

I Wilkie Clark, being of legal age, sound and disposing mind, hereby make, publish, and declare this to be my Last Will And Testament:

I have the following children now living: Charlotte A. Clark-Frieson, my natural daughter who is a product of my marriage to the late Hattie Lee Peters Clark. But, aside from my own flesh and blood child, I also have a great many other children — my children by heritage. The young hearts and minds of the black community in Randolph County, Alabama, whom I tried to lead by example and encourage with my words and deeds. These are they who were often misunderstood; these are they who could find no rational explanation for the racist conditions under which they had to live. These are they who looked to the men and women of my generation for answers and for understanding.

Sometimes lied on, cheated, talked about and mistreated, 'buked, scorned, talked about as sure as they were born. At the behest of a pseudo-integrated school system that often heaped mistreatment and abuse upon them, they needed a defender; they were up; down; sometimes level to the ground. Though I have no immense wealth to leave them — no silver or gold to leave behind — no oil wells or diamond minds; I have but one bequest — that is my glowing example of courage; the courage to continue to pursue that which is rightfully yours, regardless of how vigorously others try to deny you.

I would not dare wish upon any child, that which was heaped upon my young shoulders — to have lived all my young life without a father; to be forced to forfeit an education to go work in the cotton fields to help my mother put food on the table so my younger siblings could be fed and clothed. To my beloved grandchildren, Wilkie Sherard Frieson and Je'Lynn Mikele Frieson, I leave you something that my father did not bother to leave me — the fruit of my lifetime of labor. All my worldly possessions. In leaving you the fruit of my labor, I leave you a head-start; a fighting chance — a chance that nobody gave me, because they didn't have it to give. And all I ask you to do is to continue to tell my story to those of your generation, that they might come to know and understand the selfless sacrifices and the enormous price paid by the new black men and women of my day, so that your generation could experience a better and brighter day.

To my grandchildren, and all the children of your generation, I leave you with the scriptural admonition to "obey your parents; for it is right." I foresee many instances in which parents will be so pre-occupied with foolishness, until they will neglect to provide parental guidance. If your parents refuse to parent, I encourage you to search near and far, high and low for some one—some individual whose life you can observe and emulate, who will inspire you to spread your wings, like a mighty eagle, and fly toward your destiny of greatness.

It has been said, that if you give a man a fish, you feed him for a day; teach him how to fish, and you feed him for a lifetime. Thus, I bequeath to my impoverished black brothers, a drive to get wisdom, to become enlightened, and to pursue wisdom, knowledge and understanding, that you might be fed for a lifetime.

For those who feel you have nowhere to turn, I leave you the word of God and His precious Holy Spirit; for the fight is not over, and without these weapons, you will experience many comfortless days and nights. Remember the words of our slain martyr, Dr. Martin Luther King, Jr., who has said, "True Peace is not merely the absence of tension, but it is the presence of justice." Likewise, there will be many days and nights, wherein conditions will appear peaceful, yet, justice will stand afar off. Thus, I also leave you an example of the discerning spirit that will enable you to accurately distinguish between that which is truly genuine and that which is imaginary.

In the wake of so many illusions and disillusionments you will need a good measure of conviction to make this journey. I leave you my example of conviction. People of African descent can ill afford to live without conviction. Never forget how I stood — sustained and soothed by that unfaltering faith and trust in God; remember my belief in freedom, justice, equality, patriotism and family values. I admonish you to find something to believe in — find something to stand up for — ever mindful that men and women who refuse to stand for something, will fall for anything.

I leave you the determination to march on until victory is won....to fight on until justice rolls down like water, and righteousness like a mighty stream... to press forward until every mountain is brought down and every valley is lifted up; until the rough places are made smooth; and the crooked places are made straight; until the Glory of the Lord is revealed, and all flesh come to behold it!

As the turbulent waves of time deliberately course my ship toward the fading horizon, I bid you farewell by leaving you the greatest gift that life can bestow upon any human being — and that is the gift of HOPE.

†

I've seen the lightening flash
And I've heard the thunder roll
I've felt sin's dashing breakers
Tryin to conquer my soul
No, Never alone
No, Never alone
He promised never to leave me
Never to leave me alone

(Negro Spiritual)

†

~ *Resources* ~

Appendices

*The following pages consist of images of actual
documents issued by the Randolph County Commission
The City Of Roanoke
and the City of Five Points, Alabama
issued for the purpose of conferring
historical distinction upon
the late Wilkie Clark*

Randolph County Commission
P. O. Box 228
Wedowee, AL 36278
(256) 357-4980 or (800) 357-5133
FAX: (256) 357-2365

District #1
H. Larry Raughton
2324 County Road 498
Woodland, AL 36280
(256) 357-2353

District #2
Edward Creed, Sr.
29624 Hwy. 431
Wedowee, AL 36278
(256) 363-3443

District #3
Kevin Spears
13452 County Road 65
Roanoke, AL 36274
(256) 449-6174

District #4
T. J. "Jme" Waldrep
3585 County Road 26
Wedley, AL 36276
(334) 863-4058

District #5
Lathonia Wright
2658 County Road 65
Wedley, AL 36276
(334) 863-2500

A Proclamation Conferring Historical Distinction Upon

the late

WILKIE CLARK

BE IT RESOLVED by the Randolph County Commission, Randolph County, Alabama, that we hereby posthumously confer upon Wilkie Clark historical distinction, in recognition of his leadership in our community as a champion for civil, economic, and human rights.

BE IT FURTHER RESOLVED, that a copy of this proclamation be provided to the future African American archives center in Randolph County.

Issued this 24th day of January, 2005.

Lathonia J. Wright, Chairman

H. Larry Raughton, District I   Edward Creed, Sr., District II

Kevin Spears, District III   Thomas J. Waldrep, District IV

246

PROCLAMATION

BY THE MAYOR
OF THE CITY OF ROANOKE

WHEREAS, the late Wilkie Clark is remembered locally as a fearless civil rights champion who lived in Randolph County between March 8, 1920 until July 29, 1989; and

WHEREAS, Wilkie Clark was a leader in our community , and a champion for economic and human rights; and

WHEREAS, Wilkie Clark played a dominant role in shaping our community and took personal risk to help others.

NOW THEREFORE BE IT RESOLVED. By the Mayor of the City of Roanoke, to confer historical distinction upon the late Wilkie Clark in observance of Black History Month.

GIVEN UNDER MY HAND
And the Seal of the City of
Roanoke on this 14th day of
February 2005.

Mayor Henry V. Bonner

Office of the Mayor
Five Points, Alabama

Proclamation

THE 36TH ANNIVERSARY
OF
CLARK MEMORIAL FUNERAL SERVICE

WHEREAS, Mr. Willie Clark, a black man living during the 20th Century saw a great need to fight for Civil Rights and economic oppression, in Randolph County, Alabama; and

WHEREAS, the faithfulness and the unselfish work of this christian man has made a tremendous impact upon our Community by being the founder and owner of Clark Memorial Funeral Service; and

WHEREAS, Mr. Clark loved humanity and he always extended his hand to the poor and needy by burying the indigent; and

WHEREAS, Mr. Clark was a courageous man with a positive attitude by fulfilling his American dream to own his own business;

NOW, THEREFORE, I, Mayor Geneva Bledsoe and the Town Council of Five Points, Alabama do hereby commends the observance of the 36th Anniversary of Clark Memorial Funeral Service and I also proclaim Saturday February 19, 2005 as Mr. Willie Clark Day and I urge all Citizens to join in the celebration that has been planned.

In witness whereof I have hereunto set my hand and caused this seal to be affixed.

Geneva Bledsoe, Mayor

ATTEST: *Mary G. Moyer*

DATE: *February 19, 2005*

Bibliography

1. Copage, Eric V. Black Pearls Journal, Copyright ©1995
     William Morrow and Company
2. Hutchinson, Dr. Earl Ofari: (2000 Family Digest Media Group)
     "In Praise of Black Fathers"
3. March, Eric "The History Of The African American Funeral Di
     rector" © Batesville Casket Company
4. The Personal Effects Of Wilkie Clark
5. The Randolph Leader Archives

[1] Microsoft Encarta Encyclopedia 2000, Teachings Of Confucius

[2] Microsoft Encarta Encyclopedia 2000, Teachings Of Confucius

Just An After Thought

This book is also dedicated to the numerous other "heroes" of my community, all of which deserve a place of honor in the archives of our community. My daddy was but one out of a number of great African American men who passed this way and left their footprints on the sands of time. And if the Lord allows, I'll gladly be the one to see to it that they have their rightful place in history, too.

My beloved mother, Mrs. Hattie Lee Peters Clark
Reverend R. L. Heflin, John "Tommy" Thompson,
H. T. "Lightening" Rosser Susie Mae Rosser,
Jesse A. Terry, Velma Gertrude Heard Terry
Theodore Shumpert, H.L. Shaw, Dr. Benjamin A. Outland,
Ernest Heard, Jr., Booker T. Williams, Charlie Cameron,
Roy D. Terry, Rudolph Terry, William R. Terry
The Entire Faculty of the Randolph County Training School
From Inception To Closing

Another Book Written By
Charlotte A. Clark Frieson

Other Books Written By
Charlotte A. Clark-FriesonA Children's Book Of Wisdom

"Ancient Wisdom For Millennial Minds"

"Life Lessons For Today's Children & Youth,
Based On The Sayings Of Confucius..."

Drawing from the ancient "sayings of Confucius" a veteran teacher interprets the sayings of Confucius as a way to help youngsters understand character and virtue.

The book features a short biographical overview of Confucius' life to help children understand why he made such an impact on the world.

Kids will love and learn from this book! With its attractive custom designed red cover, vividly colored "Confucius clips" and lively print, they will not only become attached to its attractive appearance but to its contents.

From: $ 9.00
Available in hardcopy for $ 18.95
Available to Download from Website for $ 9.00

Website: http://www.wilkieclarksdaughter.net

Acknkowledgments

I acknowledge and glorify God, the head of my life, the author and finisher of my faith, along with all individuals who lent a hand in any way in the production of this my first publication. For your time, energy, and any other support you contributed, I find a mere "thank you" grossly insufficient to express the extent of my gratitude.

To my wonderful children, Wilkie Sherard Frieson, and Je'Lynn Mikele Frieson, I thank you for having me as your mother, and putting up with me. Thank you for sometimes having to be my eyes, ears, legs and feet. For reading silently; reading critically; reading orally to me; reading lovingly; and for working along with me and helping me to edit this book and make it the best book it could be. Thank you for your love, interest and diligence. In the absence of mama, I thank John C. Bell, and Lillian V. Shealey, my surrogate parents, my cousin, Gene A. Thornton and my friend and colleague, Minister Jacquelyn Cumberlander for being my writing critics.

To people like Dr. Alvin Thornton, my Uncle Beotis and Aunt Belle Clark of Augusta, Georgia, Moderator R. L. Heflin, Mr. Tommy Bridges, the Honorable Bishop Lathonia J. Wright, Mr. Jerome A. Gray, Mr. Douglas McArthur Heard, Ms. Lillian V. Shealey, Ms. Addie Sue Wilson, my friend and brother, Robert Joiner, Jr., thank you for loving and remembering daddy with a fondness that could only be exceeded by my own. And thank you for so eagerly contributing to this work with a clear understanding of my purpose for asking you to do so. I thank God for our being on one accord, when it came to putting this together.

To Gabriel S. Carr and the entire staff and management of Clark Memorial Funeral Service, likewise, I thank you for putting up with me as I labored to bear this literary child. Gabe, your steadfast loyalty, and great faith inspire me. I am blessed to have you in my life. To Dr. Kim Bond, Mrs. Etta Billingslea and the staff at Ault Academy, thank you for all your support and encouragement.

Thank you Etta, for being my friend, and for being the best boss in the world!

I love you all, and be abundantly blessed!!

About The Cover Design Concept

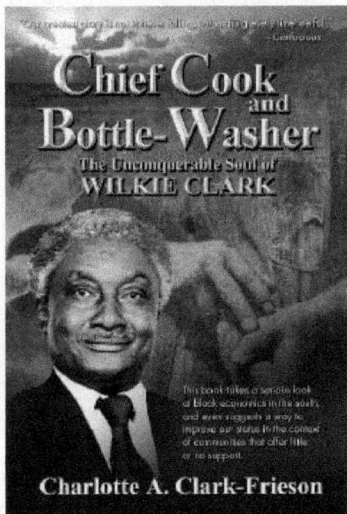

Highest praise is due to Mr. Sean Snakenberg, of Cover2Cover Designs for a dynamic and inspiring cover design concept.

The cover concept arises from a color fill of an older black and white photograph of Wilkie Clark. The designer felt it added an very interesting aspect (almost bronzed, as if preserved) as opposed to the black and white photo. The hands in the background are representative of the work Wilkie Clark did as a railroad man during that time; the two pictures together are a story of how he came from a labor background, to an independent entrepreneur and owner of his own business. The sky in the top is representative of the light he radiated in his lifetime, and continues to shine from his spirit that he left in everyone he touched with his life.

The stone grain backing added a colorful flair to the cover in contrast to the deep blue at the bottom of the cover.

About Wilkie Clark's Daughter

Charlotte A. Clark-Frieson is Wilkie Clark's Daughter. Her desire is to devote the remainder of her natural life to carrying the message of the Gospel by way of the divine lessons learned through the compelling life stories of her father and other dynamic black achievers in her community. She also seeks your support in helping her carry the message of collective consciousness to the African American communities of our nation.

Born in Roanoke, Alabama she was and is the ONLY child born to her parents. She is the widow of the late Clarence Frieson, Jr. with whom she birthed two children. She is also a proud grandmother.

She holds both the B.S. and M.Ed. from Auburn University. While at Auburn, she pledged Delta Sigma Theta National Service Sorority, as one of the first nine Deltas to be initiated there, thus establishing the first black women's sorority on the campus of Auburn University, (Kappa Upsilon Chapter), in 1974. Additionally, an honor graduate, she holds a Degree in Funeral Service from Gupton-Jones College of Funeral Service, Atlanta, Georgia. While in mortuary training, she pledged Pi Sigma Eta honorary National Mortuary Fraternity. She has devoted many years to the education profession in her neighbor state of Georgia. After the tragic death of her father, in 1989, she forfeited her teaching career to continue her father's diligent quest as an entrepreneur, serving as its resident embalmer and funeral director until she was able to mentor others including her own children, who now assist in providing services to their client-family base. She is a National Board Certified Embalmer and Funeral Director.

Entering her 50th year of life, she began to work toward her dream to devote the remainder of her life to exploring the one area of expertise wherein she believes God gifted her, and that is writing. She believes that most of today's black youth tend to show an callous lack of regard for or understanding of the civil rights struggles of African-Americans, resulting in a lack direction and purpose, thus she would like to write books to inspire them to future greatness.

Church and Community Involvement

Ms. Clark-Frieson is an active member of the Oak Grove A.M.E. Church, where she was recently appointed to serve the church as Secretary.

She has been active in the Civil Rights arena, having actively worked with NAACP, and the A.D.C. the Black Political Caucus of Alabama. In addition, in the 1980's she served on the Executive Board of the Alabama State Conference of NAACP Branches.

In 1988 after 20 years of periodic disputes over racial issues in the School system in her native Randolph County, she was elected to a seat on the Randolph County Board of Education following a Federal Court order mandating the School District to convert its method of electing officials from "at large" to "single-member districts." Ms. Clark-Frieson is now serving her 4th term, (more than sixteen years) on the Randolph County Board Of Education. As a result of the 1994 Randolph County School Controversy, she became the subject of newspaper commentary, appeared as a guest on several syndicated Radio Talk Shows, the Geraldo Show, and was featured in the May, 1995 issue of Rolling Stone Magazine.

In March of 1995, she was the recipient of the "Medgar W. Evers Award" presented at the 43rd Annual Southeast Regional N.A.A.C.P. Leadership Development Training Institute in Chattanooga, Tennessee; Later that same year, on May 20, 1995, she was the recipient of the "John F. Kennedy Profiles In Courage Award," presented at the Annual Convention of the Alabama Democratic Conference, in Montgomery, Alabama. This award read "We honor you for being a strong Randolph County School Board Member, who stood firm in 1994, even when confronted by racial threats and unrest, in calling for the dismissal of a High School Principal who sought to ban inter-racial student couples from attending a prom. Without your courage and call for a just resolution of the school crisis, buttressed by a Court Settlement, the Randolph County high School system may still be in turmoil today."

254

As of the time of this publication, she has already arrived at the strong conclusion that another extensive work is now warranted to further document through the compilation of public records, newspaper articles and personal papers, her father's innumerable activities, focusing specifically on his documented NAACP activities and the past and current racially oppressive conditions in Randolph County that warranted our past and continued activism."

Her proudest achievement to date was the February 2005 launch of Chief Cook & Bottle-Washer, The Unconquerable Soul Of Wilkie Clark, at which time, the Wilkie Clark Memorial Foundation was also launched. Since that time, the dynamic board members of The Wilkie Clark Memorial Foundation, Incorporated have undertaken many projects to promote and get the word out about the work they are trying to do. As an outgrowth of The Wilkie Clark Memorial Foundation, in August of 2005, The Clark Memorial Foundation launched *"The People's Voice,"* East Alabama/West Georgia's only black weekly newspaper, in hopes that it will become the new voice of the Southeast. The paper was launched in an effort to give "voice" to the many disturbing black conditions that persist throughout East Alabama and West Georgia. *The Peoples Voice* is published weekly by the Wilkie Clark Memorial Foundation.

Ms. Clark-Frieson will consider all requests to appear as a speaker in consideration of a generous contribution to the Wilkie Clark Memorial Foundation.

Interested persons may call or write to inquire about having Ms. Clark-Frieson appear for book signing events.

A portion of the proceeds from all book sales will benefit the Wilkie Clark Memorial Foundation.

Contact The
Wilkie Clark Memorial Foundation
Charlotte A. Clark-Frieson, Board Chairman
322 Wilkie Clark Drive, Roanoke, Alabama 36274

Website Addresses
http://www.clarkmemorial.biz
http://www.wilkieclarksdaughter.com

To Order Books: http://www.wilkieclarksdaughter.net

TELEPHONE NUMBERS
Main...334.375.7160
Email address...caclarkfrieson@msn.com

LOCAL BOARD OF DIRECTORS
Founder/ C.E.O. Charlotte A. Clark-Frieson
Wilkie S. Frieson, Je'Lynn M. Frieson, Beotis Clark, Belle B. Clark,
Reverend R. L. Heflin, Reverend William A. Dean, Reverend Jeffery
Rosser, Mrs. Mary Turner, Ms. Julia Minnefield
Mrs. Lola Mae Wright, Ms. Jeanetta Minnifield-Stevens
Ms. Frances Drake, Mr. Christopher Daniel

REGIONAL BOARD OF DIRECTORS
Dr. Alvin Thornton, Suitland, Maryland
Ms. Earnestine Thornton, Atlanta, Georgia
Gene A. Thornton, Springfield, Virginia
Mr. Jerome A. Gray, Evergreen/Montgomery, Alabama
Mr. David Baker, Anniston, Alabama (CAP, Inc.)

IN MEMORIAM
Ms. Hattie Lee Peters Clark
Ms. Lillie Thornton
Deacon John Ceroy Bell, Sr.
OTHER REGIONAL AND LOCAL APPOINTMENTS PENDING

Need More Copies Of This Book?

"Chief Cook & Bottle-Washer"
The Unconquerable Soul Of Wilkie Clark

Name _____

Address _____

City _____State _____ Zip Code _____

_____# of copies of Chief Cook & Bottle-Washer
@ 18.95 per copy....................................$_____

ALABAMA RESIDENTS ONLY
add 8% sales tax.. _____
Shipping & Handling
(Add $2.00 for the first book).................... _____
Additional Shipping & Handling Cost.................. _____
($1.00 each additional book)
TOTAL AMOUNT DUE ....$_____

Make check or money order payable to:
Wilkie Clark's Daughter Enterprises, LLC

Mail to: Wilkie Clark's Daughter Enterprises, LLC
322 Wilkie Clark Drive,
Roanoke, AL 36274
Phone: 334.375.7160
Mobile: 334.646.2056

"God is truly Good all the time...

And by the sufficiency of HIS GRACE,

Reality is something that we can ALL

Rise Above!!"

~ Charlotte A. Clark-Frieson ~

www.ingramcontent.com/pod-product-compliance
Lightning Source LLC
Chambersburg PA
CBHW032040080426
42733CB00006B/145